Text, Lies
and Cataloging

Text, Lies and Cataloging

Ethical Treatment of Deceptive Works in the Library

JANA BRUBAKER

McFarland & Company, Inc., Publishers
Jefferson, North Carolina

ISBN (print) 978-0-7864-9744-7
ISBN (ebook) 978-1-4766-3256-8

LIBRARY OF CONGRESS CATALOGUING DATA ARE AVAILABLE

BRITISH LIBRARY CATALOGUING DATA ARE AVAILABLE

© 2018 Jana Brubaker. All rights reserved

No part of this book may be reproduced or transmitted in any form or by any means, electronic or mechanical, including photocopying or recording, or by any information storage and retrieval system, without permission in writing from the publisher.

Front cover image © 2018 mars58/iStock

Printed in the United States of America

*McFarland & Company, Inc., Publishers
Box 611, Jefferson, North Carolina 28640
www.mcfarlandpub.com*

For John, always

Acknowledgments

Thank you to my family and friends (especially the poetry group) for their encouragement and support. I gratefully acknowledge my clever friend Suzanne Coffield who suggested the title. Thank you also to my colleagues, especially Ete Olson and Susan Kapost, who were understanding and supportive as I tried to balance work and writing. I am grateful to Northern Illinois University, which granted me the sabbatical that allowed me to begin this project and to the University Libraries for providing access to most of the journals and books I consulted. Finally, thank you to my husband, John Bradley, whose love, advice, and support were invaluable.

Table of Contents

Acknowledgments vi
Preface 1
Introduction 3
A Few Words about Cataloging Terms 6
Deceptive Works 9
Barriers to Accurate Cataloging 11
Codes and Standards 13

Memoirs and Autobiographies 17
   Col. Crockett's Exploits and Adventures in Texas 20
   Awful Disclosures of Maria Monk 21
   The Life of John William Walshe, F. S. A. 23
   Long Lance 24
   The Cradle of the Deep 27
   Pilgrims of the Wild 28
   The Diary of a Surgeon in the Year 1751–1752; Surgeon's Mate; Man Midwife 29
   My Sister and I 31
   The Long Walk 33
   Travels with Charley 34
   Go Ask Alice 36
   I Married Wyatt Earp; Illustrated Life of Doc Holliday 38
   The Education of Little Tree 40
   Michelle Remembers 42
   Satan's Underground 43
   Mutant Message Downunder 45
   A Rock and a Hard Place 47
   Sleepers 50
   Stoker 52
   Fragments 54
   Misha 55
   The Autobiography of Howard Hughes 57
   Jihad! 60
   The Blood Runs Like a River; The Boy and the Dog; Geronimo's Bones 62

Table of Contents

The Cage 64
A Million Little Pieces; My Friend Leonard 65
Kathy's Story 67
Three Cups of Tea; Stones into Schools 70
Child P.O.W. 72
The Road of Lost Innocence 73
Angel at the Fence 76
Love and Consequences 77
The Boy Who Came Back from Heaven 79
The Man Who Broke into Auschwitz 80

Other Nonfiction   83

Never Cry Wolf 85
In Cold Blood 87
Roots 90
In His Image 92
Arming America 93
Honor Lost 95
Ananios of Kleitor 97
The Last Train from Hiroshima 98
Imagine 100
The Embassy House 102

Fiction   105

Wild Cat Falling 108
Jack Rivers and Me 109
Famous All Over Town 110
The Hand That Signed the Paper 112
My Own Sweet Time 114
Sarah; The Heart Is Deceitful Above All Things; Harold's End 115
The Honored Society 117

Poetry   119

The Darkening Ecliptic 119
The Love Poems of Marichiko 121
Doubled Flowering 122
Saracen Island 124

Conclusion   126
Notes   131
Bibliography for Case Studies   151
Selected Bibliography for Secondary Resources   153
Index   155

Preface

> Truth is the most valuable thing we have. Let us economize it.
> —Mark Twain, *Following the Equator*

Some writers have taken Twain's advice to heart, giving us books of questionable authorship, authenticity, or veracity, sometimes for monetary gain. While these authors comprise a distinct minority in the literary world, they can cause a great deal of consternation within the library community. Selectors of materials, catalogers, and reference librarians must all be alert to works that misrepresent themselves. Librarians must ask themselves what ethical and professional standards guide their handling of deceptive works.

The purpose of this book is twofold. First, it is intended to continue a long-standing conversation about the role of the cataloger in providing useful and accurate information to the library user for these types of materials. Second, this book is a resource that identifies, describes, and discusses questionable books. Despite the focus on cataloging, many of the issues discussed will be of interest to librarians, regardless of their function, and library science students. It contains case studies of key deceptive works, limited in scope to monographs in English that were published between 1800 and the present.[1] Both well-known and lesser-known works are included. These books may be designed to intentionally deceive the reader and/or they may mislead the reader by crossing boundaries of genre. In short, the works included here are texts that often are not what they purport to be.

Inaccurate facts and false identities are addressed, but questions of plagiarism are outside the scope of this book. It also does not address works that argue against or ignore commonly accepted scientific facts. For example, books that deny climate change or evolution are not part of this discussion. We can assume that the average library user will have knowledge of and opinions about these topics that will allow him to assess such materials on his own. Nor does it include works that fly in the face of established and well-known historical events, such as books that argue that the Holocaust did not occur. In both of these cases, the books present themselves forthrightly and arguably are not designed to deceive.

Following a brief explanation of cataloging terms for the noncataloger, there is an introduction to the category of deceptive works and a discussion of barriers to accurate cataloging, after which I survey the cataloging standards and professional codes of

Preface

ethics that bear on the treatment of these works. Case studies of a selection of these problematic works follow and include relevant details of the bibliographic records describing them. The publication dates associated with the texts represent the earliest published editions and the authors listed are those that appear on the title page. Bibliographic records that are discussed represent those in OCLC with the largest number of institutional holdings attached. The case studies are organized by genre, including memoir and autobiography, other nonfiction, and fiction and poetry. Books are listed in the genre that they claim to be. Within each genre, the works are presented in ascending chronological order. I also provide my thoughts on how each book should be cataloged, but no criticism is implied if I suggest changes to the current record. I do not claim that my choices are the only valid ones, but I hope they will provide a starting point for making informed decisions. I conclude with a discussion about possible cataloging solutions for these problem books.

I have long been interested in the topic of cataloging deceptive works. I wrote an article in 2002 on this subject, and my view has largely remained the same, but I have become more concerned about the negative effects of failing to represent a book accurately to the catalog user.[2] The need for a book such as this has been reinforced for me on several occasions over recent years. *Imagine: How Creativity Works*, a book by Jonah Lehrer that came out in 2012, was quickly recalled by the publisher when it discovered that several sections were fabricated, including quotations attributed to Bob Dylan.[3] I was therefore surprised when I saw it on a shelf of new books at a major academic library, with no indication that anything was amiss. I have also noticed that questions and opinions regarding the cataloging of deceptive works have been a frequent topic on Autocat, the primary listserv for catalogers. Below is a post regarding one such book:

> I recently bought the audio book for Three cups of tea ... for our library collection. Hundreds of libraries show holdings for this book. Someone remarked that the story in this book was falsified; so I did a little searching on the Internet. Wow. How have other libraries handled this book? I thought about giving it a fiction call number, or putting the $v Fiction note after each subject heading, then thought that perhaps a note in the record stating some of the allegations about the books authenticity might be a better idea. None of the many records on OCLC say a thing about the inaccuracies in this title (It even made "60 minutes"). Any helpful hints?[4]

Because catalogers communicate with users only through bibliographic records, clear guidelines would be welcome. The issues surrounding these books, however, are diverse and the path to providing accurate bibliographic records to users varies. This book will, nonetheless, suggest a framework for navigating decisions that must be made when cataloging these materials.

Introduction

> The data describing a resource should reflect the resource's representation of itself.
> —*Resource, Description, and Access*

The above instruction appears in the most current iteration of cataloging standards, *Resource, Description, and Access* (*RDA*), and marks a continuation of an underlying principle in its predecessor, *Anglo-American Cataloguing Rules*, second edition (*AACR2*). In essence, catalogers are urged to judge books, in all their physical and virtual forms, by their covers (or title pages)—contrary to the well-known adage. We are guided by rules and standards that instruct us to take the materials that we are cataloging at face value. Our code of ethics reminds us not to be judgmental, nor to bring our personal biases to our cataloging decisions.[1] These seem like sensible guidelines, but become less clear-cut when the authorship, authenticity, and/or veracity of a book is questioned. The codes and standards in many cases raise as many questions as they answer—questions such as what are the responsibilities of the cataloger to the user when describing deceptive works? What ethical considerations, if any, are involved? Do the answers to these questions vary depending on the genre of the work or the cataloging standards being used?

Most librarians have dealt with books that are questionable in nature and many catalogers have cataloged works that are not what they appear to be. More accurately, we have cataloged books that are eventually revealed to be problematic, for librarians seldom question the way a book represents itself initially (although Truman Capote's description of *In Cold Blood* as a "nonfiction novel" demonstrates the difficulties of this approach).[2] It is only after a work has been vetted by readers that questions may surface and catalogers face a conundrum.

Interest in deceptive works has spread in recent years. It is no longer the sole domain of critics, scholars, and librarians, but has filtered into popular culture. This can be attributed, in part, to the appearance of James Frey, author of the truth-challenged memoir *A Million Little Pieces* on *The Oprah Winfrey Show* in 2005. Frey's book recounted his years as an alcoholic, drug addict, and criminal, and it was so powerful that Winfrey selected it for her influential Book Club. Soon, however, investigative journalists determined that Frey's memoir contained more fiction than fact.[3] Frey later admitted that he had embellished his story and disingenuously asserted that he never intended the book to be regarded as nonfiction.[4]

Introduction

High-profile cases such as this have raised issues of credibility in recent years, but deceptive works are not a new phenomenon. Consider that in AD 756 a document appeared that was allegedly written by Emperor Constantine in the fourth century AD It granted ownership of a large portion of the territories within the western Roman Empire to the Catholic Church. It was not until 1440 that it was declared a forgery.[5] In 1836 *Col. Crockett's Exploits and Adventures in Texas*, the purported diary of Davy Crockett, was actually written by Richard Penn Smith, unhindered by any authentic entries penned by Colonel Crockett.[6] While questionable works have become a curiosity to the general public as more and more cases have come to light, librarians must deal with them as a practical matter.

This book addresses two thorny situations that catalogers encounter. The first occurs when authorship, which is often the foundation of authenticity, is in doubt. Most authors adopt a pseudonym in order to inhabit a different identity from their real one. Their motives may vary, but unless authors later explain why they used a pen name, we cannot be certain of their reasons. They may wish to write something in a genre for which they are not well-known. For example, Gore Vidal wrote several mystery novels under the name "Edgar Box" because, he explained, the literary community was ignoring his serious fiction and he needed to make a living.[7] They may want to hide their identity in order to protect themselves, as David Cornwell, who worked for the British diplomatic corps, did when he wrote under the name John le Carré to dodge Foreign Office rules against publishing under his given name.[8] The cases discussed in this book, however, are ones where the authenticity and credibility of the work rests on the identity of the author. For example, a memoir of a Holocaust survivor relies heavily on the actual experiences of the author. If the author is not who or what she claims to be, then her account cannot be authentic.

The second situation involves challenges to the veracity of a work. While the books described in the first scenario are often lacking in veracity as well, in those cases the dubious nature of the work is inextricably linked to deceptive authorship. The second category of deceptive works does not involve questions about authorship. The fraudulent character of these books rests solely on the erroneous information they contain. They are nonfiction works that prove to be less than factual. Catalogers confront the complications that these situations create when they determine the main entry (if following *AACR2* standards) or creator(s) (if following *RDA* standards) when performing subject analysis and determining the genre and classification of a work.

Fundamental questions must be answered before she can make appropriate cataloging decisions. At what point has a verdict regarding the credibility of a book's representation of itself been rendered? What obligation does the cataloger have to act on new information? Should bibliographic records be changed retrospectively as new details come to light? The decisions the cataloger makes are in the service of one goal: providing the catalog user with the most accurate representation of the work. This book provides a framework for assessing these works in order to help catalogers decide what is ethical, practical, and necessary to accomplish this task.

The professional and ethical considerations that guide catalogers in achieving this

Introduction

goal sometimes appear to confuse rather than clarify the decisions they must make. It is therefore useful to take these considerations out of the abstract realm by examining a number of case studies of questionable works. There is no one-size-fits-all formula, but as we look at specific examples we will identify characteristics of the books that can help us navigate our way through the process of cataloging (or re-cataloging) them.

A Few Words About Cataloging Terms

Each entry describing a deceptive work will end with suggestions for possible cataloging solutions to address any unintended misrepresentation in the bibliographic record and/or authority record. Although experienced catalogers will understand the terms used, the following is for readers who are less familiar with bibliographic and authority records and the Machine Readable Cataloging (MARC) fields that comprise them. Bibliographic records describe a work, which for our purposes is a book. MARC records are composed of "fixed fields" in which information about the work (such as date and place of publication) is coded in a consistent location with a defined number of characters and "variable fields" in which the information called for by the International Standard Bibliographic Description (ISBD) standard, developed by IFLA, is entered in the appropriate numbered field tag (see figure below).

Two fixed fields are particularly relevant to deceptive books. The "Biography" field indicates if the work is an autobiography (code=a), an individual biography (code=b), a collective biography (code=c), or contains biographical information (code=d). If no biographical or autobiographical information is included in the book, the field is blank. The other pertinent fixed field describes the literary form. We are most interested in the records coded as "Not Fiction" (code=0), "Fiction" (code=1), and "Novels" (code=f).

The variable fields that are most relevant are the 100 field, which contains the author or creator of the book; field tags that begin with the number 5, which contain free-form notes; and field tags that begin with 6, which contain subject entries and genre/form terms. Although there are many fields that begin with 5, the 500 field, or general note, and the 520 field, or summary note, are the most relevant.

Another term that will appear is "added entry." In the context of this book, this is an entry in the bibliographic record for a person who is not the author or creator of the work, but has some kind of role in the creation of the work. For example, the name of the person who wrote the introduction or was the illustrator may be entered in a 700 (added entry) field.[1]

Authority records contain authorized headings (also known as controlled vocabulary), which are consistent, unique forms of subjects, names, and titles to be used in bibliographic records (see figure below). Their use is meant to disambiguate similar or identical headings. For example, if you have two authors named "Fred Smith,"

A Few Words About Cataloging Terms

you need to differentiate them. There are various ways to do this, including adding a middle initial or birth date to one of the entries. Authorized headings are also used to collocate materials that logically belong together. If you have books on the same subject, utilizing the same authorized term in the bibliographic record will assure that users will retrieve all the books on that subject when they enter that term. Authority records for names also often have cross-references to other names associated with a person. These other names may be a pseudonym, which is also an authorized heading, or they may just be a different form of the name that is not to be used in the bibliographic record because that form was not chosen as the authorized heading. For example, if we have chosen to add a middle initial to one of the Fred Smiths discussed earlier, then we need to use that form in bibliographic records that are associated with him. Source notes may also be contained in the authority record. Here catalogers record the citation for a consulted source in which information is found related to the entity represented by the authority record or related entities.[2]

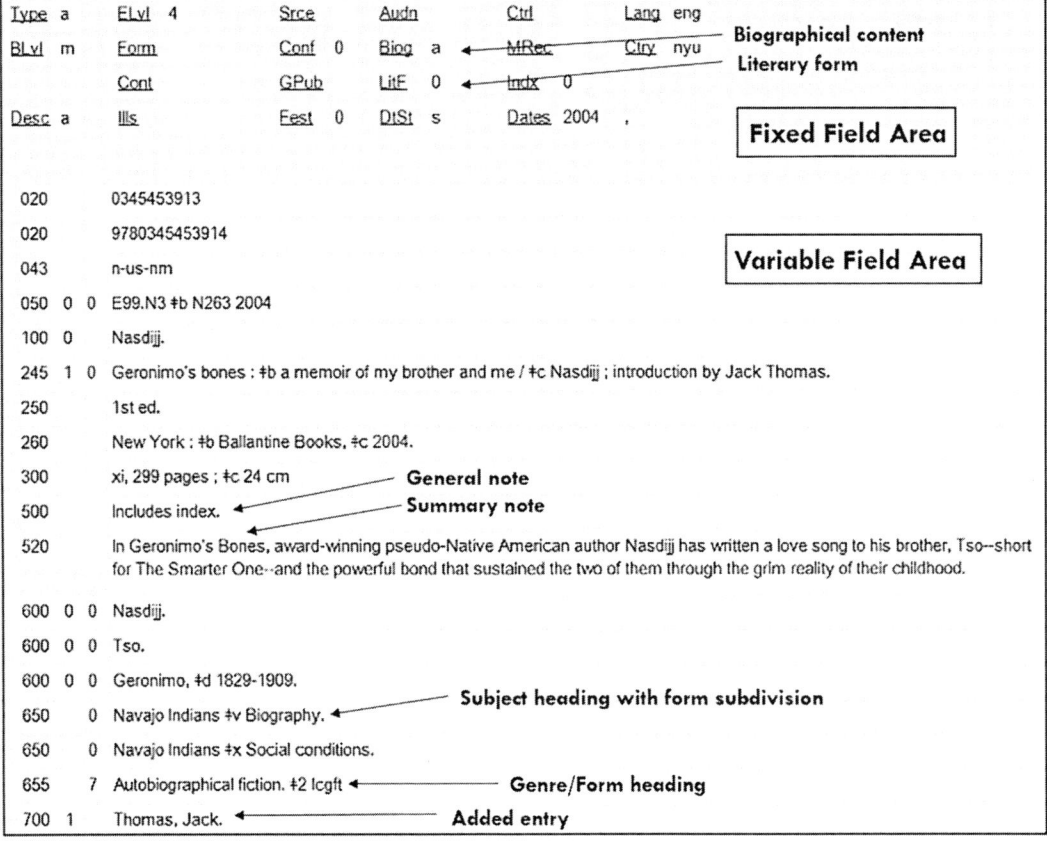

Bibliographic Record—Record has been altered for illustrative purposes. Screenshot is ©2017 OCLC, Inc., and is used with OCLC's permission. OCLC, Connexion and WorldCat are registered trademarks/service marks of OCLC.

A Few Words About Cataloging Terms

Two terms that appear frequently in the case studies are "form subdivision" and "genre/form heading," both of which are controlled by authority records. Form subdivisions are used to tell the catalog user what the book is: for example, fiction, biography, or poetry. The form subdivision usually follows a topical subject heading or a name ("Criminals–Fiction," for example, to describe a fictional account of criminals). Genre/form headings also communicate what the book is, but combines genre and form in one heading. For example, "Historical fiction" combines the genre "historical" with the form "fiction."[3]

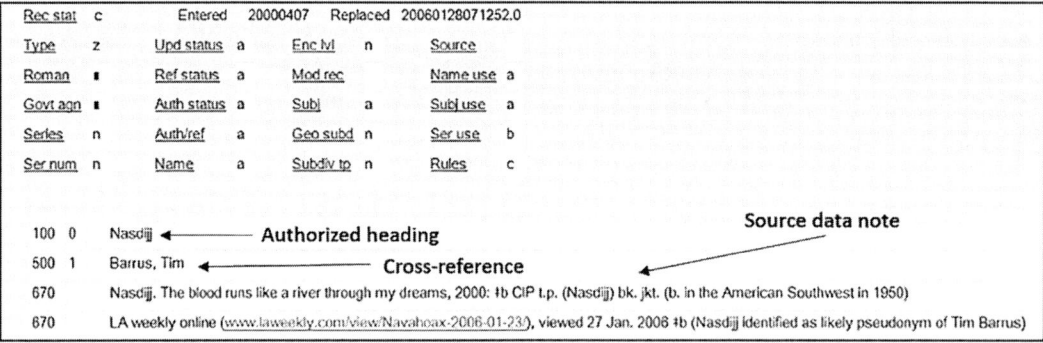

Authority Record—Record has been altered for illustrative purposes. Screenshot is ©2017 OCLC, Inc., and is used with OCLC's permission. OCLC, Connexion and WorldCat are registered trademarks/service marks of OCLC.

Deceptive Works

A variety of terms have been applied to works of questionable authorship and authenticity or veracity. These terms include literary forgeries, false memoirs, literary hoaxes, and fake literature. This book employs the term "deceptive works," a phrase that is broad enough to encompass a range of works that are not what they purport to be. While the term has a negative connotation, works labeled as such are not necessarily lacking in quality or value. In fact, in some cases the value of a work may actually be derived, in part, from the deception, as we will see later.

Authorship and Authenticity

The deceptive works included in the following case studies fall roughly into two categories, derived from the cataloging issues surrounding them. First, the person or corporate body responsible for the intellectual content of the book may not be represented accurately in the resource. The most common circumstance is one where the listed author (or authors) is not who or what he claims to be. He may write under his own name or a pseudonym, which is not usually a vexing cataloging problem, but rather a routine authority control issue. If, however, the author takes on or creates the identity of another person for the purpose of laying claim to experiences and perspectives that are not his own, that complicates the situation.

If someone writes a memoir based on a life that he did not live, that book should not be considered nonfiction. One such book was written by Tom Carew, also known as Philip Sessarego, allegedly a member of British Special Air Services (SAS). His memoir, *Jihad! The Secret War in Afghanistan*, recounts his experience training the Mujahideen during Afghanistan's civil war in the early 1980s. His knowledge of these Afghan guerrilla fighters made him much sought after by the American military during the post–9/11 invasion of Afghanistan. Unfortunately, his story did not hold up. BBC News revealed that Carew was an impostor and had never been a member of the SAS.[1] A cataloger has to grapple with determining the appropriate genre of a book such as this.

Another type of book that falls into this category is a creative work that is disassociated entirely from the actual author of the work. When Gore Vidal wrote under the pen name Edgar Box, there was no cause for alarm. Any confusion that the pseudonym may have caused has been diminished by the addition of "see also" cross-references in the Library of Congress authority records for Vidal and Box. When, however, the author assumes a false identity that lends an air of unearned authenticity to the work, controversy may ensue. Such was the case when critics discovered that author Daniel James wrote a novel about a barrio in Los Angeles under the pseudonym Danny Santiago. Although James explained that his motive was benign, he was accused of trying to pass himself off as Hispanic. One could certainly argue that the use of a name that suggested he was Hispanic changed the way many people read his novel *Famous All Over Town*.[2]

Veracity

The second category of deceptive works that are included in the case studies comprise self-described nonfiction works that are actually fiction or contain factual errors that seriously undermine the credibility of the work. Unlike memoirs, which may be allowed some creative license, these works purport to contain objective truth. *Report from Iron Mountain* is one such work, a literary hoax concocted in 1967 by three editors of *Monocle*, a journal of political satire. They were dismayed when the stock market fell due to reports that a peace accord might put an end to the Vietnam War. They wanted to make a statement about the reliance of the United States economy on war and military spending, and so they enlisted the help of author Leonard Lewin. He wrote what was alleged to be a government report asserting that the country could not afford to transition to a peace economy because the war economy was so entrenched. A cooperative publisher agreed to market it as nonfiction, but five years later Lewin confessed to the deception.[3]

Barriers to Accurate Cataloging

As noted above, catalogers depend heavily on publishers to identify the genre to which a work belongs. Is the book marketed as fiction or nonfiction? Who wrote the book? There is an unspoken assumption that publishers are as concerned about the validity of their representation as catalogers are. Indeed, the publisher is the only entity that can potentially uncover credibility issues before a book is published. Although a publisher seldom intentionally sets out to assist a writer in producing a work that is deceptive, the truth is that fact-checking is not standard practice in the book-publishing world.

Because the revelation that a book contains serious factual errors has far more negative consequences for the writer than the publisher, if anyone hires an independent fact-checker, it is the author. No reputable nonfiction author wants to be embarrassed by the discovery that her work contains one or more factual errors. She will be vilified long after the publisher is forgotten. When a book is exposed, Scott Rosenberg of MediaBugs notes that "no one looks at the publishing house's name on the book they bought four years ago when *Newsweek* exposes it as inaccurate and says, 'I'll never buy a book published by them again!' So why should the publisher care?"[1] Even if the publisher is forced to offer refunds, as Random House was in the case of *A Million Little Pieces*, the financial consequences are often negligible. Of the four million readers who purchased the book, fewer than two thousand asked for refunds.[2]

So who can the cataloger trust? We have little choice but to take the word of the publisher and author, initially. In most cases, our trust will be well-placed because most authors are honest and honor the truth and facts. In any case, it is almost certain that the cataloger will not be aware of any questions about authorship, authenticity, or veracity of the work when the book is originally cataloged. It is, however, incumbent on catalogers to be alert to revelations about fraud and misinformation in published works.

This leads us to the question of who renders a verdict on whether a work is deceptive. The responsibility for this determination does not rest with the cataloger. Typically, critics, historians, or journalists will make the argument, bolstered by concrete proof that we are dealing with a deceptive work. For example, *The Smoking Gun*, a website that posts investigative stories, revealed that *A Million Little Pieces* was a work of fiction, which James Frey, the author, grudgingly acknowledged in a second appearance on *The Oprah Winfrey Show*.[3]

It is not uncommon for authors or publishers to acknowledge charges of deception in their books in due time. Only when the facts have been well established and overwhelming consensus has been reached should catalogers contemplate ignoring the rule that instructs us to describe a resource as it represents itself. The cataloger may gain this knowledge in several ways, but at the point that the cataloger has this knowledge, she must decide how, or even if, she will communicate this to the user. Certainly, she wants to act in accordance with professional standards of conduct.

Codes and Standards

Deceptive works challenge the foundation of sound cataloging practices. How catalogers should deal with them is up for debate. Descriptive cataloging, which is simply recording information about the physical characteristics and publishing details of a work, is fairly cut and dried. There may be differences of opinion about what constitutes the title or whether to include a particular entity in the statement of responsibility, but on the whole the process is not filled with many demands for judgment on the part of the cataloger. Catalogers, however, have three opportunities to exercise their judgment that will affect how a work is presented to the user: personal or corporate name access (the entity responsible for the intellectual content of the book); subject access (what the book is about or what the genre is by assigning genre/form headings or form subdivisions); and classification (the call number that is assigned, which determines where the work is shelved). Optionally, and less visibly, notes can be added to the record.

The choice of access points, most often entries in the bibliographic record containing controlled vocabulary terms that allow the user to retrieve a record in the catalog, is a process that can be tricky under the best of circumstances. First, the cataloger must decide who or what is responsible for the intellectual content of the book. This will determine the personal name and/or corporate body entry, and the decision will be guided by the cataloging standard utilized (*AACR2* or *RDA*). Next, what is the genre? The answer to this question will dictate the choice of subject entries and call number (classification). Subject access is guided by the Library of Congress' *Subject Heading Manual* (*SHM*). Originally created as an in-house procedure for assigning subject headings, the *SHM* is consulted by many, if not most, libraries using Library of Congress subject headings to inform their subject analysis and construction of subject strings (a combination of subject headings and subdivisions).[1] Choosing what classification to assign to a book is guided by Library of Congress' *Classification and Shelflisting Manual* (*CSM*). The *CSM*, like the *SHM*, began as an internal manual for Library of Congress catalogers, but is now used by many libraries that utilize Library of Congress classification.[2]

If the publisher presents the work as fiction, this may minimize the second and third tasks of ascertaining what the book in hand is about and what classification to assign. If it is represented as nonfiction, simply perusing the work should guide subject assignment and call number. Obfuscation, however, is the hallmark of deceptive works and may lead the cataloger down the wrong path.

Codes and Standards

In determining the proper course of action, it might be instructive to take a broader view of the purpose of a catalog as set down by Charles A. Cutter, author of *Rules for a Printed Dictionary Catalog*, in 1876 and codified in cataloging standards through the present day. First, he stated that "the convenience of the public is always to be set before the ease of the cataloger."[3] This focus on the user remains the prime directive, if you will, for catalogers, and indeed for all librarians, and is a strong argument for providing the user with the most accurate record possible. Cutter identified three basic objectives of the catalog: to allow the library user to identify a known work (the finding objective); to show what the library has by a given author, subject, or kind of literature (the collating objective); and to assist in the choice of a book that meets his or her needs as to its edition (bibliographically) and character, literary or topical (evaluating objective).[4]

In 1961, recognizing the need for an international standard for cataloging to facilitate the sharing of bibliographic data worldwide, the International Conference on Cataloguing Principles authored a statement of principles, commonly known as the "Paris Principles." The theoretical foundation for these principles relied significantly on Cutter's *Rules for a Printed Dictionary Catalog*. The International Federation of Library Associations and Institutions (IFLA) approved a new statement of principles, *Statement of International Cataloguing Principles* (2016), which broadened the scope of the Paris Principles, and reinforced Cutter's focus on the user through its imperative to consider the convenience of the user first and foremost. It asserts that the objectives of the catalog are to allow the user to find, identify, and select a bibliographic resource, and to obtain access to an item described. Acknowledging the online format of modern catalogs, it also states that the user must be able to navigate and explore within a catalog. Finally, the statement includes the principle of representation, which is described as representing a resource as it appears.[5]

The current cataloging standard, *RDA* (implemented in 2013), is based on the Functional Requirements for Bibliographic Records (FRBR), which was developed by IFLA. FRBR identifies four user tasks: to find, identify, select, and obtain. Here, the user task that is most applicable to this discussion is selecting "an entity that is appropriate to the user's needs (i.e., to choose an entity that meets the user's requirements with respect to content, physical format, etc., or to reject an entity as being inappropriate to the user's needs)."[6] If we catalog a deceptive work employing misleading or inaccurate author/creator or subject entries, or inappropriate classification, we are subverting the collating and evaluating objectives (in Cutter's objectives) and the selection user task (in the *Statement of International Cataloguing Principles* and FRBR).

Librarians, like the members of other professions, are also guided by codes of ethics. The *Code of Ethics of the American Library Association* does not provide specific guidance for catalogers dealing with deceptive works. Two sections of the code, however, touch on the topic broadly. It tells us to "uphold the principles of intellectual freedom and resist all efforts to censor library resources" and to "distinguish between our personal convictions and professional duties and do not allow our personal beliefs to interfere with fair representation of the aims of our institutions or the provision of access to their information sources."[7] The Association for Library Collections and Technical

Services (ALCTS) supplemented the ALA Code of Ethics in 1994, but is only vaguely relevant to cataloging these materials. The second point in *Guidelines for ALCTS Members to Supplement the American Library Association Code of Ethics* instructs librarians to strive "to provide broad and unbiased access to information."[8] Catalogers must take special care to examine their motives when they decide not to take the work at face value. Their decision must be based on objective and compelling evidence that the book is not what it claims to be.

The ALA document *Labeling and Rating Systems: An Interpretation of the Library Bill of Rights* provides additional guidance. It states that "when labeling is an attempt to prejudice attitudes, it is a censor's tool. The American Library Association opposes labeling as a means of predisposing people's attitudes toward library materials." It goes on to say that "prejudicial labeling and ratings presuppose the existence of individuals or groups with wisdom to determine by authority what is appropriate or inappropriate for others. They presuppose that individuals must be directed in making up their minds about the ideas they examine."[9]

In 2008 cataloger Sheila Bair proposed a code of ethics specifically for catalogers. Bair states that "catalogers are responsible for two powerful areas—access and naming."[10] They create "access points," which are essentially gateways to information. This highly relevant code states that the cataloger must be "honest and truthful in the representation of resources in regards to its subject area, the identity of those responsible for the intellectual content, and its accurate description."[11] Ah, but there's the rub: who gets to decide what constitutes an "honest and truthful representation"? One would think it would be self-evident, but as we examine individual cases, we will see that it is not.

In addition to ethics codes for the profession, we can consult our cataloging standards to guide us in cataloging deceptive works. The rules of description in *AACR2* instruct us to record the information in the resource as to its title, author, etc. The deceptive nature of a book, as noted earlier, does not impact descriptive cataloging, but access points may be affected. *AACR2* instructs us to "determine the access points for the item being catalogued from the chief source of information" and to use information appearing outside of the content of the resource "only when the statements appearing in the chief source of information are ambiguous or insufficient."[12]

If we look at *RDA*, catalogers are told that "the data describing a resource should reflect the resource's representation of itself"[13] and that "the data recording relationships between a resource and a person, family, or corporate body associated with that resource should reflect attributions of responsibility, whether these attributions are accurate or not."[14] The cataloger, however, is also instructed that "the data describing a resource should provide supplementary information to correct or clarify ambiguous, unintelligible, or misleading representations made on sources of information forming part of the resource itself."[15]

To summarize our survey of professional ethics and cataloging standards, censorship and bias are to be avoided. The representations of a resource in the catalog should reflect the resource's representation of itself. Catalogers must also create accurate and truthful representations of the materials that they catalog. Finally, the very foundation of librarianship is to place the needs of the user above all else.

How is one to incorporate all of these potentially conflicting qualities into one bibliographic record? The cataloger can make a user aware of the deceptive nature of the work through subject entries, particularly form subdivisions. Form subdivisions focus on those things that are not nonfiction. If we consider a work to be poetry, drama, or fiction, we have form subdivisions for that. The absence of one of these subdivisions indicates that the work is nonfiction, as that is the default form. Classification, another signal to the user, is, of course, integrally linked to subject headings. Both of these decisions affect, in fairly direct ways, what we communicate to the user.

Less obvious to the user is information included in authority records. This is where catalogers will normally note pseudonyms, but authority records are largely hidden from users in most online catalogs in use today. Communicating through the use of general notes, both in the authority record and the bibliographic record, immediately come to mind, but does that violate the admonition to refrain from the use of prejudicial labels? Arguably, it does not because, although information in the catalog record that is in conflict with what the work presents itself as may discourage users from consulting the work, it should not stem from bias on the part of the cataloger. The cataloging standards codified in *AACR2* and *RDA* allow for, in fact *RDA* urges, the cataloger to "provide supplementary information to correct or clarify ambiguous, unintelligible, or misleading representation."[16]

There are, however, at least two reasons that notes are not an ideal solution. First, studies have shown that when catalog users were asked to rank the usefulness of fields in bibliographic records, notes were ranked lower than other elements.[17] In addition, such notes are seldom included in search interface indexes, and, depending on the display in the online public catalog, they may not even be visible to the user.[18] Second, a key justification for developing *RDA* was to move away from text-based cataloging to data-based cataloging. Rather than building citations, as libraries have done under *AACR2*, *RDA* is designed to move toward an element-based approach. By creating metadata in libraries that is structured more like metadata services for the web, their data becomes more accessible on the web.[19] The increased granularity of bibliographic data also allows it to be parsed for machine manipulation, thus increasing cataloging efficiencies.[20] General notes do not move us toward increased granularity. Nevertheless, notes may be useful when cataloging deceptive works. Indeed, it is one of the few tools catalogers have. Librarians are heavy users of the online catalog, and certainly they could benefit from general notes.

We will look at possible cataloging approaches in more depth later. First, let us delve more deeply into individual cases of deceptive works.

Memoirs and Autobiographies

> The genius of memory is that it is choosy, chancy, and temperamental.
> —David Shields, *Reality Hunger*

In recent years, the publication of memoirs has exploded. Nielsen BookScan, which tracks about 70 percent of U.S. book sales, reported that total sales of books in the categories of Personal Memoirs, Childhood Memoirs, and Parental Memoirs increased by more than 400 percent between 2004 and 2008. Memoirs are as popular, if not more so, in Britain where they accounted for seven of the top ten bestselling nonfiction hardcovers in 2007 and 2008.[1] Such statistics lead to the question: What is the lure of the memoir to readers?

Theories abound: we live in a therapeutic culture; with the rise of virtual reality, people hunger for authentic reality; memoirs have been democratized, they are no longer the exclusive domain of great men, and we can now be privy to the lives of ordinary people; much as we are drawn to reality television, we are also attracted to the voyeuristic pleasures of "misery memoirs," memoirs that chronicle the trauma and suffering of an individual.[2] One, or all, of these theories may explain the appeal of memoirs to contemporary readers.

Authors, on the other hand, may be drawn to the genre by the belief that everyone has a story about his or her life to tell, and, frankly, a good story can disguise deficiencies in literary talent. Holocaust survivor Ruth Klüger observed that the book *Fragments* was declared a masterpiece when it was presented as a memoir written by a Holocaust survivor, but was viewed less favorably when it became apparent that the story told in *Fragments* was fiction. She explained that "a passage is shocking perhaps precisely because of its naïve directness when read as the expression of naïve suffering; but when it is revealed as a lie, as a presentation of invented suffering, it deteriorates to kitsch."[3] Memoirs are easier to get published than fiction, in part because publishers are less concerned about the quality of writing in works of this genre than they are about providing a compelling story to readers. Thus, we have James Frey, author of the discredited memoir *A Million Little Pieces*, admitting that he chose to represent his book as a memoir rather than fiction because it improved his chances of getting it published. In fact, the book was rejected seventeen times when it was presented to publishers as a novel.[4]

There is no mystery as to why publishers have increased their inventory of memoirs in recent years—it sells. One writer observed, "Over the past few years, publishers have responded to declining readership by developing an insatiable hunger for books that come with 'author survivors' attached. Why? Because they know that such books are about 100 times more likely to get reviewed and featured on National Public Radio and anointed by Oprah."[5]

Memoir, however, is a tricky genre. Unlike an autobiography, which is generally thought to be an account of a person's whole life, memoir tends to focus on one aspect or period in one's life. Gore Vidal offered a slightly different perspective in his 1995 memoir, asserting that "a memoir is how one remembers one's own life, while an autobiography is history, requiring research, dates, facts, double-checked."[6] This definition goes to the heart of what makes the memoir such a challenging genre to catalog. A cataloger's main objective is to present a book honestly and objectively to the catalog user. The tools at his disposal are inadequate for expressing nuance or ambiguity when creating a bibliographic record, and memoirs are full of both. Truth, however, is no less important in memoirs than it is in autobiographies, despite Vidal's statement, which suggests otherwise.

Because the memoir tends to be the form most susceptible to the charge of fakery, it is important for the cataloger to have at least a passing knowledge of an important literary concept that is often applied to this genre. Many, if not most, memoirs fall into the category of creative nonfiction, which has one essential characteristic that is of special interest to catalogers—veracity. The great essayist and memoirist Annie Dillard writes, "The elements in any nonfiction should be true not only artistically—the connects must hold at base and must be veracious, for that is the convention and the covenant between the nonfiction writer and his reader."[7]

Memoirs, however, are based on memories, which are inherently unreliable, making the line between fact and fiction permeable. Consequently, many authentic memoirs contain factual errors, but under the rubric of creative nonfiction these are not deceptive accounts, but rather memories of events recounted by fallible narrators who may misremember, or employ certain other limited alterations in details. For example, the author may change the names of some of the people mentioned in the book to disguise their identities for personal reasons, as long as they clearly state that. Dialogue in a memoir is inherently dubious. It is doubtful that one can remember word-for-word what she or others said in the past. A memoir, however, is not a tape recording, but rather literature, and authors are allowed to use narrative tools employed in fiction, such as dialogue. The reader only has the expectation that dialogue will generally conform to what the writer remembers. Unfortunately, the application of the term "creative nonfiction" to a work has been used to excuse a multitude of factual errors, when it actually has fairly narrow parameters. Creative nonfiction is the truth told creatively.[8]

Memoirs can be divided into several broad categories. One type are memoirs written by Holocaust survivors about their experiences in war-torn Europe and they are perhaps the most fraught. Critics tend to approach Holocaust memoirs very gingerly. Accounts of such traumatic experiences are not to be taken lightly or judged rashly.

Memoirs and Autobiographies

One journalist, writing about an allegedly fraudulent Holocaust memoir explained that "to doubt its veracity would look like moral callousness."[9] It is important, however, to correctly catalog fraudulent Holocaust memoirs, even though Holocaust deniers use them to support their benighted belief, arguing that "if a single detail in a testimony is false that renders the whole thing false; if a single testimony is fake, that renders all testimonies suspect."[10] We must nevertheless accurately represent such memoirs in our catalogs, for if we fail to do so we abet the contamination of the historical record.

Another category of memoir is those works whose authors claim a racial identity that is not authentic. In particular, non-indigenous people posing as Native Americans or other aboriginal peoples. The imposter's goal may be to get published, as was the case for Tim Barrus who claimed the identity of a Native American named Nasdijj, or his motivation may reflect a desire to improve his social status, as in the case of Buffalo Child Long Lance, a black man whose prospects in early twentieth-century North America were better if he posed as a Native American. He was attempting to overcome the real or perceived limits that his authentic identity imposed on him by the cultural norms of his time.[11] We may sympathize with his actions, but catalogers should not be accomplices to his deception.

A third category of memoirs, mentioned earlier, is facetiously referred to as "misery memoirs." These works may describe a variety of traumas suffered by the author, including victimization by satanists, seduction by drugs, and escape from poverty, to name a few. They often, but not always, employ a confession and redemption story arc. St. Augustine is widely believed to have written the first memoir, *Confessiones*, in the fourth century. Jean-Jacques Rousseau, however, is credited with the transformation of confession and redemption from a spiritual exercise to a secular one in *The Confessions*, published in 1782. Confession has come to mean revealing your transgressions publicly, and redemption is bestowed by your peers (readers) as witnesses to your unburdening.[12] *New York Times* book critic Michiko Kakutani observed that many memoirs are "propelled by the belief that confession is therapeutic and therapy is redemptive and redemption somehow equals art."[13] Cathy Glass, the author of a so-called misery memoir, has a simpler explanation. "When you read them," she speculates, "you feel that your own lot isn't quite so bad."[14] Not every memoir falls into one of these three categories and some span multiple categories. There are many variations, but the following works share one quality—they are not what they appear to be.

Catalogers cannot be expected to distinguish between a fraudulent memoir and an authentic one. For that we must rely on journalists, critics, and scholars. The memoirs discussed below, for example, have all been deemed questionable, or even inauthentic by members of one or more of these cohorts. The issue for catalogers is at what point has a reasonable consensus been formed and where is the line that separates fact from fiction. Although readers (and catalogers) accept that memoirs may contain some factual errors, they trust that the person who is recounting the experience actually had that experience. If that turns out not to be true, then many readers feel betrayed, as they did when questions arose about *A Million Little Pieces*.

Although we do not have a working relationship with the author, nor do we engage in fact-checking, it might surprise you to know that some people outside the library world regard catalogers as the final arbiters of genre. One critic of three memoirs suspected of being fraudulent noted that "many libraries have now added a note to the catalogue entries for these books, classifying them as fiction."[15] Journalist Ben Yagoda, author of a book on memoirs, bolstered his argument that *Go Ask Alice*, an alleged diary of a teenage girl, is fraudulent by pointing out that it is "shelved in the Young Adult fiction section of bookstores and catalogued as fiction in the Library of Congress."[16] A critic of the book *Wyatt Earp's Tombstone Vendetta* argued that, contrary to the author's claim, the book is fiction and stated that "the most telling hint may be *Vendetta's* classification as 'Juvenile Literature' by the Library of Congress."[17] We can see that catalogers have a crucial role to play in representing works accurately to potential readers.

Col. Crockett's Exploits and Adventures in Texas: Wherein Is Contained a Full Account of His Journey from Tennessee to the Red River and Nathchitoches, and Thence Across Texas to San Antonio; Including Many Hair-Breadth Escapes; Together with a Topographical, Historical, and Political View of Texas by David Crockett (1836)

Frontiersman David Crockett's body was barely cold following his death at the Alamo when a book claiming to be based on his diary appeared. The preface of the 1836 memoir *Col. Crockett's Exploits and Adventures in Texas* contained a quotation from a letter written by Charles T. Beale who declared that he had come into possession of Davy Crockett's diary, which concluded on the day before Crockett's death. Beale sent the diary to Alex J. Dumas, the writer of the preface, with instructions to publish it if he saw fit. Dumas felt the diary was indeed worthy of publication.[1] The resulting memoir was warmly received and sold steadily in the decade following its publication.[2] In fact, it formed part of The *Autobiography of David Crockett* published in 1923, being the last of three main sections of that book. A contemporary reviewer of the autobiography, perhaps less troubled than modern audiences by the blurring of fact and fiction, acknowledged that "part three is generally considered as not being either of David Crockett's writing or dictation. Nevertheless, this part is believed to be substantially true and whether authentic or not it certainly is very entertaining reading."[3]

In 1956, one of Crockett's biographers, James Atkins Shackford, was still trying to set the record straight by including an appendix in his book *David Crockett: The Man and the Legend* that contained the recollections of A. Hart of the Philadelphia publisher Carey & Hart. According to Hart, his partner, Edward L. Carey, suggested to writer and playwright, Richard Penn Smith, that if he could get a book out quickly about Crockett's adventures in Texas it would be a huge success. Carey said that "he wanted it done in great haste, and asked [Smith] when it would be ready for the printer; his reply was,

"Tomorrow morning." Smith did not disappoint, meeting every subsequent printing deadline. While the book imprint credits T. J. and P. G. Collins with publishing the book, Shackford makes a strong case that this was part of the deception and it was actually published by Carey & Hart.[4]

Col. Crockett's Exploits and Adventures in Texas may be an entertaining read, but it should not be mistaken for a primary resource. The earliest bibliographic record for *Col. Crockett's Exploits and Adventures in Texas*, a pre–AACR2 record, attributes authorship to Davy Crockett but has an added entry for Richard Penn Smith. It contains a general note quoting bibliographer Wright Howes' description of the book as an "ingenious pseudo-autobiography." The Library of Congress bibliographic record for the 1837 edition more accurately records the author as Richard Penn Smith and includes this well-constructed note: "A pseudo-autobiography; the preface purports to be written by an Alex J. Dumas, who claims that he received Crockett's manuscript from a Charles T. Beale, who wrote the final chapter. The work is generally ascribed to Richard Penn Smith. Cf. Sabin. Amer. Bibl., v. 20, p. 471; Burton's Gentleman's magazine, Philadelphia, 1839, v. 5, p. 119–121 and Dict. Amer. Biog." Neither record, however, indicates that it is fiction. Over one hundred years after its publication *Col. Crockett's Exploits and Adventures in Texas*, catalog users still need to read between the lines to determine what this book really is and who wrote it. Patrons should be told that it is not autobiographical by the inclusion the genre/form heading "Historical fiction," the form subdivision "Fiction," and a general note, such as the one quoted, above.

Awful Disclosures of Maria Monk: As Exhibited in a Narrative of Her Sufferings During a Residence of Five Years as a Novice, and Two Years as a Black Nun, in the Hotel Dieu Nunnery at Montreal by Maria Monk (1836)

Maria Monk's 1836 account of her traumatic experiences in a convent in Montreal arrived in the midst of a fervent anti–Catholic movement in the United States. The bias against Catholics may well have been stoked by anti-immigrant sentiments since there was a perception among nativists that large numbers of mostly Catholic immigrants were flooding the country.[1]

According to Monk she had a Protestant upbringing, but entered the Hotel Dieu Nunnery to receive an education. She eventually adopted the Catholic faith and then decided to become a nun. That is when her difficulties began. Monk was instructed by the Mother Superior that she must "obey the priests in all things," which she soon discovered included satisfying their carnal desires. The children that resulted from such assignations were immediately baptized and strangled. Monk witnessed the infanticide with her own eyes and saw nuns executed for refusing to acquiesce to the priests' lustful demands. When Monk became pregnant, she fled the convent because she could not bear the thought of her own child being murdered. She ended up at the charity hospital in New York, where she asked for a Protestant clergyman to hear her story. The clergyman, shocked by what he was told, urged Monk to write an account of her experience. The clergyman was the Rev. William K. Hoyt, president of an anti–Catholic missionary society in Canada, and he soon enlisted several other clergymen to the cause, including the Rev. J. J. Slocum who later declared that he wrote down the story as it was told to him by Monk. The book was offered to Harper Brothers, and although they were tempted to publish it, they realized that their reputation might be damaged by such a blatant attack on the Catholic Church. Instead, two employees of the publisher set up a dummy publishing house under their own names, Howe and Bates. The book sold over 300,000 copies over the next few years, becoming the best-selling book in the United States until the publication of *Uncle Tom's Cabin* in 1852.[2]

Then the war of words began. *The Catholic Telegraph* asserted that Monk, by her own admission was "a murderer, a fornicator, and a liar of the most depraved character," and that her Protestant supporters were only interested in making a quick buck and defaming the Catholic Church.[3] *The New England Telegraph, and Eclectic Review* was disposed to believe Monk because "the internal evidence of Maria's narrative ... cannot fail to convince every candid mind, acquainted with the circumstances, that she has told nothing but the *truth*." They allowed, however, that if her tale proved to be false "it cannot change the features of the 'Roman Beast,' nor wash the hands of the papal priesthood of that abominable filthiness with which they have been defiled."[4]

The Christian Watchman tried to rise above the fray by reporting that they had received a copy of the book from the publisher, "but in glancing at its pages, we perceived that it contained recitals of impurities, which in our opinion, whether true or false, no uncorrupted mind should ever read."[5] Eventually, proof of the book's dishonesty was contained between its covers. Monk had described various parts of the interior of the convent in her stories. With book in hand Colonel William Stone of New York went to the convent and compared its physical layout with the descriptions in *Awful Disclosures of Maria Monk*. Colonel Stone was inclined to believe Monk's account, but when he found that the convent did not match Monk's description, he was compelled to declare that "the priests and nuns are innocent in this matter."[6] His declaration largely settled the controversy among those willing to be swayed by facts.[7]

Monk's life actually followed a much different path than the one she described in her book. Her mother insisted that, as a result of a pencil being run into Monk's ear when she was an infant, she suffered a brain injury and was an unruly child who was constantly in trouble. After becoming involved in prostitution at an early age, she was sent to a Catholic Magdalen asylum in Montreal where she continued to get into trouble and was expelled when she became pregnant at the age of eighteen. She left Canada with the help of a former lover (reported to be the Rev. William K. Hoyt), who was the father of the child she gave birth to in New York. In 1838 she gave birth to another child out of wedlock and disappeared from the public eye until 1849, when she was arrested for picking the pockets of her current boyfriend.[8]

After her death in 1849, a phrenologists explained in an article in the *American Phrenological Journal* that Monk "was not necessarily bad and criminal, but was so susceptible that she was an easy prey to the influences of others, and has thus been the instrument of designing men until she lost all self-control and self-respect, and yielded to the unrestrained and perverted sway of her lowest animal passions."[9] There was little evidence of sympathy in this small death notice in the *Montreal Pilot*, which stated that "Maria Monk died the other day in N. York, after a life of drunkenness and crime.— Our readers will remember her wonderful book of revelation respecting the convents at Montreal, which turned out to be a volume of lies from beginning to end."[10]

The bibliographic record for the 1836 edition of *Awful Disclosures of Maria Monk* identifies it as an autobiography in the fixed field and includes the form subdivision "Biography" after the topical heading "Nuns." It is disconcerting to find that the record for the 2006 facsimile edition replicates this misinformation, when it is clearly a work of fiction. The use of the genre/form heading and form subdivision "Fiction" would be accurate.

The Life of John William Walshe, F. S. A. edited and introduced by Montgomery Carmichael (1902)

In the introduction to *The Life of John William Walshe, F. S. A.*, editor Montgomery Carmichael quotes the last will and testament of his friend Philip Ægidius Walshe who bequeathed to him all his "books, letters, papers, memoranda and manuscripts."[1] Carmichael explained that "the will … has put me in possession of a large and extraordinary collection of valuable MSS., and has at the same time laid upon me a task of no little delicacy and difficulty. These MSS. are the voluminous works of his father, the late Mr. John William Walshe…. Mr. Walshe was well known to scholars as perhaps the greatest living authority on matters Franciscan: otherwise he had practically no fame."[2] Carmichael wrote in the introduction that the book is a memoir of John William Walsh written by his son, Philip, before his death, although Philip's name does not appear on the title page.[3]

John William Walshe, born in 1837, was the son of a wealthy English merchant who was interested only in business and money. The father and son were opposites, however, the younger Walshe being interested in literature, possessing a sensitive temperament, and having no interest in joining the family business, which he nevertheless was forced to do. After two or three years, Walshe escaped to Leghorn (Livorno), Italy, where he was taken under the wing of Lord Frederick Markham. Under Markham's influence, Walshe became interested in spirituality, converted to Catholicism, and lived a life of asceticism and self-mortification.[4]

The book was met with praise by some. One reviewer said, "The story of John William Walshe … is, if not stranger than fiction, at least far more attractive than fiction commonly shows itself to be nowadays."[5] Another reviewer wrote, "For its literary art, if for nothing else, this sketch of the life and character of an English Roman Catholic is well worth reading. Imaginative in a high degree, full of picturesque description and vivid characterization, it reads almost like a work of fiction."[6]

Memoirs and Autobiographies

The Life of John William Walshe, F. S. A., however, was soon exposed as a fraud. A critic declared shortly after the book's publication, "Mr. Carmichael has produced a literary counterfeit of consummate art. In its way we have never seen it surpassed. It has already deceived the best judges."[7] *The Times Literary Supplement* was less charitable. They were not appeased by the publisher's announcement that the book was a work of fiction, arguing that "we are inclined to think that the title-page should have borne a word to the same effect."[8] Carmichael, the author, acknowledged that the book was fiction, but perhaps was a bit disingenuous when he asserted, "To my great astonishment some critics have taken it to be a real biography, while it surely must obviously appear what, as a matter of fact it is—a work of imagination from beginning to end."[9]

The records for the book published in London and the book published in New York designate it as fiction in the fixed field and both have the general note "An imaginary biography." The record for the American edition also includes a quotation from *The Nation* that states that the book "is but the product of Mr. Carmichael's busy brain." Both records should contain a subject heading for the nonexistent John William Walshe, including the subfield "Fictitious character." The form subdivision "Fiction" should be also be appended to the subject heading. The inclusion of the genre/form heading, "Fictional autobiographies," would be appropriate.

Long Lance by Chief Buffalo Child Long Lance (1928)

Chief Buffalo Child Long Lance's autobiography appeared at a time when white Americans and Europeans were craving authentic Indian stories.[1] In the foreword of *Long Lance*, his accomplishments are enumerated: presidential appointee to West Point, captain in the Canadian infantry, decorated war hero, chief of one of the bands of the Northern Blackfoot Nation, and a skilled journalist.[2] Long Lance himself wrote of growing up on the plains as a Blackfoot Indian, hunting for the increasingly elusive buffalo. He described the Indians' domestic life and the powers of the medicine man. The publisher, Cosmopolitan, was so enthused about the book that it printed ten thousand copies in the first run instead of the usual three thousand. *Long Lance* was met with broad acclaim. The *Philadelphia Public Ledger* gushed that it was "a gorgeous saga of the Indian race," and well-regarded anthropologist Dr. Paul Radin declared that "I cannot think of any work that could act as a better corrective of the ridiculous notions still prevailing about the Indians than this autobiography of Long Lance."[3]

Although most of this "biographical" information was not true, Long Lance's real life was almost as interesting as his fictional one, if not as exotic. He was born Sylvester Clark Long in 1890 in North Carolina to mixed-race parents. His mother, Sallie, claimed that her grandfather was a white slaveholder and her grandmother was an illegally enslaved Croatan Indian. Sallie's mother was the progeny of this union, and Sallie's father was also a white slaveholder. Sylvester's father claimed that his mother was a Cherokee Indian and his father was a white man.[4] Although the Longs may not have had a drop of black blood, as they claimed, in the late nineteenth-century South, they were not white, which meant that they were viewed as black.

When Sylvester Long completed the sixth grade, all the public education that he was allowed as a black person, he joined the circus and became friends with some of the Indians in the Wild West Show. They taught him some Cherokee words, trick horse-riding, and archery, knowledge that would make him a credible Indian in the eyes of most white people. Long realized that taking on an Indian identity could expand his opportunities when he applied to the Carlisle Indian Industrial School in Pennsylvania, claiming to be half-Cherokee. He was admitted, and a sympathetic teacher allowed him to change his name to Sylvester Chahuska Long Lance to help him gain acceptance with the other students.[5]

At the beginning of World War I, Long went to Montreal to enlist in the Canadian Expeditionary Force. He fought on the front for several months before he was seriously wounded and sent to a hospital in England. After performing clerical work in the intelligence service in London for the remainder of the war, he was discharged to Calgary.[6]

Still claiming to be Cherokee, Long worked as a reporter for the *Calgary Herald*. He was sent on assignment to several Indian reservations, where he met Anglican missionary Samuel Henry Middleton. Long wrote an article for the *Calgary Herald* praising Middleton's work in educating the residents of the reservations, and Middleton returned the favor by asking Long to speak at a reunion at his mission school. Middleton asked Mountain Horse, the father of an alumnus, to give Long an honorary Blackfoot name. Mountain Horse complied and gave him a name that translated roughly into "Buffalo Child." Long eagerly accepted the name, incorporating it into his byline at the *Herald* and Buffalo Child Long Lance was born. After leaving the *Herald* for a free-lance writing career, Long, apparently concerned that his new moniker wasn't impressive enough, added the honorific "Chief."[7]

Long Lance made his living by writing for Canadian newspapers, in addition to well-known American magazines like *McClures*, *Cosmopolitan*, and *Good Housekeeping*. By this time, he had changed his identity from Cherokee to Blackfoot. The Blackfoot comprise a confederacy of three American Indian tribes, the Bloods, the Siksika, and the Peigan.[8] Hoping to burnish his Blackfoot credentials, Long approached Eagle Speaker, an older Blood who had fought in several war parties against the Cree. Long asked for permission to become blood brothers with Eagle Speaker's son, Mike, with whom Long had been corresponding. Eagle Speaker agreed and the ceremony took place. Mike Eagle Speaker and Long would remain lifelong friends.[9]

Long's relationship with *Cosmopolitan* led to an offer to publish a boy's adventure book about American Indians. Long signed the contract to write it in 1927, but the focus of the book quickly changed on the advice of his editor. A first-person account of Long Lance's life growing up on the plains would be more compelling, the editor reasoned. The book Long wrote was a mixture of appropriation and fiction. Having no experience growing up on the plains, Long created his autobiography, *Long Lance*, by utilizing the childhood memories that Mike Eagle Speaker had shared with him. His autobiography was basically a chronicle of Eagle Speaker's young life, anecdotes he had heard from American Indians over the years, and some legitimate insights into Plains Indian life.[10] Despite the positive reviews of the book, there were many hints that it was not authentic. His accounts of hunting buffalo were false, given that buffalo were extinct in Canada and the United States by 1883, before Long was even born. He sometimes referred to "the Indians" and "they" betraying his outsider status.[11]

Long became the toast of New York City, hobnobbing with its elite residents and giving lectures on Indian life at cocktail parties. His triumph, however, also proved to be his downfall. *Cosmopolitan* sent a complimentary copy of Long's autobiography to the commissioner of the Office of Indian Affairs, Charles Burke, and asked him to let them know what he thought of it. Before he responded, though, Burke wanted to know more about its author. The results of his investigation were evident in his response to the publisher. He graciously wrote that "through your courtesy receipt is acknowledged of a publication of fiction entitled 'Long Lance,' for which please accept thanks. The book is very interesting and quite readable." Burke had learned that Long Lance never attended West Point, as he had long claimed, nor was he a Blackfoot. He could only conclude, he reported, that the book was not factual. Long's *Cosmopolitan* editor lost interest in him and never published anything else written by Long.[12]

Before his lies caught up with him though, Long received an extraordinary offer. He was asked to star in a movie being made by young naturalist and explorer Douglas Burden. Burden wanted to make a film that would accurately portray the Indian, something that Hollywood had failed to do, in his opinion.[13] Long could not resist the invitation, even though he knew the Office of Indian Affairs was investigating him. The movie, *The Silent Enemy*, was warmly received by the critics and Long was singled out for praise. *The New York Times* noted that "he serves this picture commendably—aye, courageously. He is said to have actually killed the bull moose."[14] However, one of the other actors, Chauncey Yellow Robe, was unconvinced that Long was a Blackfoot Indian, and took his doubts to the director who conducted his own investigation and discovered the truth about Sylvester Long. Long knew that his deception had been uncovered and, devastated, he fell into a depression. In 1932 he took his own life.[15] He might have been pleased to know that his obituary in *The New York Times* gave no hint of his true identity.[16] In fact, Long might have continued using his persona for a while longer. In 1936, a belated review of his autobiography avowed that "*Long Lance* is written by a full-blood Blackfoot, with a white man's education and a good record as an officer in the Great War, who is at the same time chief of a Blackfoot band and a professional journalist."[17] It was not until 1938 that the reviewer printed a correction.[18]

The bibliographic record entered in OCLC in 1978 for *Long Lance* published by *Cosmopolitan* in 1928 leads the user to believe that this is an autobiography. The code in the fixed field tells us that it is an autobiography and the subdivision "Fiction" does not appear on the record. The authority record is much more helpful. It includes a cross-reference for Sylvester Long and notes that he "chgd. Surname to Long Lance while passing as Indian." A note in the bibliographic record explaining the true nature of the book is necessary in order to provide the best service to the catalog user. Assignment of the genre/form heading "Fictional autobiographies" and the form subdivision "Fiction" would also be appropriate since both the narrator and the events depicted are fictional creations.

The Cradle of the Deep by Joan Lowell (1929)

Joan Lowell's memoir of her childhood spent on a schooner sailing the Pacific Ocean and the South Seas was a gripping, incredible page-turner. Her mother was sickly, and so Lowell lived with her sea captain father and his crew on the *Minnie A. Caine*, a trading ship, from the time she was a baby until she was seventeen.[1] The events she related were harrowing and disturbing, but were conveyed in an amusing and jovial fashion, whether she's talking about cutting up a shark, playing strip poker with the crew, or realizing that the cook put a dead cat instead of canned beef in the soup.[2] Her publisher, Simon & Schuster, advertised it as "the straightaway story of Joan Lowell's first seventeen years."[3] The review of *The Cradle of the Deep* in *The New York Times* acknowledged some skepticism, before declaring that it does not "question the veracity of the sea-going author. But she does trundle forth the expected with such infallibility that the product seems somewhat machine-made."[4] In the *Nation*, the reviewer, Arthur Warner, noted that "Joan Lowell's story reads like a collection of all the good sea anecdotes of which she ever heard. I don't assert that it is such; I don't know."[5] Despite some doubts about the credibility of *The Cradle of the Deep*, it quickly became a Book of the Month Club selection and sold more than 100,000 copies.[6]

The truth, however, came out quickly. Within a month her family's neighbors reported that Lowell had spent most of her childhood at home in Berkeley, California. Her father was a sea captain, but she and her mother accompanied him on short trips only occasionally. When the *Minnie A. Caine*, which Lowell had claimed sank, was discovered safely docked in Oakland, the book was completely discredited.[7] Simon & Schuster, while not willing to admit they had been fooled, issued a statement that read, "A literal letter-perfect autobiography was never intended by the author, nor was it featured as such by the publishers. We now discover that there is a considerably larger element of romanticized fact interwoven with the underlying sequence of truthful narrative than we had at first realized, but after the most careful scrutiny we are still satisfied that the essential honesty of Joan's yarn remains unassailable."[8]

Nevertheless, they were sufficiently chagrined to offer a refund to all dissatisfied customers who had bought *The Cradle of the Deep* through the Book of the Month Club. Few refunds were requested and the book moved from the nonfiction best seller list to the fiction best seller list before sales plummeted. In 1939, Richard Simon and M. Lincoln Schuster admitted to *The New Yorker* "that they were completely taken in."[9] Sea engineer Felix Riesenberg, who had vouched for the book's credibility when it was published, thought it was all much ado about nothing. He declared that "the book has authentic color and the assumption on which the story is built, be it cold fact or torrid fiction, is at least novel."[10] As for Ms. Lowell, she never admitted that *The Cradle of the Deep* was untrue and had a career as an author, tabloid journalist, and actress for several years following the publication of her first book.[11]

The bibliographic record attaches no "Fiction" subdivision to its subject headings of "Seafaring life" and "Sailors," and marks the book as a biography in the fixed field. The summary note describes it as "a story of the author's early life in the South Sea on board the copra-trading schooner Minnie A. Caine." Mr. Schuster, having shelved his copy of *The Cradle of the Deep* under "Travel and Exploration" in his personal library, which was arranged according to the Dewey Decimal System, would have approved.[12] Nevertheless, this book should be clearly designated fiction in the bibliographic record through the assignment of the form subdivision and genre/form heading "Fiction." It does not contain enough factual material about the author's life to warrant the genre/form heading "Autobiographical fiction."

Pilgrims of the Wild by Grey Owl (1934)

Grey Owl told acquaintances that he was born in Mexico in 1888, the son of Katherine Cochise, an Apache, and George MacNeil, a Scot who was a scout in the Southwestern Indian wars. When he was fifteen, he left his family and moved to Ontario where he was adopted by the Ojibwa tribe and given the name of Wa-Sha-Quon-Asin, or Grey Owl. The Ojibwa taught him woodcraft, how to snowshoe, canoe, and track and trap wild game. He used this knowledge to make a living, hunting and trapping until he enlisted in in the army in 1915 to fight in World War I.[1] By 1925, Grey Owl had returned to Canada and had acquired a companion, a Mohawk woman named Gertrude Bernard, otherwise known as Anahareo. She vehemently opposed trapping animals, particularly the beaver, believing that it was inhumane. Anahareo adopted a pair of beaver kittens whose mother had been killed in a trap and Grey Owl soon became fond of them, as well. He decided never to trap another beaver, thus commencing his transformation into a conservationist.[2]

Grey Owl envisioned wildlife sanctuaries throughout the northern part of Canada and also championed the prohibition of commercial traffic in animal skins. He believed that not only would this protect the animals, but it would prevent Native American culture from becoming commercialized. He spread his vision by giving lectures in Great Britain and the United States, delighting his audience with his Native American garb.[3] He also authored four books, the second of which was his autobiography, *Pilgrims of the Wild*. In it he recounted his journey from trapper to conservationist, and lightly glossed over his origins. Not surprising, since the tales that he had told about his parents and upbringing were fabricated.[4]

Grey Owl was actually born Archibald Belaney in Hastings, England, in 1888. His father, George Belaney, was from Scotland, but immigrated to Florida with his girlfriend, Elizabeth Cox, and her younger sister, Katherine. After Elizabeth died, George married Katherine and together they returned to England, where Katherine gave birth to their son, Archibald Belaney. Archibald was left in the care of his grandmother and two maiden aunts, and as a child became fascinated with American Indians.[5] He dreamed of going to Canada to live among the Indians and fulfilled that wish when he was eighteen. His first lessons in trapping and hunting were delivered by a white man whose family had taken Belaney in when he arrived in Canada. Soon he began creating his imaginary Indian heritage. Sometime after he returned from the war he became friends with an Ojibwa family and lived with them for two or three years. Here he was indoctrinated in Indian ways.[6] After this, his story unfolded more or less as he claimed.

When it was revealed, after Belaney's death, that he was an imposter, many were outraged and believed that he had created his Indian identity to promote his books; however, he adopted his false ethnicity long before he wrote his first book. Among many white Canadians, at least, he was seen as a self-made Indian, if not an Indian by birth. His work as a conservationist was not diminished by his questionable identity.[7]

In *Pilgrims of the Wild*, Belaney was not particularly forthcoming about his early background or his ethnicity. Given this, one could speculate that he was not prepared for the attention that his literary endeavors would bring his way. If Belaney sought to deceive the reader it was through omission rather than fabrication. Information about Belaney's imaginary ancestry came from his interviews, lectures, and letters, not his autobiography.[8]

The bibliographic record for the earliest edition of *Pilgrims of the Wild* contains no subjects that suggest that it is a memoir, nor is there any indication in the fixed fields that it contains biographical information. Instead it informs us that the book is about beavers and natural history. The main entry is "Grey Owl, 1888–1938," but the authority record provides a cross-reference for "Belaney, Archie, 1888–1938." A source note in the authority record further explaining the issues surrounding Belaney's identity, would be appropriate. Although the autobiographical details in *Pilgrims of the Wild* are false, this doesn't significantly diminish the value of the book's content to readers.

The Diary of a Surgeon in the Year 1751–1752 edited and transcribed by Ernest Gray (1937); *Surgeon's Mate: The Diary of John Knyveton, Surgeon in the British Fleet During the Seven Years War, 1756 1762* edited and transcribed by Ernest Gray (1942); *Man Midwife: The Further Experiences of John Knyveton, M.D., Late Surgeon in the British Fleet, During the Years 1763–1809* edited and narrated by Ernest Gray (1946)

Ernest Gray made good use of the leather-bound journal, passed to him by a friend who was distantly related to the journal's author, John Knyveton. Gray managed to extract three books from its contents.[1] The first book, *The Diary of a Surgeon in the Year 1751–1752*, elicited mixed reviews. *The Times Literary Supplement* allows that "it contains vivid–and we dare say reasonably accurate—descriptions of the sort of thing which happened or may have happened in eighteenth-century hospitals, matters of interest mainly to medical students, since the gruesome and ghastly details of operations may not appeal to those with weaker stomachs."[2] Most reviewers were not inclined to believe that what they were reading was a verbatim transcription of Knyveton's diary, as Gray claimed.

They had good reason to be skeptical since *The Diary of a Surgeon* was filled with anachronisms. *The Times Literary Supplement* review notes that Knyveton "has a curious fore-knowledge of idioms or words in use only in the nineteenth century or, indeed at any time between, say, 1815 and the present day. A little research in the O.E.D. in this connexion will be found both profitable and amusing. Indeed, the really odd thing is that John Knyveton seems to have very little familiarity with the ordinary modes of expression common in his own day."[3] Another review of the book chides Gray on his editorial skills, saying that "an editor may at most resume, he should never under any circumstances presume. In this connection Mr. Gray appears to have gone even further and so to have 'edited' the style of the diarist as to make him use words and phrases which did not come into existence until the 19th century. It is a great pity."[4]

Other reviewers spotted more substantive errors. Knyveton was depicted using digitalis in the year 1752, but the drug was not discovered until 1776. There was a discussion about dengue fever, which was not identified until 1779.[5] One reviewer dismisses the notion of a leather-bound journal all together, speculating that "this book is apparently based on the autobiography of Thomas Denman, to which are added statements by his son-in-law Matthew Baillie as they appeared in his seventh edition of 'Practice of Midwifery.'"[6]

The second book, *Surgeon's Mate*, was sparsely reviewed, but the final book, *Man Midwife*, was met with suspicion immediately. An exchange in the letters section of *The Times Literary Supplement* was sparked by a rather flippant review in the publication that noted the anachronistic word choices ("From the linguistic point of view it is perhaps unfortunate that Knyveton's diary was not discovered a good many years ago, since it contains many interesting usages of word and phrases that anticipate their earliest occurrences as recorded in the 'Oxford English Dictionary'") and questions about its authenticity ("Is all this, however, offered to the public as a genuine document of its period, or as a curious and misconceived form of fiction?").[7] One letter writer, concerned that readers might rely on the book as a historical work, was struck, once again, by the resemblance of Knyveton's autobiography to that of Dr. Thomas Denman.[8] Gray responded in his own letter that John Knyveton was an alias used to protect the privacy of his descendants, and that the original "was written late in life, so that the author's memory is occasionally at fault" and "to correct the slips of the author's memory … [Gray] made those interpolations whose verbal anachronisms have so distressed your reviewer."[9]

This appears to be the first time that Gray acknowledged that "Knyveton" was a pseudonym. Martin Evans and Dr. Geoffrey Hooper, in their article discussing the three books, worried that "people ... have been misled into thinking they are genuine" and noted that "many libraries have now added a note to the catalogue entries for these books, classifying them as fiction. Some libraries have not yet done so."[10]

An examination of the bibliographic records in OCLC show that they provide a fair representation of the books. The record for *The Diary of a Surgeon in the Year 1751–1752* still contains the form subdivision "Diaries," but also contains the general note, "The material ... was taken from journals and diaries of that period ... [and] represents a composite picture rather than the actual writings of a surgeon of the 18th century," attributing this information to a letter from the publisher. The form subdivision "Diaries" should be replaced with the subdivision "Fiction." The addition of the genre/form heading "Diary fiction" is also warranted.

My Sister and I by Friedrich Nietzsche, translated by Oscar Levy (1951)

Was *My Sister and I*, published by Boar's Head Books and distributed by Seven Sirens Press, Inc., in 1951, the last written work by renowned philosopher Friedrich Nietzsche? Purported to be just that, the publisher claimed that Nietzsche wrote the book between January 1889 and March 1890, while he was confined in a mental asylum in the Hungarian city of Jena. Oscar Levy, an Englishman and the editor of the first collected edition of Nietzsche's writings in English, was alleged to have translated *My Sister and I* from German into English.[1] According to Levy's 1927 introduction to the first edition, Nietzsche entrusted his newly written manuscript to a fellow asylum inmate who was being released, instructing him to take it to a publisher. The former inmate did not honor Nietzsche's request and held on to the manuscript until his son, on a whim, took it with him when he immigrated to Canada many years later. The son knew that his Canadian employer, an ex-clergyman, was interested in old books and so presented the manuscript to him. The ex-clergyman was familiar with Nietzsche's work and after careful study decided that it was authentic. He sent it to Oscar Levy with the request that he translate it into English, which he supposedly did.[2]

My Sister and I detailed an alleged incestuous relationship between Nietzsche and his sister, Elisabeth. Such provocative material could not see the light of day until Nietzsche's sister died in 1935. Even then it wasn't published until after the death in 1947 of the translator, Levy.[3] When it was finally published in 1951, Nietzsche's original German manuscript had disappeared.[4] This left few options for authenticating *My Sister and I*—Nietzsche, his sister, and the manuscript's translator were all dead. The book received a favorable review by a member of the staff of the Columbia University Library who describes it as "250 pages of disjointed but surprisingly coherent paragraphs" that "are, to put it mildly, explosive." Nevertheless, the reviewer stipulates that "if—as the publishers clearly believe—this is a genuine Nietzsche work it must rank as one of the greatest literary discoveries of the twentieth century; if all concerned, including Dr. Levy, have been deceived, it is the most skillful artistic hoax since the Van Meegeren Vermeers."[5]

Not everyone was convinced. Walter Kaufmann, a Princeton philosophy professor and translator of several books by Nietzsche, was foremost among those who doubted the authenticity of *My Sister and I*. He noted the publisher's delay in releasing the book until after the translator had died. Kaufmann also questioned whether a Nietzsche scholar like Oscar Levy would have made several errors in his introduction regarding the publication timeline of some of Nietzsche's works. He conceded, however, that the book itself, rather than Levy's introduction, required the most scrutiny. Kaufmann had several questions, including, "Was it written by Nietzsche? And if not, was it forged by a German and then translated in good faith? Or is there no German manuscript at all?"[6]

There were several peculiarities that troubled Kaufmann. These included wordplay and idioms that were common in English, but unlikely to be formulated in the original German. For example, "sense and sensibility" and "horse-sense" and "horseplay" appeared in the manuscript. Even more damning, there was a reference to a book by Paul Deussen, a German Orientalist and Sanskrit scholar, that was published a year after Nietzsche's death.[7] In addition, Maud Rosenthal, Levy's daughter, wrote a letter to the *Saturday Review of Literature* stating that "my father never wrote the introduction, he never translated, annotated or knew this fantastic and clumsy concoction of nonsense."[8]

Kaufmann claimed that a man named George David Plotkin, shortly before his death, approached him and confessed that he had been hired by the owner of Seven Sirens Press, Samuel Roth, to ghostwrite the book. Although Kaufmann said that in 1965 Plotkin "gave me a long handwritten and signed statement describing how, for a flat fee paid him by the publisher, he had written *My Sister and I*," this document does not appear to be extant.[9] There were, however, a few who believed that Nietzsche wrote *My Sister and I*. Walter K. Stewart, a professor of German and philosophy, argued that it could not be disproven that the book was written by Nietzsche, which has turned out to be true, but even Stewart acknowledged that Samuel Roth "was embroiled in questionable publishing practices."[10] Psychotherapist Heward Wilkinson took a postmodern lens to the book and concluded that *My Sister and I* has value regardless of its provenance. He asserted that "what matters is no longer what opinion we definitively come to about it but that it becomes a work we wrestle with."[11]

For catalogers, this is not a satisfactory conclusion. The record for the 1951 edition does what it can to acknowledge the controversy over the authorship of this book. "Friedrich Wilhelm Nietzsche" is presented in the bibliographic record as the person responsible for the content of the book. A caveat is also included in the form of a subfield that contains the phrase "supposed author." The record for the 1990 edition also includes this subfield. The purpose of this subfield is to denote the relationship between the personal name and the work. Unfortunately, "supposed author" is not an authorized relationship subfield in *RDA*. In addition, both bibliographic records contain general notes informing users that "the authorship of this work and responsibility for the translation and editorship by Levy are under dispute," citing two sources. Since there is no definitive verdict on the veracity of this book, this is sufficient.

The Long Walk: A Gamble for Life by Slavomir Rawicz (1956)

When *The Long Walk* was published in 1956 readers were amazed by Slavomir Rawicz's chronicle of his escape from a Russian labor camp. Rawicz was a twenty-four-year-old Polish cavalry lieutenant in 1939 when he was sentenced to twenty-five years hard labor in Camp 303 in Siberia on a bogus charge of espionage. In 1941, with the assistance of the wife of the camp's commanding officer, Rawicz planned an escape, recruiting six other prisoners to accompany him. What followed was a remarkable 4,000-mile trek through a diverse terrain that included freezing wilderness, searing desert, and soaring mountains, not to mention sightings of abominable snow men. Only four of the original escapees survived the journey that ended in India. When the book was published in 1956, Nash K. Burger of *The New York Times* wrote that "the author is revealed as a literate and civilized man, with something of a poet's sensibility—but as 'The Long Walk' also proves, a poet with steel in his soul."[1]

It is somewhat surprising that *The New York Times* reviewer went out of his way to praise Rawicz's writing style since the book was openly ghostwritten by Ronald Downing, a journalist for the *Daily Mail*.[2] Questions about the veracity of the book cropped up immediately. R. D. Charques, reviewer for the *Times Literary Supplement*, was puzzled by the clarity of Rawicz's memories of being transported to the labor camp compared to the dream-like quality of his description of the journey to escape. Charques noted that it was "truly an astonishing experience, but is it possible the Mr. Rawicz, so long after the event, has not remembered the details of the escape as clearly as he remembers the march into captivity?"[3] Eric Shipton, in his review of the book for *The Geographical Journal*, conceded that memories may be cloudy, but was baffled to see that "throughout the book, there are so many improbable circumstances, so many geographical details which fail to match our knowledge of the areas travelled, that it is impossible to trace the boundary between fact and fantasy."[4]

Nonetheless, *The Long Walk* continued to attract readers and was reissued several times, most recently in 2010 when a movie based on the book was released.[5] This was also the year that Linda Willis published her book, *Looking for Mr. Smith: A Quest for the Truth Behind "The Long Walk," the Greatest Survival Story Ever Told*. Curious about the identity of one of the survivors of the journey, Mr. Smith, she wrote about her extensive research into the details contained in *The Long Walk*. Her digging revealed much more than the identity of one man. First, she discovered an official document, with the help of a Russian rights organization called Memorial, that showed that Rawicz was granted amnesty and had been released in 1942, even though his book claims that he had escaped in 1941.[6] Second, Willis discovered a questionnaire in the Hoover

Institution in California, signed by Rawicz and filled out in his own hand, that stated that he had gone to Persia, not India after he left the labor camp. Willis had to conclude that Rawicz probably had been in a Siberian labor camp, but that he had never escaped from one.[7]

Rawicz died in 2004, two years before BBC Radio 4 aired a documentary on the controversy surrounding *The Long Walk*. In addition to the evidence that Willis had uncovered, BBC Radio 4 found Rawicz's military records at the Polish Institute and Sikorski Museum in London. They clearly stated that after he left the labor camp he rejoined the Polish Army in Russia. This seemed to remove any possibility that he had walked from Russia to India with six other escapees.[8]

The story Rawicz told became even more questionable when Polish war veteran Witold Glinski claimed in 2009 that Rawicz had based his book on Glinski's experiences, although the two had never met. Linda Willis had spoken at length to Glinski and found him credible. Glinski insisted that official papers located in the Polish Embassy in London proved that he had the experiences that Rawicz had claimed as his own in *The Long Walk*. No such papers were found, however, nor was there any concrete evidence that Glinski's claims were true. Glinski died in 2013.[9]

The bibliographic record for the 1956 edition of *The Long Walk* includes a summary note telling us that the book "describes the author's 1941 escape 'from a Soviet labor camp in Siberia with six other prisoners,'" but nothing in the fixed fields or subject entries indicates that the book is autobiographical. The record for the 2010 edition unequivocally identifies the book as autobiographical through its summary note ("true story"), its use of "Biography" as a form subdivision, and the "a" coding in the fixed field indicating that it is an autobiography. Interestingly, while ghostwriter Ronald Downing's name is included on the title page of the 1956 edition of the book indicating that he wrote the book based on Rawicz's experiences, the only mention of Downing in the 2010 edition is as the author of the foreword. Consequently, while Downing has an added entry on the 1956 record, his name is completely absent from the 2010 record. Although there are many indications that *The Long Walk* is not what it is claimed to be, this judgment has not been universally acknowledged. Nevertheless, catalog users deserve a general note in the bibliographic record alerting them to the controversies surrounding the book.

Travels with Charley: In Search of America by John Steinbeck (1962)

Travels with Charley, one of John Steinbeck's last works, describes a road trip across the United States that the author and his poodle, Charley, embarked upon. Steinbeck was confined mostly to Manhattan and Long Island for the previous twenty years by his literary success, and longed to engage with the "real" America. In 1960, he and Charley took off in a three-quarter-ton truck with a camper that he called *Rocinante*, after Don Quixote's horse. Leaving from Long Island, they traveled to Maine, then across to California, and back through Arizona, Texas, and the South before returning to Long Island.[1]

In his book, Steinbeck recounted his encounters with a variety of characters: a New England farmer who expounded on Nikita Khrushchev's shoe-pounding speech at the United Nations, a Shakespearean actor camping out in North Dakota who was eager to talk about thespian John Gielgud, a group of white women screaming obscenities at a little black girl entering a newly desegregated school.[2] *Travels with Charley* was met with generally favorable reviews. Orville Prescott of *The New York Times* opined that "this is a likable and amusing book," which "contains nothing of significance about the present state of the nation."[3] It was on *The New York Times* nonfiction best seller list for a year. The veracity of this book, however, has been called into question.[4]

In 2010, a journalist named Bill Steigerwald set out to retrace Steinbeck's journey, and became convinced that Steinbeck had misrepresented dates, places, and companions in his book. According to Steigerwald's research, Steinbeck spent many more nights in motels and luxury hotels than in his camper, and Charley was not his only companion. His wife, Elaine, accompanied him on more than half of his trip. Steigerwald created a timeline using newspaper accounts, biographies, and Steinbeck's letters, and found many discrepancies between these sources and accounts in Steinbeck's book. For example, Steinbeck's conversation with the farmer about Kruschev's performance at the United Nations took place weeks before the actual event.[5] Steinbeck's son John was convinced "that he never talked to any of those people.... He just sat in his camper and wrote all that [expletive]."[6] Steigerwald asserted that Steinbeck even "dropped hints in *Charley* that it wasn't a work of nonfiction. He insisted, a little defensively, that he wasn't trying to write a travelogue or do real journalism. And he pointed out more than once that his trip was subjectively and uniquely his, and so was its retelling."[7]

This charge was met with a variety of responses. *The New York Times* accepted Steigerwald's argument that *Charley* was "shot through with dubious anecdotes and impossible encounters."[8] An editorial indignantly proclaimed that "books labeled 'nonfiction' should not break faith with readers. Not now, and not in 1962, the year *Travels with Charley* came out and Steinbeck won the Nobel Prize for literature." It went on to say that "it is irritating that some Steinbeck scholars seem not to care."[9] Indeed, when Steinbeck scholar Jay Parini was asked about the book's accuracy, he said, "I have always assumed that to some degree it's a work of fiction. Steinbeck was a fiction writer, and here he's shaping events, massaging them. He probably wasn't using a tape recorder. But I still feel there's an authenticity there."[10] An English professor in California was likewise unperturbed, arguing that "whether or not Steinbeck met that actor where he says he did, he could have met such a figure at some point in his life. And perhaps he enhanced some of the anecdotes with the waitress. Does it really matter much?"[11]

Catalogers, who work in a less nuanced world, have more reason for concern about the book's veracity. When it was first published in 1962, the subdivision "Description and travel" was used in the bibliographic record. The fixed field for biography is left blank, and a literature classification number is assigned. Records for three subsequent editions indicate in the fixed fields that the book contains autobiographical materials, utilize the form subdivision "Biography," but classify it under "United States–General–History and travel." The evidence strongly suggests that *Travels with Charley* is a mostly fictional memoir and should be cataloged as such by utilizing the form subdivision "Fiction" and the genre/form heading "Autobiographical fiction."

Go Ask Alice by Anonymous (1971)

When *Go Ask Alice* was published, the author's name, as it appeared on the title page, was "Anonymous." A note from "The Editors" advised readers that it was "based on the actual diary of a fifteen-year-old drug user.… Names, dates, places, and certain events have been changed in accordance with the wishes of those concerned."[1] Readers had no clue who the editors were either, but the publisher claimed that the book was a lightly-edited transcription of a girl's diary. It was presented as nonfiction, and was aimed at an adult audience. *Go Ask Alice* invited the reader to follow a girl's descent into drug addiction, and ended abruptly with an epilogue explaining that "the subject of this book died three weeks after her decision not to keep another diary."[2] It continues, "Her parents came home from a movie and found her dead.… Was it an accidental overdose? A premeditated overdose? No one knows, and in some ways that question isn't important."[3]

The publisher, Prentice-Hall, realized early on that the book had greater appeal to teenagers than adults and moved it to the juvenile catalog. It was wildly popular with young people, with sixty thousand copies of the hardcover sold, and the Avon paperback selling one million, four hundred thousand copies in the first year of publication.[4] Reviews of the book were positive. One reviewer called *Go Ask Alice* "perhaps the most exciting book about adolescent involvement in the drug scene published this past year."[5] Another touted it as "an important book, this deserves as wide a readership as a librarians can give it."[6] The review in *Publishers Weekly* was possibly the only one that expressed some uncertainty about the veracity of the book, stating that "whether or not this is authentic (maybe we're all too cynical on that subject these days, but it does seem awfully well written, and in any case brilliantly edited) it is a book which should be read, and once started is almost impossible to turn away from."[7] The book was also made into an ABC *Movie of the Week* in 1973, with William Shatner starring as the girl's father.[8]

And so, the book was taken at face value until 1978, when Beatrice Sparks' nonfiction book, *Voices*, was published. The cover boldly declared that it was "from Beatrice Sparks, the author who brought you *Go Ask Alice*."[9] Armed with this new information, Alleen Pace Nilsen interviewed Sparks for *School Library Journal* in 1979, but the resulting article did little to clarify Sparks' exact role in the creation of *Go Ask Alice*. Nilsen reported that Sparks was vague about the work she claimed to have done with young people, but she said that she had once held a job in a drug abuse clinic in California. There, she came to realize that young people would benefit from counseling when they first became involved in drug experimentation. She was also vague about her academic credentials, but her biography in *Contemporary Authors* states that Sparks earned a Ph.D. It does not identify the educational institution that conferred her degree.[10] Her obituary simply says, "She received her doctorate degree as a grown woman and grandma."[11]

Sparks explained to Nilsen that she was often asked to speak about her work with young people at conferences and forums. It was through her involvement in a youth convention that she came to know the troubled young woman whose diary became the basis of *Go Ask Alice*. A counselor from the convention called Sparks in the middle of the night to tell her that a girl who had drug problems was hysterical and insisted on meeting with Sparks. Sparks, the girl, and her family became friends and that was why they entrusted the young woman's diaries to Sparks.[12]

After the girl died, Sparks decided to publish the contents of the diaries to help other young people struggling with drug addiction. To appease the girl's parents, and gain permission to publish the diaries, Sparks agreed to add other incidents and thoughts she had collected from similar cases. That way, no one would know for sure which entries had been written by their daughter and which entries were from other sources. In any case, the real identity of the girl has never been revealed. Sparks also stated that the young woman's family did not share in the royalties. According to Sparks, the two diaries were locked away at Prentice-Hall. The girl, however, had also written entries on loose slips of paper, which Sparks had discarded after she was done with them. Therefore, the diaries could no longer be wholly reconstructed.[13]

In 1980, when Sparks' book, *Voices*, was republished in paperback, the nature of her involvement in the creation of *Go Ask Alice* became clearer. The cover of the book announced that Beatrice Sparks was the author of *Voices*, as well as the "author of the Multi-million-copy International Bestseller *Go Ask Alice*."[14] The picture became muddled again in 1998, however, when author Linda Glovach published a new book, *Beauty Queen*, about a girl on drugs, and claimed that she had co-authored *Go Ask Alice*.[15]

Go Ask Alice became a perennial entry on the American Library Association's list of most frequently challenged books from 1990 to 2009 because it included profanity in abundance and scenes of drug abuse.[16] Perhaps it is partly because of attempts to censor it that critics have been reluctant to address the issues that arose as the result of presenting the book as a nonfiction work. In 2013, Nilsen recalled the circumstances surrounding the publication of *Go Ask Alice*. She suggested that "it is ironic that at first *Go Ask Alice* was exempt from our criticism because we did not want to say anything negative about the 'dearly departed' [teenager]. Now the book is exempt from critical reading and discussion because we teachers have time to read and ponder only what we are teaching. And because we don't want to risk being challenged by censors, few of us would bring *Go Ask Alice* in for a full-class reading."[17]

When the book was first cataloged, it was treated as adult fiction with the subject "Drug abuse—Fiction," which is surprising since the book was marketed as nonfiction.[18] We know this because that is the way it appears in *The National Union Catalog: A Cumulative Author List Representing Library of Congress Printed Cards and Titles Reported by Other American Libraries, 1968–1972*, a print resource published contemporaneously with *Go Ask Alice*. This is a rare case when the original catalog record contradicted the edict to catalog the book as it represents itself. The author was recorded as "Anonymous," but later the author was changed in the record to "Sparks, Beatrice." In addition, the subdivision "Juvenile fiction" replaced "Fiction." Although neither Sparks nor the publishers ever explicitly acknowledged the book was a work of fiction, the evidence strongly supports that conclusion. Therefore, the bibliographic record provides an accurate representation of the book as a work of fiction. The additional genre/form heading "Diary fiction" should also be applied.

I Married Wyatt Earp: The Recollections of Josephine Sarah Marcus Earp by Josephine Sarah Marcus Earp; edited and collected by Glenn G. Boyer (1976); *Illustrated Life of Doc Holliday* by Glenn Boyer (1966)

I Married Wyatt Earp received positive reviews when it was published and was a welcome addition to the pantheon of Wyatt Earp literature. It contained what many viewed as the definitive account of the 1881 gunfight at the O.K. Corral in Tombstone, Arizona, that made Earp a legend. The memoir was even referred to as the "Dead Sea Scrolls of the West." Touted as the recollections of Earp's common-law wife, Josie Earp, it made a valuable contribution to an emerging field of study: women in the American West. Enhancing the memoir's credibility, it was published by a respected university press and edited by leading Earp authority, Glenn G. Boyer, who had by this time written one book and several articles about Earp.[1]

By 1999, University of Arizona Press had sold 36,000 copies, making it one of the press' best sellers, but by then many people were beginning to question the authenticity of the book.[2] Historians were troubled by, among other things, the epilogue Boyer included in the book that described the complicated nature of his task, and suggested that he had chosen to apply some questionable methods. He wrote that it involved "merging two manuscripts, which contained vastly different materials presented in widely varying styles.... To establish a conversational standard for the combined first-person narrative, I interviewed and corresponded with many people who were intimately associated in life with both Wyatt and Josie.... From directions and clues picked up from such informants, I was able to arrive at a vocabulary and syntax that closely approximated the speech of the living Earps."[3] No one doubted that Josie Earp composed one of the manuscripts, with the help of two female Earp relatives. The other manuscript, known as the Clum manuscript, was allegedly written by Josie Earp with the assistance of a Tombstone journalist and former mayor named John Clum. Curiously, no one other than Boyer has ever seen this document.[4]

About half of the book, Josie's Tombstone years, was based on the Clum manuscript, according to Boyer. Boyer claimed that he had lost the manuscript, but gave different accounts of how this came to pass. In 1985, he told a researcher that he lost it when he moved from Hawaii to Arizona, about four years before *I Married Wyatt Earp* was published in 1972. In 1998, he said that he had lied in 1985 and that he lost the manuscript in 1972, but found it again before the memoir was published, only to lose it again later. In 1995, Boyer wrote a letter to a history association saying that the manuscript was "alive and well." When he was asked about this in 1998, he pointed to his scalp and said, "It is alive and well—in my head."[5] As if his changing story about the manuscript had not raised enough doubts, he told journalist Tony Ortega in 1998, "So, I put words in [Josephine's] mouth! So what?"[6]

This was not Boyer's only foray into controversy. In 1966, he published the *Illustrated Life of Doc Holliday*, which proclaimed on its cover that it contained "sensational photo discoveries from Doc's past."[7] A note after a transcribed letter in the book explained that "the material ... is actually in Doc's letters which are extant, in the possession of parties who are not willing to be identified with Doc.... In due time this material will probably be made available to some historical society or university library where the entire collection may then be consulted by students of Western Americana."[8] He re-released the book in 1989 with an introduction tipped in, explaining that the book was actually "a clever satire" in the "best tradition of Western journalistic hoaxes," intended to trip up "history fakers."[9] In fact he bragged that Paula Mitchell Marks, a respected academic historian, was his "latest victim" when she cited the *Illustrated Life of Doc Holliday* in her nonfiction book *And Die in the West* (1989), an account of the gunfight at the O.K. Corral.[10]

The University of Arizona Press played a large role in shaping *I Married Wyatt Earp*. Letters written by the press director at the time, Marshall Townsend, revealed that he repeatedly encouraged Boyer to put "more of yourself" into Josie's account.[11] Associate editor Kit Schiefele, who first handled Boyer's manuscript, however, chastised Boyer for taking out a line in his introduction that disclosed that Josie Earp's voice was a composite of several sources and not a literal memoir. She wrote that "in your earlier draft of the Introduction, you made clear that the manuscript you have presented is not solely the first-person writing of Mrs. Earp, and that you have written a first-person account based on her memoirs and other material as well. In your new Introduction you no longer make this clear. This is not fair to the reader—nor is it sound scholarship."[12] Boyer did not make the suggested change. Despite the discomfort of his editor, the University of Arizona Press published the book. Scheifele's successor, Karen Thure, said that she doubted the credibility of Boyer's sources from the beginning, stating that "I think it's a shame that anyone took *I Married Wyatt Earp* literally. It's somewhere between history and historical fiction."[13] By 2000, Boyer acknowledged that he was not a historian, but rather a "novelist, and a damn good one," and was calling his book "creative non-fiction," although this was not an accurate use of the term.[14]

When University of Arizona president Peter Likins was asked about the controversy, he stated: "It's not as though [Boyer] presents the book as being a lost manuscript. He presents the book as being a creation that is synthesized from a variety of source materials. And you know there's a lot of that now in contemporary historical accounting. And it's controversial as a class of activity, when you write in a kind of fictional format, using your imagination blended with historical information. And then the poor reader ...

has no way to separate what in the text is based on well-researched material and what in the text is kind of an interpolation, you know what I'm saying? But that's a scholarly dispute."[15] At first the press asserted that they stood by the book as a work of nonfiction. Christine Szuter, then the interim director of the press, wrote in a letter to the university president in 1999 that the press "as a scholarly publisher, does not examine primary sources for the books we publish."[16] Nevertheless, they were "looking for ways of changing the copy on the cover to actually reflect what is in the book."[17] In 2000, however, the press announced that it would no longer publish or sell the book.

By then, the damage was done. Gary L. Roberts, a Georgia college professor and historian, lamented that "the record has been poisoned. There is a great deal of material out there that relied on Boyer's falsehoods for source material. People who accepted him in good faith took him as a reliable source and unwittingly perpetuated the hoax. He's left behind a mess that has to be cleaned up."[18]

As distressed as historians were by the inauthenticity of *I Married Wyatt Earp*, catalogers should be equally troubled. The bibliographic record for the 1976 edition treats the book as an autobiography in the fixed field code, and "Earp, Josephine Sarah Marcus" is entered as the author/creator. The summary note tells us that the book "presents the memoirs of Josephine Sarah Marcus Earp, in which she recalls the adventures she experienced as the wife of legendary lawman Wyatt Earp, a marriage that lasted close to fifty years." The record for *Illustrated Life of Doc Holliday* likewise represents the book as nonfiction. The "mess" Boyer created will continue to grow as the record lures the next unsuspecting historian. To remedy this, Boyer should be designated as the author/creator. The form subdivision "Fiction," and the genre/form heading "Historical fiction" are appropriate for both books.

The Education of Little Tree by Forrest Carter (1976)

The Education of Little Tree is a book beloved by many a child (and adult) both in and out of the classroom. This autobiography, which took place in the 1930s, recounted Forrest Carter's life with his Cherokee grandparents after his parents died when he was five years old. Readers were moved by Carter's account of his gentle education in the ways of the Cherokee conducted by his wise grandparents. He learned that they lived amicably with nature, but not so harmoniously with white people, in particular the government. White people were a mystery and the government interfered in Carter's family's life in undesirable ways.[1] So appealing was the book to a broad range of readers that a review in the journal *Teaching Sociology* in 1991 encouraged teachers to incorporate it into their curriculums, stating that "it would also be useful in courses on Native Americans, race, ethnicity, gender, family, childhood, education, aging, death, and the environment."[2]

First published by Delacorte Press in 1976, the book's authenticity was challenged before it was even released. Carter had written a novel earlier, *The Rebel Outlaw: Josey Wales* (also published under the title *Gone to Texas*), that Clint Eastwood turned into

The Education of Little Tree

a film that was released in 1976. The attendant publicity for the movie included the fact that Carter had written an autobiography about his childhood with his Cherokee grandparents that was soon to be published. People who had known a man named Asa Carter in his native Alabama were sure that he was the same person who now wrote under the name Forrest Carter. When Carter appeared on the *Today* show, any doubts were dispelled. Bill Baxley, the Alabama State Attorney General asserted that "my chief investigator who has known Asa Carter since the 1960s saw Forrest Carter on the *Today* show. He positively identified him as the same person."[3] The copyright application for the book *The Rebel Outlaw: Josey Wales* also listed the same address as the one where Asa Carter had resided. Writing under a pseudonym is perfectly acceptable, except that Carter was not Cherokee, but rather a well-known white supremacist. Asa Carter wrote speeches for Governor George Wallace, including the address with the famous lines, "Segregation now! Segregation tomorrow! Segregation forever!" He had taken his pen name, Forrest, from the Confederate general Bedford Forrest, the first imperial wizard of the Ku Klux Klan.[4] Carter died in 1979, but the controversy lived on.[5]

The Education of Little Tree sold moderately well for Delacorte Press, but when it was republished by the University of New Mexico Press in 1986, its perceived message of environmentalism and multiculturalism struck a chord. It remained on *The New York Times* paperback best seller list for fourteen weeks. As of December 1997, the University of New Mexico Press had sold 600,000 copies.[6] The republication of the book attracted the attention of fans and critics alike. One of these critics, Dan T. Carter (no relation to Asa Carter), then a Southern history scholar who taught at Emory University in Atlanta, wrote an op-ed piece that was published in *The New York Times*. Professor Carter once again revealed that Forrest Carter's real name was Asa Carter, a man who had "carved out a violent career in Southern politics as a Ku Klux Klan terrorist, right-wing radio announcer, home-grown American fascist and anti–Semite, rabble-rousing demagogue" in addition to being George Wallace's speech writer.[7] Although some of Carter's acquaintances claimed that his mother was part Cherokee (a claim denied by his brother Doug), he was not raised by Cherokee grandparents.[8] Clint Eastwood wrote a letter to the *Times* in response, arguing that "if Forrest Carter was a racist and a hate-monger who converted to being a sensitive, understanding human being, that would be most admirable."[9] Such a transformation, however, would not make *The Education of Little Tree* any more authentic. Shortly thereafter, *The New York Times* moved the book from its nonfiction best seller list to its fiction list. *The Times* stated that "Mr. Carter's widow recently confirmed her husband's true identity, which he denied."[10]

In 1997, a film version of the book was released to good reviews. Many notable directors, including Steven Spielberg, had been interested in making the movie, but were uneasy about the controversy that had surrounded the book. Richard Friedenberg, the screenwriter and director who finally took it on, acknowledged Carter's disturbing history, but said that he believed that "his apology was in his troubled literature."[11] Friends who knew Carter near the end of his life, however, maintained that he remained a bigot until his death.[12]

The bibliographic record for the 1976 Delacorte Press/Eleanor Friede edition utilizes the subject entry "Cherokee Indians–Fiction." The 1976 University of New Mexico Press record employs the form subdivision "Biography," and indicates in the fixed field that the book is autobiographical. The form subdivision "Fiction" should replace "Biography." The book should also be classified in literature, rather than history as the University of New Mexico Press record indicates, in order to collocate Carter's works of fiction. The genre/form heading "Fictional autobiographies" should also be used in both records. The authority record for Forrest Carter is a little more informative. There is a cross-reference for Asa Earl Carter, and a note identifying him as a "Ku Klux Klan leader, segregationist speech writer, and later famed western novelist."

Michelle Remembers by Michelle Smith and Lawrence Pazder (1980)

In 1979 Thomas B. Congdon, Jr., part-owner of publisher Congdon & Làttes, eagerly awaited the release of what he hoped would be "the biggest nonfiction book I've ever published ... 'Michelle Remembers,' the true story of a little girl given by her parents to the Satanic Church as the subject of a ritual."[1] Although we don't know if his hopes were realized, there is no doubt that *Michelle Remembers* succeeded in starting a panic. Before the book's publication, the phrase "satanic ritual abuse," or SRA, did not exist. After its publication, the floodgates opened, and scores of people claimed to have endured such abuse.[2]

Michelle Smith consulted psychiatrist Larry Pazder in 1976 after she experienced a terrifying dream in which hundreds of tiny spiders exploded out of a scratch in her arm. Eventually, Smith began remembering disturbing ordeals that she was subjected to as a child by her mother. These memories included sexual abuse, satanic ritual, infanticide, and a battle between the devil and the Virgin Mary.[3] Smith did have a difficult childhood. Her mother died when she was fourteen, and her father placed her in the custody of her maternal grandparents.[4] Was satanic ritual abuse another burden that she had to bear?

Although Pazder looked for medical records from Smith's childhood to corroborate her story, he found none. Nevertheless, he was thoroughly convinced she was telling the truth, stating that "in the beginning I wondered if she had made things up, but if this is a hoax, it would be the most incredible hoax ever."[5] Smith and Pazder later wed. Smith, anxious to be of help, offered to cooperate with religious and secular investigators. There was talk of a movie and Pazder and Smith suggested casting Christopher Plummer as a satanist priest and Dustin Hoffman as Pazder. Although no movie was ever made, *Michelle Remembers* earned a $100,000 hardcover advance and $242,000 in paperback sales.[6]

It was also a very influential book, ushering in the era of satanic ritual abuse, which ended, by most accounts, in the early 1990s. During this period, newly recalled memories of SRA resulted in thousands of accusations of satanic abuse. One of the most high-profile cases began at the McMartin Preschool in Manhattan Beach, California.

A parent of a child who attended McMartin claimed that her son had been sexually abused there. Although the district attorney declined at first to prosecute the owner or staff due to a lack of evidence, the chief of police sent a letter to the parents of the children enrolled in the preschool informing them that the charges had been dropped, but warning them to be alert. After the police pressured parents of the children at the preschool to question their children about satanic activities, several of the youngsters recalled witnessing animal sacrifice, and being flown to Palm Springs in hot air balloons for satanic events. The prosecutor asked for, and got, indictments against the owner of the preschool and several staff members. It took seven years for all of them to be exonerated.[7]

The media feasted on the juicy details of SRA. Stories about Smith's satanic experiences appeared in *People Weekly* and *National Enquirer*. The high (or low) point of the frenzy was Geraldo Rivera's two-hour television special on satanism, *Devil Worship: Exposing Satan's Underground*, which was viewed by about twenty million people in 1988.[8]

More repressed memories surfaced. A national random sample survey of clinical psychologists who were members of the American Psychological Association was conducted in 1990 through 1991. The 802 psychotherapists surveyed reported almost 3,000 cases from 1980 to 1990 that they defined as satanic ritual abuse. Following publicity about the McMartin Preschool case, the panic spread with new accusations of abuse coming from many states and cases were even popping up in Great Britain, Canada, Australia, New Zealand, and Wales.[9]

By 1990, the hysteria was subsiding. As of 1998, no law enforcement agency or research study had uncovered any physical evidence that would support a single account of satanic ritual abuse.[10] *The Mail on Sunday* published an investigative report that included refutations by Smith's family and neighbors of the abuse she claimed to have suffered. Her father, Jack Proby, asserted that his wife was a good mother who was never involved in satanic worship. Their family doctor, Andrew Gillespie confirmed that he remembered her mother as a "kindly woman." One of their neighbors agreed and argued that "a little girl could not have been tortured without someone hearing." Even Smith's psychiatrist and husband, Pazder, seemed to equivocate. When asked if it mattered if her story was true or not as long as she believed it happened, he replied that "we are all eager to prove or disprove what happened, but in the end it doesn't matter."[11]

It does matter to librarians, however. The earliest bibliographic record treats the book as nonfiction. Neither the publisher nor the authors have stated that the book is fiction and while the evidence suggests that it is, it is not conclusive. Therefore, it would be rash to replace the subject entry of "Satanism Case studies" with the subject entry "Satanism–Fiction." A general note cited from a reliable source summarizing evidence that her claims are questionable, however, should be added.

Satan's Underground by Lauren Stratford (1988)

Lauren Stratford was a troubled young woman, but then that was to be expected if you believed her account of the satanic ritual abuse she suffered throughout her childhood.

Memoirs and Autobiographies

In her 1988 book, *Satan's Underground*, she told a shocking story of the physical and psychological abuse she was subjected to from the time she was four years old until she was in her early twenties. She was raped, tortured, and forced to participate in the sacrifice of babies. This horror began when Stratford's mother allowed a day laborer to rape her when she was six years old, in lieu of paying him for his services. Her mother also coerced her into posing for pornographic photographs and introduced her to bestiality when Stratford was eight. She fled her mother's home and went to live with her father, but her mother was still able to convince Stratford to report to a pornographer's studio where her abuse continued. Victor, the pornographer, soon immersed Stratford in the world of satanism, forcing her to attend satanic rituals and demanding that she participate in rituals of child-sacrifice. When she refused, Victor told her that he would ritually kill a baby each week until she agreed. After four weeks she was locked in a metal drum with the dead bodies of the four babies who had been sacrificed. She finally acquiesced and, on a Halloween night, participated in her first, and last, child-sacrifice ritual.[1]

Stratford's experiences debilitated her physical and emotional health to such an extent that she was hospitalized forty times during one eight-year period. During that time, she received the counseling that she needed to begin healing, and helping others. Stratford claimed that she had personal knowledge of the McMartin Preschool ritual child abuse case in Manhattan Beach, California (see entry for *Michelle Remembers*). Although the parents involved in that case wanted to believe Stratford when she said she had been trapped in the McMartin abuse ring, her story was maddeningly vague. She said she feared for her life if the ring found out that she was talking about her experiences with them. Stratford finally agreed to be taped while recounting her story by one of the parents if her face was obscured. The McMartin parents, who viewed the tape or were present when it was being made, were not convinced that Stratford was telling the truth. One parent, Leslie Floberg, said, "That's just it. She [Stratford] seemed to be telling us exactly what we wanted to hear.... She described most things in very general terms. The only things she described in detail were incidents that had already been described in detail on a recently aired CNN television special about our case."[2] Stratford also claimed in the tape to have had a lesbian relationship with Virginia McMartin, one of the defendants in the preschool satanic-ritual trial. Despite having misgivings, one of the McMartin parents introduced Stratford to Johanna Michaelson, the Christian author of *The Beautiful Side of Evil*. A few months later Michaelson's publisher, Harvest House, published Stratford's book, *Satan's Underground*, with Michaelson's strong backing.[3]

Stratford's tale, incredible to begin with, was almost totally lacking in details, such as dates, places, and names. *Cornerstone Magazine* published an investigative report after the book was released, in which they reported being told by Harvest House that it "possessed documentation more than sufficient to prove her story."[4] *Cornerstone*, however, discovered that Stratford's given name was Laurel Willson and that the publisher had never talked to any of her relatives to verify details in her book. In addition, although Willson/Stratford claimed that she had given birth to three children, all of whom had been ritually murdered, no one who knew her at those times remembered noticing that she was pregnant. Harvest House cited three reasons that they believed Stratford was telling the truth. First, she had told the same story consistently to several staff members at various times, and she seemed sincere. Second, they had spoken to experts who confirmed that such things had happened to others. Finally, they had gathered character references from her supporters.[5] Despite this "evidence," the publisher subsequently withdrew her book in 1990. Pelican Publishing, however, reissued *Satan's Underground* in 1991 and also published two subsequent books Stratford wrote, *I Know You're Hurting* and *Stripped Naked*.[6]

If there were any doubts about the fictitious nature of *Satan's Underground*, Stratford put those to rest when she reemerged in 1997 as a different person, a Holocaust survivor named Laura Grabowski. Grabowski was the surname of her Polish Catholic maternal grandparents. She insinuated herself into the Child Holocaust Survivors Group of Los Angeles, and while she didn't write a book about her alleged Holocaust experience, she did copyright a poem, "We Are One," portraying herself as a Jewish survivor. In 1997 Grabowski contacted another Holocaust survivor, Binjamin Wilkomirski, who had recently published the best-selling book *Fragments: Memories of a Wartime Childhood*, in which he chronicled his childhood internment in Auschwitz-Birkenau (see entry for *Fragments*). He claimed that he remembered Grabowski from the camp and later an orphanage. Grabowski also insisted that she remembered Wilkomirski.[7] After it was revealed that Wilkomirski was not a Holocaust survivor, however, their common recollection was moot.

The bibliographic record for *Satan's Underground* indicates in the fixed field that it is an autobiography and the use of the subdivision "Biography" confirms this. This is also true for the record for the 1991 republished edition. However, the subdivision "Fiction" and the genre/form heading "Fictional autobiographies" would be more accurate since there is verifiable evidence that Stratford is a fictional identity and that her story is also fiction. Also, a general note citing a reliable source regarding the deception should be added to the bibliographic record, and a note documenting her multiple identities should be included in the authority record.

Mutant Message Downunder by Marlo Morgan (1991)

Marlo Morgan wrote *Mutant Message Downunder* to convey an important message to the world. Morgan was a health-care professional in Missouri in 1985 when she was invited by an Australian she met at a conference to come to Brisbane for three or four months to become acquainted with the Australian health-care system and do volunteer work at a pharmacy. While there, Morgan also worked with a group of indigent Aboriginal youths, and she assumed that this was why she was invited to a tribal conference two thousand miles away, on the other side of the Australian continent.[1] Instead, she claimed that she was kidnapped by the "Real People Tribe" and forced to go on a "walkabout" in an undisclosed location with them. She was told that she had been specially selected to carry their message to the outside world and she adopted the name "Traveling Tongue." Morgan learned that the tribe had decided to stop procreating and die out because the Earth's environment was being destroyed. She was to warn her people to turn away from their Western materialism before it was too late.[2]

When she returned to the United States, Morgan took her mission seriously, giving lectures and self-publishing a book in 1991 detailing her experiences. She printed 350,000 copies, selling most of them for ten dollars, but also giving away 100,000 copies. She sent the manuscript, unsolicited, to Stillpoint Publishing, part of the Stillpoint School of Advanced Energy Healing. They were interested in publishing her book, but Errol Sowers of Stillpoint recounted that he started getting a lot of phone calls from Australia, questioning the veracity of the book. Stillpoint asked Morgan to authenticate five or six details having to do with location, time, and individuals. When this verification was not forthcoming, Stillpoint sold the rights back to Morgan for a fraction of their estimated investment.[3]

In 1994, a literary agent named Candice Fuhrman read Morgan's self-published book and quickly convinced Morgan to let her represent her. HarperCollins beat out Bantam and two other rival publishers, paying $1.7 million for the publishing rights. HarperCollins, however, made some significant changes. They removed most of the numerous typographical errors, and corrected cultural inconsistencies, such as Morgan's claim that she borrowed a quarter (a currency that does not exist in Australia) to make a phone call when she emerged from the desert. The biggest change that they made, however, was that they classified *Mutant Message Downunder* as fiction, unlike the self-published version that was marketed as a true story. Morgan, however, wanted to have it both ways. She claimed that she and her publisher had decided on this classification, because she wanted to protect the Aboriginal people she took her lessons from, and refused to divulge specific information that might make them identifiable. At the same time, Morgan maintained that everything in the book had actually happened.[4]

As the book deal was being finalized, Morgan also sold the movie rights for the book to United Artists, who wasted no time gearing up for production. Both Goldie Hawn and Susan Sarandon were approached to play the lead role. By March 1995 reports revealed that the movie had been scripted and they were seeking a director, but by 1997 talk of the film evaporated.[5]

This was perhaps because the Aboriginal Australian community's doubts about the veracity of *Mutant Message Downunder* were being heard. The book came to the attention of Robert Eggington, the coordinator of the Dumbartung Aboriginal Corporation, a Nyoongah (an Australian Indigenous peoples) arts advocacy organization. Dumbartung organized a series of meetings with Aboriginal communities and it soon became clear that none of them had any knowledge of Morgan, nor had any of them heard of the "Real People Tribe." Dumbartung also commissioned Dr. John P. Stanton, from the Berndt Museum of Anthropology at the University of Western Australia, to prepare a report on the book.[6] He concluded "that it demonstrates more of the author's imagination than any first-hand experience of living with, and knowledge of desert Aborigines beyond that available in any popular text."[7]

After the Dumbartung report came out, a delegation of eight Australian Aboriginal people traveled to the United States to confront Morgan. During a telephone conference call between the delegation in Los Angeles and Morgan in New York, Australian and international media reported that Morgan had apologized and promised to share a written apology within forty-eight hours. No written apology ever appeared, however, and she refused to meet with the delegation again. The controversy did not affect the public's interest in the book, however. It remained on *The New York Times* best seller list for thirty-one weeks, and Perennial, a HarperCollins imprint issued an anniversary edition in 2004.[8]

Even though the 1991 self-published edition of *Mutant Message Downunder* represented itself as nonfiction, the bibliographic record treats it as fiction with its assignment of the form subdivision "Fiction." The record for the first HarperCollins edition also utilizes the "Fiction" subdivision and classifies it as fiction. Both records contain the same summary note: "An American woman's fictionalized account of her life with the Aborigines of Australia." The genre/form heading "Fiction" would also be an appropriate addition.

A Rock and a Hard Place: One Boy's Triumphant Story by Anthony Godby Johnson (1993)

This book's saga began before it was written. In 1991 Paul Monette, the author and gay activist, received a letter from a thirteen-year-old boy named Anthony Robert Johnson (later known as Anthony Godby Johnson). It expressed the boy's admiration for Monette's books *Love Alone* and *Borrowed Time: An AIDS Memoir.* Young Tony admitted that he "sat with the dictionary to read your book, but ... learned *lots* of new words." He included a photo of himself.[1]

Monette began a correspondence with Tony and soon he became so charmed by the boy that he spent hours talking to him on the phone. Tony told him in these conversations that he had suffered greatly in his short life. Tony's father was a New York City policeman, but he was also a sadist who beat Tony and pandered him to a ring of pedophiles. He had no bed, no winter coat, nor even a toothbrush. When, at one point, depression overcame him, he called a national hotline and spoke to Earnist Johnson, a black man from the South, who encouraged Tony to contact child-welfare services in Manhattan. He spoke to a woman named Vicki who arranged for him to go to the hospital where they discovered that he had fifty-four broken bones that had healed badly and that he also had syphilis. Vicki soon took Tony in to live with her. Meanwhile, Johnson came to visit Tony and ended up falling in love with Vicki, marrying her, and adopting Tony as well as Vicki's two daughters from a previous marriage. Tony's policeman father and his biological mother were prosecuted and sentenced to twenty-five years to life in jail. Tony's travails were not over, however, as he was diagnosed with AIDS in 1991 and subsequently lost a leg and a testicle to the disease.[2]

Tony's adopted mother, Vicki, reached out to Jack Godby, a leader of the AIDS

Memoirs and Autobiographies

Mastery Workshops, to counsel Tony over the phone. He and the boy became so close that Tony took Godby as his middle name. Monette remained Tony's constant confidant and advisor in their nightly telephone conversations. He encouraged Tony to write down his story and referred him to his editor at Crown Publishing, David Groff.[3] Tony's circle of friends eventually expanded to include Fred Rogers of *Mr. Rogers Neighborhood*, Keith Olbermann of ESPN, and author Armistead Maupin. All were enchanted by Tony's mixture of innocence, wisdom, and strength and developed close friendships with him, especially Maupin. When Tony's memoir, *A Rock and a Hard Place*, was published in 1993 by Crown, Monette and Maupin wrote blurbs for the book and Rogers wrote the afterword.[4]

One by one, however, Tony's dear friends became troubled by the fact that they were never allowed to visit him. He was always too weakened by the tuberculosis that he had contracted, or the fever that he constantly ran. One day Maupin's partner, Terry Anderson, chatted on the phone with Tony and Vicki and after he hung up he remarked on the similarity between Vicki's and Tony's voices. Although the pitch was different, the cadence and rhythm were the same.[5]

Newsweek reporter Michelle Ingrassia was also suspicious. She thought it was strange that there was no photograph of Tony on the jacket of his memoir and some of the sentences didn't sound as if they had been written by a teenager. For example, it seems unlikely that an adolescent would write that "diseases were a means of financing sports cars for cocky physicians who thought they had the world by the short hairs by virtue of their prescription pads." Also, she couldn't track down any of the people Tony mentioned in the book. Ingrassia lamented that "trying to find the real Tony is like getting trapped in a page of 'Where's Waldo?'"[6] She noted that although Tony had TB and his lungs had been damaged by pneumonia, Tony never wheezed or coughed in a recent radio interview. She could find no evidence that Tony's parents had been prosecuted and jailed as he claimed. Nobody at Crown had ever seen him, nor had any of his telephone confidants. Ingrassia was convinced that Tony did not exist and speculated that Paul Monette had actually written the book, remarking that "both loathe book reports and love plush afghans" and used similar phrases in their writing.[7] When her story appeared in *Newsweek* in 1993, Monette and his agent vehemently denied the charge, as did Crown Publishing.[8]

Monette, however, was beginning to have doubts himself. He tried to arrange a press conference for Tony, but Vicki gave multiple excuses that made such an event impossible: she had no car, Tony was too sick, she didn't want the press in her home. Although a press conference was out of the question, Vicki invited Associated Press reporter Leslie Dreyfous, who she judged to be sympathetic, to visit Tony at their Union City, New Jersey, home. A second A.P. reporter interviewed Dreyfous and wrote the story, which confirmed that Dreyfous had met Tony in person. His face was swollen and he wore sunglasses, but the voice was the same one she had heard when she spoke to him on the phone.[9]

The A.P. story calmed some of the suspicion that the *Newsweek* story had raised. HBO wanted to turn *A Rock and a Hard Place* into a cable movie and had already paid

Tony an advance of twenty-five thousand dollars, but its insurers wanted reassurance that Tony existed. They wanted him to meet with the screenplay writer before they proceeded. Although Tony would have received an additional $100,000 if he agreed to the meeting, Vicki said no and the HBO movie was cancelled.[10]

In 1995, a television producer named Lesley Karsten read Tony's book and wanted to incorporate his story into a documentary about children that she was working on for ABC. Tony agreed and in 1997 the documentary *About Us: The Dignity of Children* aired. Tony narrated his story, but did not appear in the documentary. Instead, a child actor played his part, a detail that was only revealed in the credits. By 1998, Tony was no longer living with Vicki. According to him, Vicki and Earnist Johnson had divorced and she had moved to Illinois with her new husband. Tony revealed that he had begun living with Lesley Karsten, but remained elusive. Karsten claimed that Tony was at death's door, and personal contact was out of the question.[11]

Keith Olbermann, however, had been convinced by the *Newsweek* story that Tony did not exist and ceased communication with the boy. Armistead Maupin was also growing skeptical, but was reluctant to accept that the boy he deeply cared for did not exist. Seeking a creative outlet for this dissonance he signed a six-figure contract with HarperCollins in 1994 to write a novel inspired by his relationship with Tony. For three years, however, he found himself unable to write about it. Meanwhile, he continued to talk to Tony on the phone and in 1997 he made one last-ditch effort to meet him in person. When Maupin was again thwarted, he called Tony and told him about his plan to write a fictional account of Tony's story. Tony had no problem with that because he said, "I know you love me and I can trust you."[12] When Maupin's book *The Night Listener* was published in 2000, however, Maupin received a call from Vicki who was furious and claimed the he had "trashed" Tony. They never spoke again.[13] Six years later *The Night Listener* was adapted for a movie with the same title. At that time Maupin speculated that "maybe Tony was her [Vicki's] imaginary friend. He certainly was mine."[14]

Maupin's novel sparked the interest of a journalist named Tad Friend who wrote an investigative story about Tony for *The New Yorker* in 2001. His conclusion that Tony was Vicki's creation was supported by a total lack of evidence that he actually existed. Friend discovered that Vicki's maiden name was Vicki Fraginals, and although she had lived in Union City, New Jersey, as she claimed, none of her neighbors recalled seeing either her husband, Earnist Johnson, or Tony. Vicki's family acknowledged that they had heard of Tony, but had never actually seen him. The Manhattan district attorney's office had no record of a trial of a policeman who had abused and prostituted his son. Crown editor David Groff, perhaps unwilling to entertain the thought that he had been duped, continued to profess that Tony existed even though he had never seen him. The few people who claimed to have seen Tony communicated with Friend in letters or e-mails, but none were willing to meet Friend in person.[15]

Despite the compelling evidence that Friend cites that appears to substantiate that Tony was not a real person, it is still baffling that two real women, Karsten and Fraginals, claim that they were his surrogate mothers. Could both women have embraced the same imaginary son? On the other hand, could a child really have survived all the ailments that Tony was said to have suffered? Neither Tony (if he exists) nor the publisher of his book has ever backed down on their claim that he is a real person.

It is therefore not surprising that the bibliographic record for *A Rock and a Hard Place* includes the subdivision "Biography," nor that the fixed field code indicates that it is an autobiography. Nevertheless, Tony's existence is so questionable that a note with a reference to the *Newsweek* and *The New Yorker* articles should be included in the bibliographic record.

Sleepers by Lorenzo Carcaterra (1995)

Publishers Weekly described *Sleepers* as "a memoir that reads like a novel."[1] Tom De Haven in his *Entertainment Weekly* review concluded that "*Sleepers* is a good story, all right—ugly as sin but fascinating. Truth be told, though, I don't altogether believe it."[2] The *Los Angeles Times* review acknowledged that it was "tough to figure out whether 'Sleepers' is really a memoir, as the author insists ('This is a true story,' he writes, 'about friendships that run deeper than blood') or a novel thinly camouflaged as autobiography."[3] The degree of skepticism expressed about the veracity of a book so soon after its publication was certainly unusual.

Sleepers is the story of Lorenzo Carcaterra's hellish experience in a juvenile reformatory in the late 1960s after a youthful prank went tragically awry. He and three friends stole a hot-dog cart, which subsequently got away from them and crushed an old man against a wall, severely injuring him. As a consequence, Carcaterra and his friends were incarcerated in the Wilkinson Home for Boys in upstate New York, an institution that, as one reviewer noted, "makes that Turkish jail in *Midnight Express* seem almost tolerable."[4] The boys were beaten and molested, emerging emotionally scarred and bitter, but Carcaterra and one other boy managed to build productive lives for themselves. In fact, the other boy, called Michael Sullivan in the book, became a lawyer in the New York City district attorney's office. It was in this capacity that he was able to help the two remaining boys, who hadn't fared as well, when in the 1980s they were arrested and charged with murdering one of the former guards at the Wilkinson Home for Boys. Having been appointed to prosecute the case despite his inexperience, and viewing the murder as totally justifiable, Michael Sullivan decided to handle his duties so ineptly that his childhood friends would be acquitted.[5] In addition, he persuaded the neighborhood priest, Father Bobby, to perjure himself by testifying that the two defendants were with him the night of the murder. Sullivan's plan succeeded when he failed to win guilty verdicts and his friends were set free.[6]

Sleepers was an alternate selection of the Book of the Month Club and rights were purchased for two million dollars for a future film to be directed by Barry Levinson. Despite this initial success, doubts about the book's veracity were growing in the book industry. New York youth agency spokesman, Jim Cotter, admitted that cases of abuse had been known to occur in juvenile homes, but the conditions at the homes were not as Carcaterra described. The boys' quarters were bedrooms, not cells, and isolation "holes" had never been used, contrary to Carcaterra's claims. Furthermore, Cotter doubted that first-time juvenile offenders would have been sent away to a reformatory, in the first place. Carcaterra wrote in the book that allegations of abuse at the Wilkinson Home for Boys were later heard by a board of inquiry, in part because of the author's efforts. Forty-seven witnesses were called and a complete overhaul of the reformatory was recommended. Cotter said no one at the youth agency remembered a scandal like the one described, "and this is not the kind of thing you'd forget."[7]

The Manhattan District Attorney's office also said that the trial described in the book was unbelievable, and no one could recall a case that resembled the one Carcaterra recounted. In addition, "no six-month prosecutor would ever handle a homicide, let alone get it assigned to him," said a spokeswoman for the District Attorney. Carcaterra was unfazed by the denials from the District Attorney's office and the Division of Youth, asking, "What are they supposed to say?"[8] The editor in chief of Ballantine, the book's publisher, said, "We know this book is true. We've had legal readings. We've had it vetted." Anyone casting doubt on its veracity would "wind up with egg on their face."[9]

When Ballantine first published *Sleepers*, Carcaterra's prologue explained that most of the names and dates had been changed "to protect the identities of those involved."[10] Less than a month after its publication, Ballantine went further, saying that "locations" and "identifying characteristics of people and institutions" had also been changed. For example, their statement said, the murder of the guard did not take place in Manhattan.[11] Carcaterra added that "the what, where and when these things happened were not as important to me as the fact that they did happen."[12]

If the facts were unimportant to Carcaterra, the Catholic Church was very concerned with the truth. *Sleepers* put the Sacred Heart of Jesus Church and its elementary school in a terrible light. There was no doubt that this was the school Carcaterra attended, and that he claimed later altered their records so that there was no hint that he and his friends had been away from school for an extended period as they served their time in reform school. Sacred Heart was the home of the priest that Carcaterra claimed in *Sleepers* lied under oath in court in order to protect his former students. The parochial school maintained that Carcaterra was a good, well-behaved student who missed no more than twenty days of school in all the time he was at Sacred Heart. Furthermore, according to the pastor of Sacred Heart and a priest who worked there at the time of the alleged crime, no priest had testified at a murder trial.[13]

No time was wasted in getting the film version of *Sleepers* to the big screen. The 1996 movie starring Brad Pitt, Robert DeNiro, and Jason Patric was the number one film the weekend it opened. Barry Levinson, the director, was nevertheless perturbed by questions about the credibility of the source material. "You would hope that this doesn't overwhelm what we've done," he fretted. He went on to state that "I don't know what is this big quest for the truth, with four boys no one ever heard of. What's this big thing we need to get into? There are no historical figures here."[14]

Obviously, Levinson was never a cataloger. Literary license may flourish when one is making a film, but truth (or lack thereof) is deeply relevant to librarians. Ballantine and Carcaterra maintain to this day that *Sleepers* is substantially true. Without solid evidence to the contrary, catalogers should err on the side of caution and treat it as a memoir. In the bibliographic record the subdivision "Case studies" is used under "Criminals" and "Gangs." An extensive summary note resembles a publisher's statement, describing the book as a "true story." The addition of a general note regarding questions about its veracity would not be inappropriate.

Stoker: The Story of an Australian Soldier Who Survived Auschwitz-Birkenau by Donald Watt (1995)

Donald Watt, an Australian, enlisted in the Australian Imperial Forces in 1940. Three months later, he was shipped to Northern Africa and then Crete as World War II commenced. In Crete, in June 1941, Watt was captured by the Germans.[1] First, he was taken the Hammelburg in North Bavaria, where he was held with other prisoners of war from Australia, New Zealand, and England, but he tried to escape. After he was recaptured, he was sent to Bergen-Belsen and held for two or three months. Finally, Watt was sent to Auschwitz-Birkenau in July of 1944 and remained a prisoner there until liberation in April of 1945. While he was there, he became a furnace stoker (a member, he claimed, of the *Sonderkommando*), whose job it was to stoke the fire used to burn the bodies of the victims of the gas chambers. For forty-four years Watt never spoke of this experience, not to the men in the British tank brigade that liberated him, nor to his wife.[2]

Stoker detailed Watt's sickening experiences in Auschwitz-Birkenau. He described stoking the wood-burning furnaces prior to the arrival of hundreds of bodies from the gas chambers. Watt estimated that during the seven months he was there, five thousand bodies were disposed of every twenty-four hours, seven days a week in Crematorium two and three alone.[3]

After Watt disclosed his war experiences he was hailed as a hero. He was honored at war reunions and commemorations, such as the VE Day fiftieth anniversary celebration at the Sydney Opera House. There was talk of a movie, and a play titled *The Singing Forest*, based on Watt's book, was produced in 2001. *Stoker* had three print runs in Australia and was also published in Great Britain before critics began to question Watt's story.[4]

In 1996, a German publisher was considering publishing Watt's work, but wanted to make sure the book was authentic. It enlisted the assistance of the Fritz Bauer Institute, which in turn contacted Konrad Kweit, a director of the Centre for Comparative Genocide Studies at Sydney's Macquarie University School of History, Philosophy and Politics at the time. Kweit's analysis of the book was pointed. Watt claimed to have seen Jews wearing the Star of David in Hammelburg, Germany in the summer of 1941, but Kweit argued that Jews were not ordered to wear the yellow stars until the autumn of 1941. In addition, by Watt's own account, his papers were processed when he arrived in Auschwitz-Birkenau, but not a single reference was found documenting the arrival and imprisonment of an Australian POW named Donald Watt. This was a notable lapse on the part of the Nazis who were renowned for their meticulous record-keeping.[5]

Gideon Greif, who was employed in the education department at Yad Vashem, the distinguished Holocaust museum and research center in Jerusalem, asserted that "after I read the two chapters [of Watt's account of Auschwitz] thoroughly, I could ascertain that the author at no time was a member of the *Sonderkommando* in the Auschwitz-Birkenau. Doubtful also is the fact that under any circumstances he was a prisoner there."[6] Greif, considered by many to be the foremost expert on the history of the *Sonderkommando*, took issue with almost every sentence Watt wrote about his experience in Auschwitz-Birkenau. Watt wrote that Jews, gypsies, and communists, who arrived daily, were sent directly to the gas chambers, but Greif said that they were never taken as a group, but rather were selected individually.[7]

Additional discrepancies were noted by other Holocaust scholars. For example, although Watt described the work of a stoker as one who stokes the fires at the crematorium, the stoker's job was actually to strip the waiting bodies before they were burned. Watt also identified wood as the fuel for the crematoria fires, but they were, in fact, fueled with coke and coke gas.[8]

Kweit offered up a possible motive for Watt's decision to share the story of his Holocaust experience after concealing it for so many years. In 1987 the Australian government announced that it would compensate veterans who had been "illegally interned in a concentration camp" and "subjected to brutal treatment." With his wife's encouragement, Watt filed an application for compensation, but it took some time for the Concentration Camps Committee to authorize it due to the fact that his military records lacked any supporting documentation. In 1990, however, he was granted the compensation based on his medical records, which listed symptoms that were consistent with harsh treatment. In 1991, Watt produced a self-published, fifty-page booklet titled *I Was There Too* recounting his ordeal in Auschwitz, which preceded the Simon & Schuster edition of *Stoker* published in 1995.[9]

Although most critics do not dispute that Watt was a POW, the story told in *Stoker* has been convincingly discredited. The preponderance of evidence presented by leading experts is persuasive, although neither Watt nor his publisher ever acknowledged that the book was factually challenged. The bibliographic record represents the book as nonfiction, utilizing the subdivisions "Biography" and "Personal narratives," and designating it an autobiography in the fixed field. Catalogers have few options in terms of form subdivisions. Because the book has some truthful elements about Watt's wartime experience, the subdivision "Fiction" is no more accurate than the subdivisions that appear in the record, "Biography" and "Personal narratives." Perhaps the inclusion of all three subdivisions is the only way to communicate the fuzziness of the genre. The genre/form heading "Autobiographical fiction" would be an appropriate addition. Regardless, a general note should be added describing the fictional elements of *Stoker*.

Memoirs and Autobiographies

Fragments: Memories of a Wartime Childhood by Binjamin Wilkomirski (1996)

In 1996 a noteworthy Holocaust memoir appeared on the American literary scene. *Fragments*, an unorthodox autobiography, recounted the horrifying experiences of a three-year-old boy in Nazi concentration camps. The story was told from a child's point of view, in a fragmented style that mirrored the disjointed way that memories emerge. *Fragments*, written in German and translated into fourteen languages, including English, won the American National Jewish Book Award for autobiography and memoirs, the *Jewish Quarterly* literary prize for nonfiction in Britain, and the Prix Mémoire de la Shoah in France.[1]

The reviews were almost uniformly glowing. Jonathan Kozol raved that "this stunning and austerely written work is so profoundly moving, so morally important and so free from literary artifice of any kind at all that I wondered if I even had the right to try to offer praise."[2] *The New York Times* book review exulted that "his extraordinary memoir ... recalls the Holocaust with the powerful immediacy of innocence, injecting well-documented events with fresh terror and poignancy."[3] Wilkomirski addressed conferences on the Holocaust in several countries, and was sent on a speaking tour in the United States by the Holocaust Museum to help raise money.[4]

In his speeches, Wilkomirski's shared his memories, which were the hazy recollections of a child. He remembered that his father was killed in the ghetto in Riga, Latvia, and that he fled Riga with a woman and some other boys, ending up in Lvov, in western Ukraine. There he was spotted by a woman in uniform who took him to the concentration camp Majdanek. He was later sent to Auschwitz, from which he and other camp survivors were eventually freed. Wilkomirski was transported to Switzerland, where he was put in an orphanage until he was sent to live with foster parents, Dr. and Mrs. Doessekker. They eventually adopted him and he was given the name Bruno Doessekker.[5]

People in Zurich who had known Doessekker since he was a child believed that he was Protestant and were surprised to hear that he claimed to be a Jewish orphan who had survived the Holocaust. When Wilkomirski's German publisher, Suhrkamp-Verlag, began hearing troubling rumors about his identity, they asked for a birth certificate, adoption papers, and any other documents that would verify his account in *Fragments*. Instead they got testimonials that his story was true from psychologists who had befriended or treated Wilkomirski, and statements from Holocaust experts that affirmed that his account was very plausible. When Wilkomirski offered to add an afterword, which explained that "as a child, I received a new identity, another name, another date and place of birth," Suhrkamp moved forward with publication.[6]

Any concerns about the veracity of *Fragments* did not faze the American publisher, Schocken Books, an imprint of Random House. Schocken relied on Suhrkamp-Verlag's impeccable reputation when it published the American edition in 1996. *The New York Times* included *Fragments* on its list of notable books for 1997.[7]

Wilkomirski became something of a celebrity in Switzerland, and Swiss journalist Daniel Ganzfried was commissioned to write a profile of him. His investigation revealed several discrepancies. Wilkomirski's adoption records documented that his birth name was Bruno Grosjean, and that he was the illegitimate son of a Swiss Protestant woman named Yvonne Grosjean. He was later taken into custody by Swiss authorities and adopted, as Wilkomirski stated, by a Zurich doctor named Kurt Doessekker and his wife.[8] His records gave a birth date of 1941, which conflicted with the subtitle that appeared on most foreign editions of the book, *Fragments: A Childhood 1939–1948*. Wilkomirski brushed these details aside, stating that "this date has nothing to do with either the history of this century or my personal history. I have now taken legal steps to have this imposed identity annulled." No legal steps were ever taken.[9]

Other conflicting information surfaced. Wilkomirski claimed that he was circumcised, but his ex-wife and his girlfriend refuted this. When Ganzfried asked him whether he had a tattoo from his time in concentration camps, Wilkomirski said that he did not because he had been part of a medical experiment. He also explained that the account set down in his book was the result of memories recovered during therapy.[10] A DNA test could have resolved most of the questions about identity, but Wilkomirski refused to submit to one.[11]

The German and American publishers stood behind the book, even after *Granta* and *The New Yorker* published detailed articles corroborating Ganzfried's charges. Wilkomirski's literary agent, Eva Koralnik commissioned Swiss historian Stefan Mächler to investigate, and Blake Eskin, an editor for *The Jewish Daily Forward* at the time, began writing a book about the case.[12] Arthur Samuelson, editorial director for Schocken conceded that "I believe he believes what's in the book, because it's largely based on recovered memory, and it's possible he's wrong," but he argued that "we don't have fact checkers. We are not a detective agency."[13] By the fall of 1999, however, the investigation conducted by Mächler for Wilkomirski's agent concluded that *Fragments* was fiction. The German publisher quickly withdrew its hardcover editions, and Schocken suspended publication. *Jewish Quarterly* also withdrew the 1997 nonfiction prize they had awarded Wilkomirski.[14] Wilkomirski himself said, "It was always the free choice of the reader to read my book as literature or to take it as a personal document. Nobody has to believe me."[15]

Bibliographic records in OCLC illustrate this possibility. The 1996 Schocken edition is cataloged as fiction, but the summary note refers to *Fragments* as a memoir. The 1997 Schocken edition record contains the subdivisions "Biography" and "Personal narratives." With reliable evidence that *Fragments* is not factual and its withdrawal by Schocken, the use of the form subdivision "Fiction" and the genre/form heading "Fictional autobiographies" is warranted. The authority record for "Wilkomirski, Binjamin" includes a note stating that per "email from IsJJNL, Jan. 21, 2003 (not a concentration survivor; his memoir is a fake)."

Misha: A Memoire of the Holocaust Years by Misha Defonseca (1997)

Misha was presented as the true story of a Jewish Belgian girl's struggle to survive the Holocaust. After her parents' arrest by the Germans in 1941, Misha Defonseca, age seven, was taken in by a foster family and given a new name (Monique De Wael) and Christian identity. Terrified that her foster family would turn her over to the Nazis, she ran away to search for her parents. For the next four years Defonseca wandered through Europe until the end of the World War II when she was reunited with her Belgian foster grandfather.[1]

A Holocaust memoir from a child's point of view is unusual enough, but the most intriguing element of her story involved her relationship with wolves that she encountered when she slept in the forests. Defonseca recounted that she curled up with them on cold nights, and shared regurgitated meat with wolf pups. Other aspects of her tale were almost as incredible. Although she was just a young child, she found a dead rabbit, skinned it, and lined her shoes with the fur. Despite her hunger, she had the moral fortitude to throw away candy given to her by an SS soldier.[2]

Published by tiny Gloucester, Massachusetts publisher Mt. Ivy Press in 1997, *Misha* did not sell particularly well in the United States, although hundreds of American libraries own a copy. It was, however, translated into eighteen languages and was very popular in Europe where it was adapted as an opera in Italy and was the basis of a film called *Surviving with Wolves* in France.[3] Perhaps because the book was not a best seller in the United States, reviews in English are hard to find. One review that appeared in *People* in 1997, however, noted that "some of the narrative strains credulity."[4] We learned that the reviewer was on to something when, in 2008, Defonseca admitted that, although her parents had been arrested and killed by the Germans, she was not Jewish and that she lived safely in Brussels during the war.[5]

Nevertheless, when the book was first published it contained blurbs from famous Holocaust survivor and author Elie Wiesel and from the head of the North American Wolf Foundation. There were also skeptics, however, including historian Deborah Dwork and literary scholar Lawrence L. Langer, both of whom were asked to write blurbs for the book. They each declined and told the publisher that *Misha* was fantasy, but their warnings were ignored.[6] Other historians pointed out factual errors in dates and locations, while naturalists were not convinced that wolves would behave in the manner that Defonseca described. When Vera Belmont, the director of the French film *Surviving with Wolves*, was confronted with these doubts, however, she told the Israeli newspaper *Haaetz*, "That is exactly like the people who deny the existence of concentration camps. This is a true story. Everything that happened during the Holocaust is unbelievable and impossible to grasp, and people therefore also find it difficult to believe this story."[7]

When Defonseca was confronted with irrefutable proof that her story was not factual by the Belgian newspaper *Le Soir*, she issued a statement through her lawyers revealing that "yes, my name is Monique De Wael, but I have wanted to forget it since I was four years old. My parents were arrested and I was taken in by my grandfather, Ernest De Wael, and my uncle, Maurice De Wael. I was called 'daughter of a traitor' because my father was suspected of having talked under torture in the prison of Saint-Gilles. Ever since I can remember, I felt Jewish."[8] In 2014 she was found guilty of fraud and ordered by a Massachusetts judge to return $22.5 million to her publisher.[9] Determining if she set out to deceive her readers is complicated by her statement that "there are times when I find it difficult to differentiate between reality and my inner world. The story in the book is mine. It is not the actual reality—it was my reality, my way of surviving."[10]

The bibliographic record attaches the form subdivision "Fiction" to the subject headings. The summary note, however, describes the work as an "autobiography of Misha Defonseca, who found herself alone in Nazi occupied Belgium at age seven, explaining how she managed to survive and evade capture for four years while crossing Europe on foot." The authority record for Misha Defonseca has a cross-reference for "Monique De Wael," as well as source data notes indicating the fictional nature of the book. The addition of the genre/form heading "Fictional autobiographies" would be appropriate since both Defonseca and her memoir are inventions.

The Autobiography of Howard Hughes by Clifford Irving (1999)

In 1970, Howard Hughes was one of richest and most mysterious men in the country. He had led an eventful and prosperous life before he withdrew from public view in 1958. Born into new wealth in Houston, Texas, he was orphaned at the age of eighteen and inherited a major share of the Hughes Tool Company, which held a patent for rock-drilling bits. The Hughes bit was the best one available, and was always rented, never sold. Accused of holding a monopoly on drill bits, Hughes denied the charge asserting that "people who want to drill for oil and not use the Hughes bit can always use a pick and shovel."[1] By the time Hughes disappeared from public life he was the sole trustee of the Howard Hughes Medical Institute in Miami, which was financed by the profits of Hughes Aircraft, a major supplier of electronics equipment to the United States defense industry. He was a real estate mogul who owned huge tracts of land in California, Arizona, Texas, and Nevada. Hughes was also the majority shareholder in Trans World Airlines, the world's second largest international airline at that time. He was believed to be worth between $1.3 billion and $2 billion.[2]

Howard Hughes had many other claims to fame. He produced movies, such as *Hell's Angels*, *Scarface*, and *The Outlaw*, and owned RKO studios. He filled his Hollywood days dating a string of famous actresses including Katherine Hepburn, Olivia de Havilland, Ginger Rogers, Loretta Young, Lana Turner, Ava Gardner, and Yvonne DeCarlo before he married Jean Peters in 1957, when Hughes was fifty-one. He loved airplanes and survived four airplane crashes. In 1941, he ordered his airplane division, Hughes Aircraft, to design and build an air freighter in anticipation of the United States' entry into World War II. It was the largest airplane in the world, and because of a shortage of metal, it was built of wood. It became the butt of unkind jokes, with some people calling it the "Flying Coffin," or the "Spruce Goose." Few believed that it would ever fly, but Hughes did indeed take it for a mile-long flight, and then permanently stored it in a hangar in Long Beach, California.[3]

Memoirs and Autobiographies

Hughes was a private man, and some might say, a paranoid one. He was convinced that his business rivals were trying to "bug" all of his conversations, a notion that was not without some foundation. Therefore, he held business conferences in parked cars and airplane cockpits. He maintained twenty Chevrolets with twenty individual drivers in order to make eavesdropping more difficult. In addition, he was phobic about germs. He rarely shook hands with anyone, wiped doorknobs with his handkerchief, and insisted that couriers wear white cotton gloves when they delivered documents to him. His germ phobia became more severe as he got older.[4]

What biographer wouldn't jump at the chance to write about such an accomplished and secretive man? The dilemma, of course, was what biographer would the very reclusive Howard Hughes consent to work with? McGraw-Hill seemed to have solved that problem when, on December 8, 1971, they announced that they had purchased world publishing rights to a 230,000-word transcript of the taped reminiscences of Howard Hughes. A book, based on the tapes, was to be published March 27, 1972, and *Life* magazine would serialize the book in three installments beginning with the March 10 issue. McGraw-Hill explained that Hughes had spent the last year working on the memoir with novelist Clifford Irving. Their work resulted in one hundred taping sessions together. Still, a high executive at McGraw-Hill acknowledged privately that nobody at the company had seen Hughes and that the negotiations had been handled exclusively by Irving.[5]

After the announcement by McGraw-Hill, a spokesman for Hughes Tool Company denied that an autobiography existed. A spokesman for *Life* was sanguine about the denial, explaining that "we never dealt with the Hughes Tool Company. It doesn't surprise us that they know nothing of this since Mr. Hughes was totally secretive about the project. We are absolutely certain of the authenticity of this autobiography and we wouldn't put McGraw-Hill's and *Life's* name behind it if we weren't."[6]

Hughes uncharacteristically agreed to a phone interview with seven reporters to deny that the memoir was authentic. He maintained that he was baffled by the claim that he had collaborated with Clifford Irving on an autobiography and that he had received payment for the forthcoming book. None of these things transpired according to Hughes. McGraw-Hill and *Life*, meanwhile, were equally adamant that the book was authentic. In a written statement, they said that "it is alleged that Howard Hughes made a telephone call Friday repudiating this material and the man who worked on it with him, Clifford Irving. We cannot accept this. McGraw-Hill and *Life* have in their possession, among many documents, a ten-page handwritten letter from Howard Hughes to Harold W. McGraw Jr. dated Nov. 17, 1971" granting McGraw-Hill and Time, Inc., the right to publicly announce the book, provided that Irving receives final payment simultaneously from the publishing house and that Mr. Irving, in turn, makes payment to Hughes.[7]

McGraw-Hill and *Life's* publisher, Time, Inc., according to their statement, made the payment and had in their possession the checks endorsed by Hughes. Both the checks and the handwritten letter were submitted to a reputable handwriting-analysis firm that compared them to known documents written by Hughes. The firm certified that the documents were written by the same person. The publishing house concluded its statement by asserting that they "have substantial written and verified documentation authorizing this autobiography. Finally, we have a completely convincing manuscript; no one who has read it can doubt its integrity, or, upon reading it, that of Clifford Irving."[8]

By January 21, 1972, however, Irving's claims began to fall apart. Credit Suisse, the bank where the checks to Hughes had been deposited and later withdrawn, announced publicly that it was a woman, not the industrialist Howard Hughes, who had made the transactions. The day before the bank issued its statement, the publishers had announced that publication of the book would be delayed, but did not explain why. Irving admitted to his lawyer and representatives of the New York County District Attorney that his wife, Edith, using the name "Helga R. Hughes" and a fake passport, had deposited the checks made out to H. R. Hughes from McGraw-Hill. She later withdrew the money from the account, but Irving insisted that this was done at the direction of Howard Hughes. To bolster his claim, Irving, in an affidavit, described his first meeting with Hughes in Mexico. Shortly thereafter, however, a Danish singer named Nina Van Pallandt told reporters that she had been with Irving on the Mexican trip and that he was not away from her long enough to have had a meeting with Hughes.[9]

Meanwhile, excerpts from Irving's manuscript began to trickle out. The anecdotes related in the text were accurate, but had actually appeared in other works. At least two dozen of the tales paralleled those that appeared in freelance writer James Phelan's unpublished book about Hughes' relationship with Noah Dietrich, who was the chief executive officer of the Hughes Tool Company for thirty-two years. Another strongly resembled, in form, a Hughes anecdote included in a book by Ben Hecht, *A Child of the Century*. Time, Inc. now said that they believed that somehow in 1971 Irving had gained access to Phelan's manuscript.[10]

On February 12, 1972, McGraw-Hill announced that they were turning over evidence that supported the claim that Irving's Howard Hughes autobiography was a fraud. They laid a great deal of blame for the publisher's misplaced confidence in the authenticity of the book at the doorstep of the handwriting-analysis firm Osborn Associates. By now, upon reconsideration, Osborn had rendered a supplementary opinion that contradicted their original "overwhelming" conclusion. They now declared that the check endorsements and a letter allegedly written by Howard Hughes were forgeries. Time, Inc. also announced that it was canceling the original plan for a serialization of the Hughes autobiography. They went on to say, "In our further coverage of the Irving affair, we may well refer to the passages from the Irving manuscript. We're not going to publish any of this as the autobiography of Howard Hughes—which it clearly is not."[11]

On June 1972, Irving was convicted on charges of conspiracy to defraud, forgery, using the federal mail to defraud, and perjury, and was sentenced to two and a half years in prison. His wife, Edith, was sentenced to two years in prison, but only served two months. Irving returned most of the money to McGraw-Hill. In order to recoup some money he had spent, Irving made an arrangement with the U.S. attorney to be allowed to write an account of the hoax before he began his prison term. This resulted in the book, *The Hoax*, which was made into a movie in 2006. Ironically, Irving insisted that his name be removed from the movie credits because it took too many liberties.[12]

The Hughes "autobiography" finally became a reality in 1999 when a start-up Internet publisher, Terrificbooks.com, released it as an "imaginative biography."[13] Despite all the publicity surrounding the book twenty-seven years earlier, the bibliographic record utilizes the form subdivision "Biography," with no hint in the bibliographic record that anything is amiss. In 2008, John Blake Publishing issued the book under the title *Howard Hughes: The Autobiography: The Most Famous Unpublished Book of the 20th Century—Until Now.* The bibliographic record for this edition contains a lengthy summary note explaining some of the unsavory history of the book.

The note is needed, but *The Autobiography of Howard Hughes* presents a dilemma for catalogers. It has been thoroughly discredited, but many, if not most, of the facts it contains may well be true, even though they were "borrowed" from other researchers. It does not fall under the scope of the genre/form headings "Biographical fiction" or "Autobiographical fiction" because there is no evidence that fictional characters are intermixed with fictional events. The only option for catalogers, it seems, is to include a general note in the bibliographic record stating that it is not an autobiography based on interviews with Howard Hughes.

Jihad! The Secret War in Afghanistan by Tom Carew (2000)

Tom Carew, British Special Air Service veteran, described being summoned to an office near Buckingham Palace in the summer of 1980 and offered a mission to go to Pakistan to train the Afghan Mujahideen resistance movement to fight the Russians. Russia had invaded Afghanistan and this became the front in a cold war battle between Russia and the West. Carew described his experience setting up a training camp for the Mujahideen in Pakistan's North-West Frontier Province, after which he was dispatched to Afghanistan to assess what training and supplies they needed.[1]

Carew was exposed as a fake on a BBC *Newsnight* broadcast aired on November 14, 2001. A former SAS officer claimed that "this man is a complete charlatan."[2] He was never in the SAS and Tom Carew wasn't his real name. He was actually Philip Anthony Sessarego. He had served for two years in The Royal Artillery and tried, but failed, to pass the rigorous SAS selection test. Instead he was invited to join a troop of soldiers who had narrowly failed the SAS test and were stationed at the Hereford, England, headquarters where they posed as the enemy in training exercises. In 1975 Sessarego was discharged from the army. That's when he began posing as an SAS veteran.[3]

Using knowledge that he picked up from time spent in pubs with SAS men, he found work on the mercenary circuit. He worked in Afghanistan, Sri Lanka, the Maldives, the Balkans, Latin America, and southern Africa, claiming that some of the operations were on behalf of British and U.S. intelligence agencies. It appears that he did engage in dangerous, deniable operations, although it is unclear if they match the exploits described in his book. In 1991, Sessarego faked his own death when he was allegedly killed in a bomb explosion in Croatia. He took the name Philip Stevenson and was eventually discovered to be alive and well. Although he claimed that British Intelligence had given him a new identity, some sources assert that he was simply trying to avoid child support payments.[4]

In 2000 he re-emerged under the pen name Tom Carew when his book *Jihad! The Secret War in Afghanistan* was published. The book, which was actually ghost-written by Adrian Weale, a former military intelligence officer, sold modestly until it was serialized in the *Sunday Times* (London). On September 10, 2001, it was published in paperback. In the wake of the September 11, 2001, al-Qaeda attack on the World Trade Center in New York City, sales of the book climbed.[5] Carew became the media's go-to expert on Afghanistan. A reporter for a *Newsweek* article, for example, solicited Carew's opinion on how to fight in Afghanistan. Carew advised that it would perhaps be better "to stay out of the country as much as possible and arm the Taliban's own enemies, the Northern Alliance. On their own territory, it may take Afghans to defeat Afghans."[6]

After he was exposed as a fake SAS veteran on BBC *Newsnight*, he disappeared from sight. In 2009 his body was found in a garage in Antwerp, Belgium, where he apparently died from carbon monoxide poisoning. While there was speculation that he had been killed by a member of the SAS, his death was apparently accidental. Some even wondered if he was actually dead, given his history of faking his own demise.[7]

The most passionate criticism fell on Carew's claim that he had been a member of the SAS, but this lie cast doubt on everything in his book. His publisher, Mainstream Publishing, defended Carew, issuing a statement shortly after the broadcast that "obviously we have to reconsider minor parts of *Jihad!* which require changes in light of this investigation, but the main gist of the story concerns the account of what it's like to fight alongside the west's most recent enemy."[8] It is doubtful that the truth about Carew's deeds will ever emerge from the murky world of mercenary operations.

The bibliographic record includes a summary note that consists of extensive quotations from the book jacket. The subject entries, lacking "Fiction" form subdivisions, indicate that the book is nonfiction, and utilizes the form subdivision "Personal narratives, British." Coding in the fixed field also conforms to nonfiction materials. The authority record for Tom Carew states that he "worked on a freelance basis for the US Defense Intelligence Agency and for the US Drug Enforcement Administration, currently lives, under false identity, in Belgium." There is no mention of Philip Anthony Sessarego, his given name. There are no hints of any questions about the identity of the author or the authenticity of the book.

The events in the book appear to be a mixture of fiction and fact. There are no easy answers regarding what form subdivision should be applied. Is this truly a personal narrative or is it fiction? Perhaps it is a mixture of both. The author, however, was not a member of the SAS and this should be noted in his authority and the bibliographic records and the genre/form heading "Autobiographical fiction" should be added.

Memoirs and Autobiographies

The Blood Runs Like a River Through My Dreams: A Memoir by Nasdijj (2000); *The Boy and the Dog Are Sleeping* by Nasdijj (2003); *Geronimo's Bones: A Memoir of My Brother and Me* by Nasdijj (2004)

"My son is dead. I didn't say my adopted son is dead. He was my son. My son was Navajo. He lived six years. Those were the best six years of my life."[1] So began the excruciating and moving article that appeared in *Esquire* in 1999. Written by a half-Navajo man named Nasdijj, the story had arrived unsolicited at the magazine's office and *Esquire*'s editor in chief, David Granger, was immediately taken with it. It told the true story of the short life of Nasdijj's adopted son, Tommy Nothing Fancy, who had fetal alcohol syndrome. Nasdijj, the son of an alcoholic Navajo mother and a brutal white cowboy father, suffered from the same affliction. The article was sent to the magazine's research department for fact-checking where medical experts were consulted and verified that the symptoms of fetal alcohol syndrome described in the article were possible. Details about the Navajo reservation where Nasdijj lived at the time were confirmed. At *Esquire*'s request Nasdijj provided two small photographs of Tommy along with some official-looking identification papers.[2]

"The Blood Runs Like a River Through My Dreams" was a finalist for a prestigious National Magazine Award, and Houghton Mifflin quickly offered Nasdijj a contract for a full-length memoir with the same title.[3] Published in 2000, the book received uniformly favorable reviews. "Some writers know how to write from life experiences, others do not. Those who do not slide by on attempts of explaining their lives, finding a meaning to what needs no explanation. But those who are truly meant to write are those whose lives have been so chaotic, so episodic, it only makes sense to write. Nasdijj is one of these ambiguously gifted writers," asserted reviewer MariJo Moore.[4] *The New York Times* book review mused that "his book reminds us that brave and engaging writers lurk in the most forgotten corners of society."[5] In *Salon*, Maria Russo exalted that "its singular language blends Native American mythological rhythms and imagery, stirring Whitman-esque catalogs and unadorned observations about life on and around the reservation."[6] *The Blood Runs Like a River Through My Dreams* was a *New York Times* Notable Book, a finalist for the PEN/Martha Albrand Award, and winner of the *Salon* Book Award.[7]

Nasdijj's second book, *The Boy and the Dog Are Sleeping*, recounted his experience with his second adopted son, Awee, who was dying of AIDS. Living in rundown hotels near large hospitals, Nasdijj did the best he could to get his son treatment. A review of this book declared that "poet-healer Nasdijj is an American treasure. Booksellers, prepare: readers who find their way to this gem will want his first book, too."[8] *The Boy and the Dog Are Sleeping* won a 2004 PEN/Beyond Margins Award.[9]

Geronimo's Bones: A Memoir of My Brother and Me, his third book, was met with similar accolades. No less harrowing than his first two books, this one chronicled his childhood spent with his beloved brother and a cruel father who rained physical, sexual, and emotional abuse on the two boys after their mother died.[10] The *Kirkus Review* spoke of going "back to the land of pure evil that Nasdijj revisited previously ... for no other word can describe his youth. Yet here, readers will also witness an incantational summoning, as in a streaming prose poem, of the lifelines that saw Nasdijj and his brother Tso through."[11]

There was, however, some growing discomfort lurking beneath the abundant praise. Well known Native American writer Sherman Alexie later revealed that when he read *The Blood Runs Like a River Through My Dreams* he felt his own story had been appropriated by Nasdijj. Alexie recalled that "the whole time I was reading I was thinking, this doesn't just sound like me, this *is* me."[12] Alexie was born hydrocephalic and, like Tommy Nothing Fancy, had suffered chronic seizures throughout his childhood. He had also published a story in *Esquire* in 1993, which featured "an autobiographical character ... who suffers a brain injury at birth and experiences visionary seizures into his adulthood, [and it] was a finalist for a National Magazine Award."[13] Alexie approached Nasdijj's publishers "and told them his book not only was borderline plagiarism but also failed to mention specific tribal members, clans, ceremonies and locations, all of which are vital to the concept of Indian identity. They took me seriously, but they didn't believe me."[14]

It was not until 2006 that Alexie was vindicated. An article in *LA Weekly* revealed that Nasdijj was not Native American at all. His real name was Timothy Patrick Barrus and he was raised in Lansing, Michigan, by parents of European descent. After he and his first wife divorced, he moved to San Francisco, where he began to write for the gay magazine *Drummer*. He later moved to Key West, Florida, where he published his first book, *Mineshaft*, a pedestrian attempt at erotica. Sometime after this he adopted the name Nasdijj, which he claimed meant "to become again" in Navajo Athabaskan. According to a full-blooded Navajo professor of literature and Navajo studies named Irvin Morris, however, no such word exists in the Navajo language. Three days after the *LA Weekly* article appeared, Barrus' publisher, Ballantine, announced that it would no longer ship copies of *The Boy and the Dog Are Sleeping* or *Geronimo's Bones* to booksellers and would allow retailers to return unsold copies.[15]

A few months after the *LA Weekly* article appeared, *Esquire* decided to interview the man who called himself Nasdijj. The head of research, Andrew Chaikivsky, spent three days with Barrus, who admitted he had adopted a Native American persona, but was alternately apologetic and defiant. Chaikivsky asserted that other than Barrus' admission, he did not "believe much of what he [Barrus] tells me [Chaikivsky]. The levels of deception can run from white lies and wild exaggerations to matters that touch our most fundamental illusions—how we try to convince ourselves that we are wiser, more strong-willed, braver, more significant."[16]

All three books, however, are cataloged as straightforward memoirs, with the fixed fields coded for autobiography or collective biography, and the use of the form subdivision "Biography." There are no general notes suggesting to the catalog user that these books are actually fiction. There should be notes, and the subdivision "Fiction" should replace "Biography." A genre/form heading for "Fictional autobiographies" is also warranted. The authority record for Nasdijj contains a cross-reference for Tim Barrus and states that "Nasdijj identified as likely pseudonym of Tim Barrus," but again there is no clue that this information raises serious questions about the authenticity of his books.

The Cage by Tom Abraham (2002)

Tom Abraham admitted that he wasn't much of a reader, but he wrote a book about his experiences as a soldier during the Vietnam War that was direct, compelling, and filled with tension. His was the unusual true story of a British citizen who lived in the United States and enlisted in the U.S. Army. Abraham served in the 1st battalion of the 7th Cavalry, engaged in fierce combat, became a second lieutenant, and received the Silver Star for gallantry. Of this, there was no doubt.[1] There was, however, considerable skepticism over Abraham's additional claim that he was captured by the Vietcong, half submerged in a bamboo cage in a rat-infested lake, and managed to escape two days later.[2]

According to Abraham, this experience contributed to his post-traumatic stress disorder and explained his problems when he returned home: his drinking and driving arrest, his attack on his wife with a knife, and his separation from his family. The publication of *The Cage* invited even more trouble into his life. As Vietnam veterans became aware of his claim that he was a POW, many forcefully objected, asserting that this was untrue.[3] The chief of public affairs for the United States Defense Prisoner of War/Missing Personnel Office (DPMO), Larry Greer stated that "[Abraham] did serve in the US army, he did win the Silver Star for gallantry, but [there is] no record of his being held captive. We have searched every scintilla of his military record and it's not there."[4] Mary Schantag, the spokeswoman for the Missouri-based organization POW Network, reported that "many genuine ex-POWs have contacted us about Mr. Abraham's book, all of whom are telling us that he is a phoney [sic]." She went on to say, "Every single prisoner of war from Vietnam was thoroughly documented and debriefed after their ordeal. Abraham does not appear on any record of POWs or those reported as missing in action during the entire war."[5]

Abraham's ex-wife recalled that he had written to her every day when he was in Vietnam, but did not mention his capture by the Vietcong. She mused that "oddly enough, the only thing in the book that I didn't understand were the 48 hours when he wrote he had been captured and put in a cage. In none of his letters did he say anything to me about this experience. I've been meaning to ask him about it but I had no reason to disbelieve him."[6] Abraham's agent, Mark Lucas, had no doubts, but his support came with caveats. He explained that "when somebody walks through my door I don't immediately put my people on to investigate what he says. I cannot produce a signed affidavit from Tom's torturer, but I am completely convinced by his account." Lucas did not, in any case, think the book's merit depended on the disputed claim of Abraham's captivity, suggesting that "if you like, this story is more about the cage of memory."[7]

Abraham's editor at Bantam, Bill Scott-Carr, asserted, somewhat defensively, "When you buy a book like this from an agent, you buy it as a package and you have to assume that some checking has taken place."[8] Nor has Abraham ever yielded in his assertion that the events in the book were true. He argued that "a lot of the criticism is simply, factually, wrong. Some of the critics do not seem to understand even where we fought and I wonder if some of the criticism revolves around the fact that they cannot believe that a British guy served as an officer in the U.S. Army." Then he made an odd statement, allowing that "I also made clear in my book at the time that these are my memories. I do not claim that the book is a work of history. It is based on my memories."[9]

The bibliographic record provides no hint that the book might not be totally factual. It utilizes the subdivision "Personal narratives, British." The cataloger faces a dilemma when a predominantly factual book includes sections that are demonstrably untrue, as is the case with *The Cage*. Including a general note about the fictional elements of the work and assignment of the genre/form heading "Autobiographical fiction" might be the only option.

A Million Little Pieces by James Frey (2003); *My Friend Leonard* by James Frey (2005)

James Frey has become the poster boy for fraudulent memoirs. If Americans know one thing about this phenomenon it is that *A Million Little Pieces* is fiction, but it had a much more auspicious beginning. Author Pat Conroy called the book "the 'War and Peace' of addiction," and film director Gus Van Sant compared Frey's voice to those of Dave Eggers and David Foster Wallace.[1] Reviews of Frey's account of his descent into addiction and crime, and his successful struggle to rid himself of his demons were passionate.

Critics mostly loved it, conditionally, or they hated it. Jeff Turrentine wrote in the *Los Angeles Times*, "Autopathographies—memoirs that ascend the bestseller list by vividly detailing their authors' descent into the hell of dysfunction—are too often book-length exercises in apologia. What distinguishes Frey's memoir from so many others in the genre is his refusal to blame his addiction on genetics, bad parenting, cultural ennui or anything but his own nihilistic appetites."[2] Other reviewers also admired this quality. *Entertainment Weekly* reviewer Jennifer Reese wrote that "too many contemporary autobiographies outline all the ways the vagaries of life (Daddy, race, sexual abuse) shape character. Frey believes that character shapes life, and believes it with a vengeance."[3]

Sarah F. Gold, in a *Publishers Weekly* review, displayed mixed feelings, pointing out that "the prose is repetitive to the point of being exasperating, but the story with its forays into the consciousness of an addict, is correspondingly difficult to put down."[4] Returning to Turrentine's review, he asserted, "'A Million Little Pieces,' while a great story, doesn't necessarily herald the debut of a great storyteller. It represents a triumph of the human spirit, not of literature."[5]

Janet Maslin in *The New York Times* was having none of it. In fact, she had some doubts about the book's authenticity. She noted that "Mr. Frey is reported to have originally presented this material as a novel when he looked for a publisher.... Little problem: This story is supposed to be all true." She goes on to lament that "although every detail of it may be accurate, it powerfully and sadly resembles pulp fiction."[6] For his part, Frey told *The Cleveland Plain Dealer* in July 2003, "The only things I changed were aspects of people that might reveal their identity. Otherwise, it's all true."[7]

Then in September 2005 Oprah Winfrey selected *A Million Little Pieces* for her influential Book Club. Previous Book Club selections greatly benefited from the publicity that it generated, and Frey's book was no exception. Within a day of Winfrey's announcement *A Million Little Pieces* was number one on Amazon.com, and within four days bookstores sold about 85,000 copies.[8] The book was the first work of nonfiction that Winfrey had ever chosen for her Book Club and she called it "a gut-wrenching memoir that is raw and it's so real."[9] Frey's good fortune did not last long, however. *The Smoking Gun* website published an exposé of Frey in January 2006, claiming that they had evidence that he had lied about a number of the events in his book. By this time, 3.5 million copies of *A Million Little Pieces* had been sold and it had been on *The New York Times* nonfiction best seller list for fifteen weeks. In addition, director Gus Van Sant was negotiating with Frey for film rights.[10]

The investigative website *The Smoking Gun* determined that Frey's claims of multiple arrests on serious drug charges were greatly embellished. He did have a substance abuse problem and he did go the Hazelden for rehab, but he spent a few hours in jail, not three months, and he wasn't wanted in three states as he recounted in his book. He also did not undergo root canal surgery without anesthesia. In fact, he was nothing like the hardened criminal he portrayed himself as in the book.[11]

Three nights after *The Smoking Gun* story appeared, Frey was invited to defend himself on the *Larry King Show*. He told King and his audience, "My side is I wrote a memoir. I never expected the book to come under the type of scrutiny that it has. A memoir literally means my story, a memoir is a subjective retelling of events."[12] He went on to claim that even though it contained blatant falsehoods "the book is 432 pages long. The total page count of disputed events is 18, which is less than 5 percent of the total book. You know, that falls comfortably within the realm of what's appropriate for a memoir."[13] At that point Winfrey was still in Frey's corner and called into the show, telling viewers that "the underlying message of redemption in James Frey's memoir still resonates with me, and I know it resonates with millions of people who have read this book.... To me, it seems to be much ado about nothing."[14]

Soon, however, Winfrey reconsidered her support of the book. She invited James Frey and his publisher, Nan A. Talese, the head of Random House's Doubleday division, to her show on January 26, 2006. Winfrey did not go easy on Frey, telling him that "it is difficult for me to talk to you because I feel really duped. But more importantly, I feel that you betrayed millions of readers."[15] Frey tried mightily to explain the embellishments and untruths contained in his book, but acknowledged that *The Smoking Gun* report "was pretty accurate."[16] Winfrey then turned to Talese and wondered why, prior to selecting *A Million Little Pieces* for her Book Club, her producers were reassured by Doubleday that the book was accurate. Talese replied that "an author brings his book in and says that it is true, it is accurate, it is his own. I thought as a publisher, this is James' memory of the hell he went through and I believed it."[17] She went on to say that the publisher checks nonfiction books to make sure that no one is defamed or libeled, but it does not verify the truthfulness of the account. Doubleday also said they were delaying the printing and shipping of any more copies of *A Million Little Pieces* so that they could include statements from the publisher and Frey acknowledging that "a number of facts have been altered and incidents embellished."[18]

Within a month, book sales had fallen by more than half, but in September 2006 *A Million Little Pieces* remained at number twenty-four on *The New York Times* nonfiction paperback best seller list. Some readers were decidedly unhappy with Frey, however, and filed lawsuits against Frey and Random House claiming that they had been defrauded. The various lawsuits were consolidated and the defendants agreed to a full refund of the cost of the book to qualified purchasers.[19]

The revelation also reflected negatively on Frey's sequel to *A Million Little Pieces*, *My Friend Leonard*, which was published in 2005. The second book picked up where *A Million Little Pieces* left off, with Frey completing the three-month jail sentence that he admitted in 2006 had not occurred. It described his post-rehab relationship with the mafia boss surrogate father he met there, Leonard. The authenticity of this book was dismissed after *A Million Little Pieces* was discredited.[20]

Despite the undeniable truth that *A Million Little Pieces* is a novel (albeit with some facts sprinkled in), the bibliographic record for the first edition uses the form subdivision "Biography." The fixed field for biography, however, is blank. There is a general note quoting the publisher, "Memoir is a personal history whose aim is to illuminate, by way of example, events and issues of broader social consequence.... In the case of Mr. Frey, we decided 'A Million Little Pieces' was his story, told his own way, and represented to us that his version of events was true to his recollections." The summary note simply states that the book is "a memoir of drug and alcohol abuse and the rehabilitation experience examines addiction and recovery through the eyes of a man who had taken his addictions to deadly extremes, describing the battle to confront the consequences of his life." This is a case where the original record has apparently been edited to include updated information, but the catalog user is still left to contend with a great deal of ambiguity.

The record for *My Friend Leonard* unambiguously represents the book as an autobiography, assigning the subdivision "Biography," and neglecting to include any general notes that might suggest that the book is not factual. The records for *A Million Little Pieces* and *My Friend Leonard* should both be edited, removing the form subdivision to "Biography" (although this is not totally satisfactory) and adding the genre/form heading "Autobiographical fiction."

Kathy's Story: A Childhood Hell Inside the Magdalen Laundries by Kathy O'Beirne (2005)

In 2006, the *Irish Independent* wrote, "After another week spent in the British nonfiction best sellers list, Kathy O'Beirne's book *Don't Ever Tell* (released here last year under the title *Kathy's Story: A Childhood Hell inside the Magdalene Laundries*) has now sold nearly 300,000 copies between here and the UK. Not bad for a book that has a major question mark hanging over its authenticity."[1] *Kathy's Story* recounted O'Beirne's monstrous mistreatment at the hands of Catholic nuns and priests in a workhouse run by the Irish Magdalene Sisters, where she was sent at the age of twelve by her abusive father. Here she was beaten and raped during her fourteen years in the Magdalene Laundries. O'Beirne claimed that when she rebelled, she was transferred to a mental hospital where she was given drugs. When she was thirteen she gave birth to a child who was conceived as the result of sexual assault. The baby was taken away from O'Beirne by the nuns, and later died.[2]

From the mid-nineteenth century until 1996, when the last laundry was closed, the Magdalene Laundries, a network of ten institutions, were run by four religious orders: the Sisters of Mercy, the Sisters of Charity, the Sisters of the Good Shepherd, and the Sisters of Our Lady of Charity of Refuge. There, "fallen" girls and women were locked up and forced to labor for free in the facilities that served both the clergy and commercial clients. Often these young women were brought to the laundries by their families who were ashamed of their daughters' behavior and wanted to hide them away. Little attention was paid to the laundries until 1993, when the nuns at High Park, one of the facilities, sold some of the land to developers. The land, unfortunately, held the graves of 155 women who died while working at the laundry. The remains were relocated, but the public took notice, and Ireland was finally forced to confront the sordid history of the Magdalene Laundries.[3]

The story of the laundries captured the imagination of a diverse group of artists. Joni Mitchell wrote a song called "The Magdalene Laundries," which appeared on her album *Turbulent Indigo* in 1997. Diane Fenster, an American photographer and artist, created an installation on the subject in New York. In 2002, Scottish actor Peter Mullan directed the film, *The Magdalene Sisters*, which was condemned by the Vatican, attracting even more attention to the shameful episode. Into this milieu O'Beirne's memoir arrived, fortunate timing to be sure. Oprah Winfrey was reported to be anxious to interview her and at least one film company wanted to buy the rights to the book.[4]

The first challenge to the claims in her book came from the Sisters of Our Lady of Charity who denied that O'Beirne had ever spent time in either of their laundries and asked the Minister for Justice to investigate her story.[5] O'Beirne, the oldest of nine children, was also denounced by five of her siblings. Her younger sister asserted that "our sister has a self-admitted psychiatric and criminal history, and her perception of reality has always been flawed."[6] Contrary to O'Beirne's claims, her siblings said that their father had never hit them, but that their sister had made their parents' lives miserable. They acknowledged that O'Beirne had spent six weeks in a children's home, but produced her birth certificate to counter her claims that she was adopted. To back up their story, O'Beirne's brother Oliver agreed to take part in a television program that used Magnetic Resonance Imaging of the brain to determine if people were telling the truth. A psychiatrist evaluating the results was convinced that Oliver was being truthful in his responses to questions about O'Beirne's childhood. O'Beirne initially agreed to submit to the test herself, but backed out at the last minute.[7]

Three former residents of the Sherrard House Hostel in Dublin, a voluntary shelter for homeless girls, remembered that she spent three years there in her mid- to late teens. They said that she never spoke of having any children or being in a Magdalene Laundry. Members of the Justice for Magdalenes, a group that was seeking compensation for former inmates, asserted that O'Beirne's account of her years with the nuns got many facts wrong and that she did not speak nor sound like a Magdalene. One of O'Beirne's oldest friends was perplexed and outraged by her claims. She said that O'Beirne was never pregnant and she claimed that O'Beirne asked her to commit perjury by testifying that she had witnessed her being raped by a priest in 1969. One of the priests that O'Beirne accused of assaulting her was Father Fergal O'Connor, a well-respected university lecturer and founder of Sherrard House Hostel. Father O'Connor, however, had been crippled by arthritis since his early twenties, and he could not even shake hands because it was too painful.[8]

For her part, O'Beirne contended that her family had ulterior motives for contradicting her claims. After the death of their parents, their father's will stipulated that the family home was supposed to be sold and the proceeds divided among the nine children. O'Beirne, however, claimed that their father, her alleged abuser, had promised that she could stay in the home for life, in exchange for her looking after him and her mother, who had health problems. A Circuit Court ruled in favor of O'Beirne. The siblings appealed in 2008, but at the last minute an agreement was struck with O'Beirne, which resulted in the home being sold.[9]

O'Beirne also claimed to have documents supporting her story, including her daughter's birth certificate and a letter from the nuns that stated she was in the Magdalene Laundries, but she never provided the evidence. Michael Sheridan, her ghostwriter (O'Beirne could not read or write), claimed that he spoke extensively to another woman who remembers being in the Magdalene home with O'Beirne. Unfortunately, she died in a psychiatric hospital some time after they spoke.[10] Representatives for Mainstream Press, her publisher, continued to support the book, saying, "We have used every possible effort to establish the truth of Kathy's memoir. We invited comments and corrections from the Church and we received no substantive response."[11]

At the time, *Kathy's Story* was the most successful work of nonfiction by an Irish author. Mainstream bid for the rights to publish the sequel, but lost out to Hodder Headline, which published *Always Dancing* in 2009. Only eleven libraries worldwide hold the sequel, and it is no longer available on Amazon. The bibliographic records for both books represent them as autobiographies in the fixed fields and in the assignment of the subdivision "Biography." Although there is some evidence that the books are not factually accurate, neither the author nor the publishers have ever retreated from their assertion that they offered a true story of O'Beirne's experiences. A general note in the bibliographic record, alerting the catalog user to the controversy surrounding them, should be included.

Memoirs and Autobiographies

Three Cups of Tea: One Man's Mission to Fight Terrorism and Build Nations—One School at a Time by Greg Mortenson and David Oliver Relin (2006); *Stones into Schools: Promoting Peace with Books, Not Bombs, in Afghanistan and Pakistan* by Greg Mortenson (2009)

Three Cups of Tea and its sequel *Stones into Schools* chronicle Greg Mortenson's quest to build schools in Pakistan and Afghanistan. In *Three Cups of Tea*, he writes that he was inspired by an encounter in 1993 that was the result of an unsuccessful attempt to climb K2, the world's second highest mountain. Exhausted and sick, Mortenson wandered into the small village of Korphe in northeast Pakistan. There he was nursed back to health and he vowed to build them a school to repay their generosity. This was only the beginning of his philanthropy, however. In 1996 Mortenson founded the Montana-based Central Asia Institute (CAI), a charitable organization created to fund the building of schools in Pakistan and Afghanistan. Donors included President Obama, who gave $100,000 of his Nobel Peace Prize award to the organization.[1]

Three Cups of Tea and *Stones into Schools* were inspiring to those (and they were legion) who read them. The paperback edition of *Three Cups of Tea* resided on *The New York Times* best seller list for over four years. In 2011, however, two controversies related to the book emerged. Jon Krakauer, one of CAI's donors and himself a bestselling nonfiction writer, published *Three Cups of Deceit*. In this book he claimed that the financial records for CAI were sloppy and that a large portion of the charity's funds went to promoting sales of *Three Cups of Tea*, for which, by its own admission, the charity received no income or royalties.[2] Even before Krakauer's exposé, The American Institute of Philanthropy revealed the worrisome mingling of Mortenson's personal business interests with those of CAI.[3] Mortenson has since been ordered by the Montana's attorney general to pay one million dollars back to CAI. A *60 Minutes* story on Mortenson and CAI reported that the 2010 CAI tax return listed 141 schools that it claimed to have built or supported in Pakistan and Afghanistan. *60 Minutes* visited thirty of them, and while some were performing well, about half were empty, built by somebody else, or not receiving support at all.[4]

Krakauer's *Three Cups of Deceit* also contained allegations that cast doubt on the truthfulness of Mortenson's books. Krakauer claimed that he discovered many inaccuracies in Mortenson's books and stated that "the first eight chapters of *Three Cups of Tea* are an intricately wrought work of fiction presented as fact."[5] According to an interview that he conducted with Mortenson's climbing partner, Mortenson did not spend several weeks recovering in the village of Korphe as he claimed. Instead he spent a few days, after his attempted climb, in Khane visiting the cook for the expedition with whom he had become friends. When he learned that the village had no school, Mortenson vowed to return the following year and build one. Krakauer's investigation found that Mortenson did not spend a long period recovering from the travails of his climb in Korphe or anywhere else, and the village that he promised a school to was Khane.[6] Mortenson also claimed to have been kidnapped by the Taliban and taken to South

Waziristan, which came as a surprise to his Pakistani host, who told Krakauer that Mortenson was treated graciously and had a wonderful time. His account is bolstered by photographs of Mortenson relaxing and smiling during his "captivity," and the fact that at the time of his "kidnapping" in 1996 there were no Taliban operating in that area of Pakistan. Most disturbing, however, are the questions about the success of his projects. It is unclear how many schools have actually been built, and whether those schools that have been built are in operation. *60 Minutes* concurred with the allegations in *Three Cups of Deceit*, interviewing many of the same people that Krakauer had.[7]

Unaware that Mortenson's books had serious credibility issues, the U.S. military embraced them for their supposed lessons about winning hearts and minds to shape strategies in the war on terror. Mortenson's central theme in his books is that he built schools in areas known as breeding grounds for terrorists, displacing madrassas where children were trained to be insurgents. In reality most of the schools were built in areas where the Taliban have little or no influence. Then top commander, General Stanley McChrystal, impressed by Mortenson's claim about the beneficial effect of schools and by his knowledge of Pakistani and Afghan culture as chronicled in *Three Cups of Tea* was convinced that potential insurgents could be subdued by understanding, communication, and aid.[8] The revelations about the veracity of his books don't inspire a great deal of confidence in Mortenson's insights, however. Scholarly articles were also written about *Three Cups of Tea* based on the assumption that the book was credible.[9]

The publisher of these books vowed to conduct a review of *Three Cups of Tea* and its contents with Mortenson after the *60 Minutes* story in 2011.[10] No results of the review have been released and the book is still for sale on Viking's website with no indication that any controversy surrounds it. Mortenson acknowledged that "the time about our final days on K2 and ongoing journey to Korphe village and Skardu is a compressed version of events that took place in the fall of 1993."[11] Mortenson's most egregious offense was his role in the mishandling of donations to CAI, and the falsehoods in his books kept the money pouring in from unsuspecting donors. This financial misconduct, however, has little bearing on the work of catalogers and our charge to accurately represent *Three Cups of Tea* and *Stones into Schools* in bibliographic records. It should, however, give us pause when we consider that Mortenson's mendacity misled not only casual readers, but influenced serious military strategies and academic research.

How were these books cataloged? The bibliographic records for both include summary notes, which quote the publisher's glowing descriptions of the books. They include fixed field codes that designate them as "not fiction." The subject entries include no form subdivisions that indicate that they are anything other than nonfiction and there are no notes alerting users to the questionable nature of the books.

The records for these books are not accurate representations in light of what has been alleged and the evidence that has been presented to support the charges. Therefore, a general note in the bibliographic record making catalog users aware of the controversy is in order. Because it is unclear what portion of the books are invented, and since the publisher and author have not acknowledged any major credibility problems with the books, it would not be prudent to add the form subdivision "Fiction" to the record.

Memoirs and Autobiographies

Child P.O.W.: A Memoir of Survival by A. L. Finch (2007)

Using her maiden name, A. L. Finch wrote an account of her internment in Japanese prisoner of war camps in the Philippines, China, and Japan. The year was 1942, and Finch was eight years old. Because she had contracted polio in the Philippines, Pan Am Airlines refused to allow her to fly back to the United States.[1] Finch explained that "my mother and I had gone to Manila to visit my Aunt Alice, who was an army nurse stationed there at the time. I developed polio nearly as soon as we got there and was not allowed to be transported back out of the country. Doctors didn't know as much about how the disease was transmitted back then. They didn't want me using public transportation to exit the country for fear that I would transfer polio to the general public."[2] As a consequence, she was captured by the invading Japanese and interned with her mother for a little over three years. They were poorly treated and experienced great brutality. After the book's publication, Finch's cousin Shannon Lamarche decided that she wanted to produce a movie based on the story. By 2012, *Child P.O.W.* (the film) had a director and a cast and was scheduled for release in December.[3] No movie has ever been released, however.

By 2010, critical reviews of the book began appearing. J. Michael Houlahan, a retired U.S. diplomat, who was stationed at the American Embassy in Manila from 1989 through 1992, wrote a particularly scathing review that pointed out numerous factual errors.[4] Among these, there was no major, the rank that Finch claimed her Aunt Alice held, in the U.S. Army Nurse Corps. The highest ranking officer was a captain named Maude Davison. The Bay View Hotel, which Finch characterized as "second rate" and to which she and her mother were initially transported, was actually a luxury hotel. There, Finch described seeing piles of dead women and children. Houlahan reported, however, that there was no violence at the hotel during the time that Finch was there. Finch also related a story of a camp commandant who forced internees, including Finch and her mother, to watch decapitations of other prisoners. This execution story was not found in any other wartime accounts of Japanese abuse.[5]

Finch further maintained that this camp commander "became a mega-millionaire" and a member of the Japanese Diet following the war.[6] She also claimed that the American government protected him from prosecution because it needed people to run the new Japanese government. In addition, General Douglas MacArthur placed this man at the head of an immense American electronic corporation, which MacArthur helped establish. This would have been quite a scandal, but Finch identifies neither the Japanese man nor the corporation. Finch cites two reasons for her lack of specifics. First, she feared retaliation, although it was unlikely that any war criminals were still alive to threaten her when her book came out in 2007. She also claimed that she was forced to sign a nondisclosure agreement by the American government. Other civilian internees insist that they were never asked to sign such an agreement.[7]

Finch also reported that she and her mother were moved from the Bay View Hotel to a Japanese officers' brothel in the resort city of Baguio. She described it as "near the former summer home of the Philippine emperors."[8] Houlahan asserted, however, that there was no evidence that this brothel ever existed and the Philippines was never home to any emperors. Finch also wrote that an Australian friend, Lennie, was beheaded in front of her and her mother in Fukuoka, Japan. A photograph that appeared in the book included a link to the Australian War Memorial website (https://awm.gov.au/). The website identified it as a famous photograph of Sgt. Leonard George Siffleet being decapitated on a beach in Aitape, New Guinea, not in Fukuoka, Japan. Finch never claimed to be in New Guinea, but she said she was shuffled from the Philippines to Foochow, China, before being sent to Fukuoka, Japan, and then back to the Philippines. According to Houlahan, no other accounts of prisoners being moved to so many different locations exists.[9]

Another critical reviewer was Sascha Weinzheimer Jansen, a former child internee in the Philippines and an active member of the American Ex-Prisoners of War Group. She cited additional discrepancies in *Child P.O.W.* Finch claimed that after she contracted polio in 1941 she was sent to a hospital, Nuestra Senora de Socorro de la Santa Spiritu, where the doctors and nurses were ignorant of how to treat polio. Jansen pointed out that no such hospital ever existed in Manila. In addition, in 1934 she herself had also contracted polio in the Philippines, and the Filipino and United States Army doctors had no problem treating her. Finch's account of the brutality she witnessed at the Bay View Hotel conflicted with Jansen's personal recollection of a calm transition at the hotel as it came under Japanese authority. According to Jansen (and historical records) civilian prisoners of war were transferred from the hotel to Santo Tomas, one of the Japanese internment camps in the Philippines.[10] Why would Finch and her mother have been sent to a brothel in the Baguio area that, in any case, did not appear to exist? Jansen ended her review by stating that "in my opinion, Finch's disgraceful memoir is a fabrication that would only be recognized as such by actual victims of war, true historians, researchers and scholars. She makes a mockery of the truth and puts a blight on the real history of veteran POWs of that war. Shame!"[11]

Despite this, the bibliographic record indicates in the fixed field that *Child P.O.W.* is an autobiography and utilizes the "Biography" form subdivision in the subject entries. Neither record contains any notes that would alert readers to questions of credibility. Although neither the author, nor the publisher has acknowledged any fabrication, the evidence indicating that this work contains serious factual errors and misrepresents Finch's experience is overwhelming. Replacing "Biography" with the form subdivision and the genre/form heading for "Fiction" is warranted. Whether *Child P.O.W.* is an "Autobiographical fiction" or just "Fiction" is unclear. A general note should also be added.

The Road of Lost Innocence: The True Story of a Cambodian Childhood by Somaly Mam (English edition 2007)

Somaly Mam was a star in the anti-human trafficking community, and she had a compelling story of her own. Mam was born in 1970 or 1971 (she doesn't know her exact age) in a mountain village in Cambodia. Her parents and grandmother disappeared during the Khmer Rouge era. When she was nine or ten, a man claiming to be her grandfather took her to another village where she became his domestic slave. Although she was later adopted by a couple who sent her to school, her alleged grandfather was still a presence. First, he sold Mam to a Chinese merchant and, when she was fourteen, he forced her to marry a violent soldier. At about the age of sixteen, she was sold to a brothel in Phnom Penh. In 1991, Mam met her future husband, a French biologist named Pierre Legros, who helped her escape the world of prostitution. The couple moved to France for a few years, but returned to Cambodia in 1994 when Legros took a job working for Doctors Without Borders. There, Mam, along with her husband and a friend, created a nonprofit nongovernmental organization called AFESIP (*Agir pour les Femmes en Situation Précaire*, or Acting for Women in Distressing Circumstances) to help girls escape brothels and provide a safe shelter for them.[1]

In 1998, a France 2 documentary gave the organization significant exposure, and as a result Mam was chosen as one of seven women to receive the Prince of Asturias Award for International Cooperation. AFESIP's fundraising efforts succeeded as never before, and Legros realized that media attention was the reason. To capitalize on the organization's higher profile, AFESIP opened satellite offices in Laos, Thailand, Vietnam, France, and Sweden, and Legros encouraged his wife to write a memoir. Several publishers were interested in such a project, and in 2005 the French edition of *The Road of Lost Innocence* (*Silence de l'Innocence*) was published. English editions were published in England and the United States in 2007 and 2008, respectively.[2] Mam's memoir was well received, with *Booklist* noting that her "voice is humble, matter-of-fact, and wrenchingly real."[3]

By then, Legros and Mam had separated, and Legros severed his relationship with AFESIP. In 2007, Mam co-founded the Somaly Mam Foundation, a nonprofit charity based in the United States, that was designed to provide funding to AFESIP and other anti-trafficking organizations.[4] She continued to collected awards and accolades. She was named a CNN Hero, *Glamour's* Woman of the Year and included in *Time Magazine's* 100 Most Influential People, *Fortune's* Most Powerful Women, and *Fast Company's* League of Extraordinary Women. *New York Times* columnist Nicholas Kristof wrote the foreword to her book, calling her "the Harriet Tubman of Southeast Asia brothels," and featured her in his documentary, *Half the Sky*. She had other high-profile supporters such as Susan Sarandon, Angelina Jolie, Facebook COO Sheryl Sandberg, and Hillary Clinton's former chief of staff Melanne Verveer.[5]

In April of 2012, Mam told a U.N. panel that in 2004 the Cambodian military killed eight girls in a raid on AFESIP's center in Phnom Penh. Cambodian police questioned the claim and Mam hastened to clarify that "some of my comments were ambiguous and my intention was not to misrepresent the course of events in 2004.... I had in no way intended to allege that the girls were murdered during the shelter raid."[6] This was only the beginning of questions about Mam's truthfulness. Nicholas Kristof had written about one of the girls that Mam had rescued. Long Pross was kidnapped and sold to a brothel where she was beaten, forced to undergo two crude abortions, and had an eye gouged out with a piece of metal by a pimp. The eye had become infected and was crudely removed. Her parents and eye surgeon told a different story, however. Dr. Pok Thorn recalled that Pross' parents had brought her to him when she was thirteen to remove a nonmalignant tumor covering her right eye.[7] An Australian newspaper spoke to Pross' father in 2013 and he confirmed that "she had a disease and I took her to the hospital myself."[8] Meas Ratha, another girl allegedly rescued by Mam, told a horrifying tale on French television in 1998. She had been sold to a brothel and held against her will. In late 2013, however, Ratha confessed that the story was fabricated. She had auditioned and won the "role" of a former sex slave, rehearsing for her television appearance under the tutelage of Mam. Although Ratha was reticent to portray herself as a child prostitute, according to her "Somaly said that … if I want to help another woman I have to do [the interview] very well."[9]

Mam's own life story was also questioned. Simon Marks, a reporter who wrote for *The Cambodia Daily* newspaper and *Newsweek*, interviewed Mam's childhood acquaintances, teachers, and local officials in the village where she grew up. A former commune chief, Orn Hok, recalled that she moved to the village with her parents, and did not remember any cruel grandfather. A classmate remembered that Mam first attended the school in the village in 1981 and received her high school diploma in 1987, a story that was corroborated by the director of Khchao High School, as well as the commune chief. This contradicted Mam's version of events, but Mam also contradicted herself on various occasions. Mam, speaking at the White House in 2012, claimed that she was sold into slavery at age nine or ten and spent a decade in the brothel. On *The Tyra Banks Show*, she said that she spent four or five years in the brothel, while in *The Road of Lost Innocence*, she stated that she was trafficked when she was about sixteen years old.[10]

Mam also asserted that her daughter, Nieng, was kidnapped in 2006 in retaliation for Mam's work, but her ex-husband, Legros, contended Nieng was Mam's niece and that she ran away with her boyfriend. When Legros was asked why he was speaking out, he said, "I kept silent so far because I do not really think this debate over Somaly's lies is of interest. When you work in this world, you know fabricated stories are used by everyone to get funding. But I received death threats from Somaly and her entourage, telling me not to speak. I do it for my children, for the truth to be restored and to denounce the logic of a failing system praising 'development.'"[11]

If what Legros said was true, then it was not surprising that several of the people who claimed that Mam coached them to lie later retracted their claims, perhaps in fear for their lives or livelihood. The magazine, *Marie Claire*, published Mam's side of the story in 2014, and made the argument that the allegations of Mam's dishonesty were inaccurate. They re-interviewed several of the people that reporter Marks had talked to for his original article and their stories changed. The high school director, who by that time was working for AFESIP, said that Mam left school after seventh grade. Dr. Pok Thorn, the surgeon who removed Long Pross' right eye, could no longer remember her.[12]

Nevertheless, the Somaly Mam Foundation retained a law firm in March 2014 to investigate the allegations of Mam's dishonesty, and by May of that year Mam had resigned from the foundation. The details of the report were never released, and it is not known if the report was the impetus for her resignation.[13] Her champion Nicholas Kristof admitted in *The New York Times* that the article by Marks "makes a strong case."[14] He conceded that "sorting out the facts will take time, and we may never know for sure what is true or false in Somaly Mam's past. I now wish I had never written about her, given my doubts."[15] The Somaly Mam Foundation announced in October 2014 that it was closing its doors, and many believed that Mam's reputation was damaged beyond repair. In February 2015, however, Mam co-founded The New Somaly Mam Foundation.[16]

Neither the bibliographic record for the United Kingdom publication, nor the record for the American version include any indication that *The Road of Lost Innocence* has been challenged on its veracity. The record for the American edition of the book includes a description from the publisher in a summary note. Although a designation of fiction may be premature, a general note describing the questions surrounding the book would be appropriate.

Angel at the Fence: The True Story of a Love That Survived by Herman Rosenblat (2008)

Angel at the Fence is a book with a tangled history. It was favorably reviewed prior to publication in *Kirkus* where it was described as Herman Rosenblat's account of his internment as a child and teenager in a Nazi concentration camp during World War II.[1] The dark story was leavened by Rosenblat's description of encounters he had at the camp's fence with a girl who lived nearby. She tossed apples and bread to him, thus supplementing his meager diet and saving his life. Miraculously, they met again on a blind date twelve years later in Coney Island where they both then lived. Herman Rosenblat and Roma Radzicki eventually married and celebrated their fiftieth wedding anniversary in 2008.[2]

Although the book was never selected by Oprah Winfrey for her coveted Book Club, the Rosenblats appeared twice on her television show prior to the projected publication date. Winfrey enthused that their romance was "the single greatest love story" that she had seen in her twenty-two years on her show.[3] Inspired by this interview, Laurie Friedman wrote a children's book based on the love story that was published by Lerner Publishing.[4] Atlantic Overseas Pictures also announced its plan to produce a film based on Rosenblat's book.[5]

Kenneth Waltzer, the director of Jewish studies at Michigan State University, did not set out to discredit Rosenblat's account. He was working on a book about an underground rescue operation inside Buchenwald that had saved the lives of 904 boys. He interviewed hundreds of survivors, including some who were with Rosenblat. They told Waltzer that Rosenblat's story could not be true. First, the fence he referred to was visible to the SS barracks and anyone loitering by it would have been spotted. In addition, the fence was electrified and civilians outside the camp were barred from walking along the road that bordered the fence. Waltzer verified these claims with maps, and also discovered that Roma Radzicki and her family were hidden at a farm 210 miles away from Schlieben, the camp where Rosenblat was held. Waltzer was one of several scholars and family members to dispute the veracity of the book.[6] At first, Berkley Books, the publisher, and Rosenblat denied the accusations. Rosenblat protested that "I was a young child at the time my family was caught up in the Holocaust, and I saw things through a young child's eyes. But I know and remember what I saw."[7]

Soon, however, the publisher was backing away, cancelling publication of the book and demanding that money advanced to Rosenblat and his agent be returned. His agent, Andrea Hurst, stated that "Herman revealed to me that part of his memoir was not true. He'd invented the crux of this amazing love story—about the girl at the fence who threw him an apple—which drew my attention when I read it in a major magazine [*Guideposts*] two years ago. All of the story about Herman in the concentration camps and the love and survival of him and his brothers, he states is true."[8] Rosenblat apologized, but explained, "Why did I do that and write the story with the girl and the apple, because I wanted to bring happiness to people, to remind them not to hate, but to love and tolerate all people."[9] In addition to the cancelled publication of *Angel at the Fence*, the publisher of the children's book, *Angel Girl*, canceled pending reprints and offered a refund for any returned books.[10]

Rosenblat's story did not disappear, however. Atlantic Overseas Pictures, which was producing the movie based on Rosenblat's story, said it would proceed with the film portraying "the fictional elements of the love story." Atlantic said that as a condition to moving forward, Rosenblat had agreed to donate all profits of the film to Holocaust survivor charities.[11] The movie, *Flower at the Fence,* has yet to materialize. Soon after the deception was revealed, York House announced that it would release the book as a work of fiction. A version of the book titled *The Apple: Based on the Herman Rosenblat Holocaust Love Story* was published in 2009, but it had morphed into a different genre. While the bibliographic record clearly indicates that this is a work of fiction, the author, Penelope Holt, contended that the book "went to press as creative non-fiction."[12]

Despite the aborted publication of the Berkley Books edition of *Angel at the Fence*, OCLC shows that eighteen libraries hold it and the bibliographic record gives no indication that it is not a biography, as its subdivisions claim. There is really no suitable form subdivision given what we know about the book, but the genre/form heading of "Autobiographical fiction" should be included along with a general note explaining the deception.

Love and Consequences: A Memoir of Hope and Survival by Margaret B. Jones (2008)

Love and Consequences offered a unique perspective on life in South Central Los Angeles in the late 1980s and early 1990s. Margaret B. Jones was a mixed-race white and Native American who grew up in a callous foster care system. She found some refuge when she was sent to live with Big Mom, a tough, religious African American woman who also cared for her own four grandchildren. Jones grew up among gangbangers in Blood territory. Two of her foster brothers joined the gang and she followed them, cooking crack and running drugs to pay the water bill. Fortuitously, a teacher saw promise in Jones and encouraged her to apply to college. After she was admitted to the University of Oregon and graduated, her life took a dramatic turn for the better.[1]

In another lucky twist of fate, a creative-writing professor in Oregon admired the stories Jones had written in class about her life in Los Angeles, and asked her to speak to author Inga Muscio, who was writing a book on racism. Muscio used some of Jones' accounts in her book and introduced Jones to her agent, Faye Bender. In 2005, Bender sent about one hundred pages of Jones' writing to four publishers. Riverhead Books gave Jones an advance of less than $100,000 and she worked closely with editor Sarah McGrath for three years.[2]

Love and Consequences was published in 2008 to rave reviews. The *Library Journal* review marveled that "this conversationally written, exquisitely detailed book is as close to a living experience of the American ghetto as one can get."[3] *The New York Times* noted that "what sets Ms. Jones' humane and deeply affecting memoir apart is not just that it's told from the point of view of a young girl coming of age in this world, but also that it focuses on the bonds of love and loyalty that can bind relatives and gang members together."[4]

Jones' downfall, however, came as the result of a profile in the House & Home section of *The New York Times.* Reporter Mimi Read visited her in her four-bedroom bungalow in Eugene, Oregon, where she lived with her daughter who was born while Jones was in college. Read described her as a single mom with a rocky past and a warm heart, still, for the disadvantaged. Jones told Read that she had recently started a gang truce organization called International Brother/SisterHood to help young people escape gang life.[5] Unfortunately for Jones, the article caught the attention of her sister, Cyndi Hoffman, who notified the publisher that the story Jones told in her book was untrue. Her real name was Margaret Seltzer; she was white, and she had grown up in the affluent Sherman Oaks section of Los Angeles with her biological family. Seltzer graduated from Campbell Hall School, a private school in North Hollywood, but had not graduated from the University of Oregon.[6]

Riverhead Books immediately recalled 19,000 copies of *Love and Consequences*, offered refunds to book buyers, and canceled Seltzer's book tour.[7] Seltzer remorsefully admitted that the account of her personal experiences in the book was fabricated, but insisted that much was based on the experiences of close friends she had met while working to reduce gang violence in Los Angeles. She explained that "for whatever reason, I was really torn and I thought it was my opportunity to put a voice to people who people don't listen to. I was in a position where at one point people said you should speak for us because nobody else is going to let us in to talk."[8] It is doubtful, however, that Seltzer did much, if any, work with gangs, and the gang truce organization she claimed to have founded did not appear to exist.[9] Hoffman, Seltzer's sister, was dismayed at the whole affair, declaring, "I don't know how [the publisher does] business, but I would think that protocol would have them doing fact-checking."[10]

For her part, Sarah McGrath, the Riverhead editor who worked with Seltzer, was stunned. She and Seltzer had worked together on the book for three years, although she had never met her personally. She knew that Seltzer was using a pseudonym, but McGrath said that she trusted her, in part, because she had come to McGrath through "a respected literary agent."[11] Another agent who was not involved with *Love and Consequences* explained that book publishing "is not an industry capable of checking every last detail, so to present yourself as something you are not betrays all the trust."[12]

In this case we see directly the harm that such false tales can do. A legitimate author, Inga Muscio, included Seltzer's lies in her book on racism. Such a thing could happen again if a catalog user relies on the bibliographic record for *Love and Consequences* as it stands. The record is coded as an autobiography in the fixed field and the subdivision "Biography" is assigned. There is no indication that the book is fiction, either in the bibliographic record or the authority record for Margaret B. Jones, although there is a cross-reference to her given name. The bibliographic record should be edited to reflect that the book is fiction by replacing the form subdivision "Biography" with "Fiction" and adding the genre/form heading "Fictional autobiographies."

The Boy Who Came Back from Heaven: A Remarkable Account of Miracles, Angels, and Life Beyond This World by Kevin and Alex Malarkey (2010)

The Boy Who Came Back from Heaven is the inspirational true story of Alex Malarkey, a six-year-old boy who was critically injured in a 2004 car accident. When he regained consciousness, after a two-month coma, he was a quadriplegic, but had an incredible tale to tell. He had visited heaven and had seen angels and met Jesus.[1]

Alex attracted the attention of the media in 2009, when he became the youngest person to receive a "diaphragm pacing system," which was installed by the same surgeon who treated actor Christopher Reeve after his horse-riding accident. An Associated Press reporter suggested to Alex's father, Kevin, that he write a book, but did not specify what it should be about. Four months later Kevin had a literary agent and *The Boy Who Came Back from Heaven*, purportedly co-written by Kevin and Alex, was published by Tyndale House in 2010, and reissued in 2014.[2] The Christian book publisher described the book as "the true story of an ordinary boy's most extraordinary journey. As you see heaven and earth through Alex's eyes, you'll come away with new insights on miracles, life beyond this world, and the power of a father's love."[3] Although the book was not widely reviewed, it spent many weeks on the *New York Times* nonfiction best seller list in 2011 and sold over a million copies.[4]

In January of 2015, however, a sensational confession was revealed by both the mainstream and Christian press. Alex confessed in an "open letter to Lifeway [the religious bookstore] and other sellers, buyers, and marketers of heaven tourism … [that] I did not die. I did not go to Heaven. I said I went to heaven because I thought it would get me attention. When I made the claims that I did I had never read the Bible. People have profited from lies, and continue to. They should read the Bible, which is enough."[5]

This, however, was not Alex's or his mother's first attempt to set the record straight. In August 2011, Alex left a comment under his own name on the Facebook fan page for the book stating that this was "1 of the most deceptive books ever."[6] The comment was removed, perhaps because no one believed that Alex had actually posted it. As early as 2012, Alex's mother, Beth, contacted the publisher complaining of inaccuracies in the book that were the result of this being Kevin's story, not Alex's story, and it did not truly reflect Alex's experience.[7] All parties seemed to agree that Alex did not help write the book, despite the fact that his name was on the title page. Alex never signed a contract with the publisher and his father had applied for and received sole copyright. Beth also asserted that Alex did not receive "monies from the book nor have a majority of his needs been funded by it."[8]

Despite this, the book's publisher, Tyndale, claimed on January 15, 2015, that "this was the first time Tyndale had been told that Alex fabricated the story. We were alerted to his public statement on January 14, 2015, and have since confirmed Alex's retraction with his father, Kevin Malarkey."[9] In response, Tyndale "immediately put the book and all ancillary products into out-of-print status," and informed retailers that they could return any unsold books if they chose to.[10]

Tyndale also acknowledged a controversy among Christians regarding the sub-genre of real-life tales of paradise, also known as heavenly tourism, stating that "Tyndale goes through an extensive vetting process and exercises discernment to ensure that the books we publish are consistent with biblical principles. At the same time, we recognize that there are many different perspectives as to what does or does not conform to biblical truth."[11] They were, perhaps, responding to a resolution passed in the summer of 2014 by the Southern Baptist Convention declaring that books and movies describing afterlife experiences are "antithetical to Scripture," and reaffirming "the sufficiency of biblical revelation over subjective experiential explanations to guide one's understanding of the truth about heaven and hell."[12]

In the bibliographic records for the 2010 and 2014 editions, there is no hint of any controversy surrounding this book. The fixed field in the record for the 2010 edition indicates that it contains biographical information. Neither record utilizes the form subdivision "Fiction." The summary notes consist of straightforward synopses of what the book purports to be about, a description of heaven based on Alex's experience. Given Alex Malarkey's confession and the actions of the publisher, the form subdivision "Fiction" is warranted, as is the genre/form heading "Fiction autobiography." There should also be a note describing the controversy surrounding the book.

The Man Who Broke into Auschwitz: A True Story of World War II by Denis Avey with Rob Broomby (2011)

Denis Avey kept his most significant experience in a World War II German prisoner of war camp secret for almost sixty-five years, which was odd because he had a very important and unique tale to tell. Avey enlisted in the British Army in 1939, and in

The Man Who Broke into Auschwitz

1940 he was shipped to Egypt where he nearly died. He was part of the crew in a gun carrier that was hit by a grenade and his best friend was killed. In 1941 he was taken prisoner in Libya and eventually arrived at a work camp called E715, which was a short distance from Auschwitz III (also known as Monowitz). Here, prisoners assigned to forced labor at a rubber works owned by the German conglomerate I.G. Farben were housed. Auschwitz II, or Auschwitz-Birkenau, was about six miles from E715 and was the camp where the Nazis perfected their gas chambers and where most of their prisoners were killed.[1]

While working in the POW camp, Avey became acquainted with Jewish laborers also assigned to work there, although communication between prisoners was prohibited. He befriended a prisoner named Ernst Lobethal, to whom he provided smuggled cigarettes, a valuable commodity in the camps. Avey also became acquainted with an Auschwitz prisoner named Hans, but he could not recall his last name. He became obsessed with bearing witness to the brutality that surrounded him and to that end he convinced Hans to trade places with him so that Avey could gain first-hand exposure to life in a concentration camp. He and Hans switched clothes and identities on two occasions, despite the extreme danger this posed for both men if they were discovered. Avey described what he saw and experienced in Monowitz (Auschwitz III) in *The Man Who Broke into Auschwitz*. He saw a dead body hanging from gallows and smelled the foul odor coming from the crematorium and dead bodies. He walked under that notorious sign that proclaimed *Arbeit Macht Frei* ("Work Sets You Free") and slept with lice-ridden inmates. Avey and Hans somehow avoided detection and certain death. Avey's heroic acts earned him the British Hero of the Holocaust Award in 2010.[2]

Some people, however, were puzzled by discrepancies between his account in the book and accounts he had provided in earlier interviews. He told the *Daily Mail* in 2009 that he had switched places with Ernst Lobethal, not Hans, and that he had infiltrated Auschwitz II, not Auschwitz III. Even more troubling, Avey had given a five-hour interview to the Imperial War Museum in 2001, in which he never mentioned smuggling himself into either Auschwitz III or Auschwitz II. He did, however, mention being in Auschwitz II and trying to contact an Australian prisoner who was forced to stoke the crematorium. Later, Avey discovered, the Australian had published a book about his experience called *Stoker*, which he managed to find and read (see entry for *Stoker*). Unfortunately, *Stoker* was discredited as a false account in 1997 when investigators could find no evidence that its author, Donald Watt, had ever been incarcerated in Auschwitz II.[3] There were other problems with Avey's account in the book. Brian Bishop who was also held captive in E715 asserted that "to do something like that [switch places with a Jewish inmate] you need to have several people helping on both sides—our side and the Jewish side."[4] This would have been almost impossible given the number of spies in the camp.

Avey's claim that he walked under the infamous "Work Sets You Free" sign as he entered Auschwitz III was also factually untrue. The sign was at the entrance of Auschwitz I.[5] Avey's reference to Jewish inmates infested with lice made no sense to former prisoner Sam Pivnik who stated, "We were made to be scrupulously clean at all times in Auschwitz III work-camps, and you risked a severe beating if you got dirty."[6] Perhaps most damning was that Avey's story was almost identical to one told by another former POW in camp E715 named Charles Coward. Coward testified in a post-war trial that he had infiltrated Auschwitz by switching places with a Jewish prisoner. The story was widely discredited by Holocaust scholars, but was included in a 1954 book about Coward's supposed ordeal called *The Password is Courage.* The book jacket refers to him as "The Man Who Broke into Auschwitz," the title that appeared on Avey's book.[7]

Avey and his co-author Rob Broomby, a journalist for the BBC, maintained that the events depicted in their book were true. Broomby stated that "this poor man had the supreme misfortune to end up a witness to the most supreme injustice of all time. Those around him had no idea who would survive to tell what happened. The Jews said to him, 'Please, if you get home, tell the world. Tell the world.' He did what he could."[8] Why, then, did Avey wait until 2011 to respond to their plea? According to Broomby, Avey "was not a well man. When he came back, he was questioned by military officers, and he sensed that people didn't want to hear about it. So he just shut down."[9] Peter Black, senior historian at the United States Holocaust Museum, was troubled by the claim that the military did not want to hear about his experiences. "That would surprise me. Right at the end of the war, the British and US military were looking for evidence of atrocities and for suspects to indict. They were very eager. It could well be that if Avey's story wasn't credible enough, they didn't want to hear more from him," Black stated.[10]

The publisher, Hodder & Stoughton did not back away from the book, stating that it was "proud to publish [it]" and that "we have never doubted Mr. Avey's testimony."[11] Avey, responding to growing skepticism, stated, "I am disappointed and sorry that they have doubted my word. This sort of thing is deeply unpleasant.... I did what I did and that is it. In war everything you do is more extreme. I stand by my account. It is a fact."[12] Yad Vashem, Israel's official memorial to the Jewish victims of the Holocaust, however, issued a statement that it would not honor Avey with the title "Righteous Among the Nations," an award given to Gentiles who saved Jews during the war, because it was unable to verify his account of the prisoner swaps.[13]

The bibliographic record for the British edition utilizes the form subdivisions "Personal narratives" and "Biography." Records for both the British and American editions include summary notes that describe the book as "a true story." No doubt *The Man Who Broke into Auschwitz* is partially true, but Avey's central claim of trading places with a Jewish inmate in Auschwitz III is very questionable. A general note to this effect should be included.

Other Nonfiction

> But the trouble with a lie is that it's easier to believe than the truth.
> —Denis Johnson, *Fiskadoro*

Memoirs are one genre of nonfiction, but this section will look at nonfiction books that are not memoirs. While memoirs are based on memories, these are works that are presented as historically or empirically accurate, and include the genre of biography. Nonfiction writers must conduct sound and responsible research that catalogers and the general public expect to be reliable. It is not surprising then that we assume that a book that is presented to the reader as nonfiction is factual. Unfortunately, that faith is sometimes misplaced. Craig Silverman, author of a book on media accuracy, explains, "A lot of readers have the perception that when something arrives as a book, it's gone through a more rigorous fact-checking process than a magazine or a newspaper or a website, and that's simply not the case."[1] Although journalists are obliged by their professional standards to fact-check their articles, no such principle applies to authors and publishers. Contrary to popular belief, fact-checking has never been standard practice in the book-publishing industry. Nevertheless, National Book Award winning author Ron Chernow notes that "people tend to accept more uncritically what they read in a book than what they read in a magazine or newspaper."[2]

Nonfiction book contracts offered by publishers typically require an author to stipulate that every fact is true and that the accuracy of the book is the sole responsibility of the writer. There are certain processes that the publisher will perform. A copy editor checks basic names and dates, and the publisher's attorney will review the book for potential libel or copyright infringement. "What about the editor?" you might ask. The relationship between the editor and the author is based on trust that is developed over the months it takes to write and edit a book, and the editor serves as the author's advocate within the publishing house. This role is not conducive to a critical examination of the book's accuracy. If a fact-checker is employed at all, the author himself usually hires her and pays for the service. Despite numerous examples of nonfiction books that have serious factual errors, there does not seem to be any movement toward more fact-checking by publishers.[3]

There are several reasons for this. First, publishers do not consider fact-checking to be their responsibility. David Rosenthal, former executive vice president and publisher at Simon & Schuster, explained, "We place the onus, contractually in fact, on the author.... We do not do a line-by-line check; we rely on the warranties of the author, as well as the author's bona fides, which we regard as critical in commissioning a book."[4]

Publishers also claim that fact-checking is not cost-effective. Former Random House publisher Daniel Menaker argued that "it would be impossible for publishers to check all their books and still create an economy of scale."[5] Another, former publisher of Soft Skull Press Richard Nash added, "If fact-checking was involved, we'd all publish far fewer books, and that isn't going to add to the store of human knowledge."[6]

Finally, publishers are not subject to any long-term consequences for publishing a fact-challenged book. Few people remember who published *Arming America*, the discredited history of gun ownership, for example. There was no movement to boycott them or punish them in any way. Only rarely are books recalled by the publisher and refunds given to purchasers.[7]

Virtually all nonfiction books contain some errors. Author Jean Strouse acknowledged that mistakes are unavoidable because "there's no way in a great big project that you're going to get everything right unless you spend 40 years on it."[8] A research editor for *The New York Times Magazine* put it more bluntly, saying, "It's impossible to write 50, 60, 70,000 words and not screw up somewhere."[9] When errors are discovered after publication, publishers do not have the option to just run a correction in the next issue. Most publishers quietly correct mistakes in the next edition.[10] Very few publishers would be willing to publish nonfiction if it was deemed reasonable to label a book fraudulent because it contains a handful of minor errors.

What is the harm in a few factual errors slipping through the writing and editing process? Often, on the face of it, not that much. Chernow, however, argues that even small errors can have large consequences. He says, "The historical error can be very much like the virus that spreads from book to book."[11] Fact checkers and authors usually consider books in print to be authoritative and rely on them to verify information. Thus, a factual error can gain credence through its repeated use in other books.[12]

Consider the book *Arming America* by historian Michael Bellesiles, published in 2000. It was based on what turned out to be shoddy research about gun ownership in eighteenth-century America. It supported the "collective right" interpretation of the Second Amendment of the Constitution, and was the basis of Amicus Curiae briefs submitted to the U.S. Fifth Circuit Court of Appeals by gun-control advocates in U.S. vs. Emerson. We will look at this book more closely, but suffice to say that the "facts" drawn from *Arming America* could have led to a court decision that was based on erroneous information.[13]

Although comedian Stephen Colbert facetiously argued that "truthiness" is an acceptable standard in today's world, and *Oxford Dictionaries* selected "post-truth" as the international word for 2016, facts still matter.[14] Catalogers clearly have a responsibility to accurately represent questionable nonfiction that is allegedly based on research, not memories. The consequences of ignoring this obligation are too great to shrug off. Notable librarian Will Manley asserts, "As librarians we are the reader's last line of defense against this kind of deceit."[15]

The following books have been judged by experts in their discipline to be, if not fraudulent, at least significantly inaccurate. This presents the cataloger with a dilemma. Referring to *The Last Train from Hiroshima,* a book with enough serious errors that the publisher stopped printing and shipping it, one librarian asserted, "I think merely by including something in our collections, that somehow lends credence to it."[16] Another librarian argued that it still might have value to readers, if only for curiosity's sake.[17] Both arguments are worth considering, but if a library chooses to retain such a book, it is imperative that it be cataloged in such a way that the user understands what it is.

Never Cry Wolf by Farley Mowat (1963)

When Farley Mowat died in 2014, he was lauded as a Canadian national treasure. He had published forty-five books that were translated into over twenty languages in more than sixty countries around the world, and garnered a number of literary awards.[1] Mowat also had managed to stir up his share of controversy, particularly with his popular work of nonfiction, *Never Cry Wolf.*

Never Cry Wolf was a book that anthropomorphized wolf behavior based on Mowat's study of their effect on the caribou population in the Canadian tundra. He portrayed wolves as playful, family-centered animals that he gave names like "George" and "Angeline," and even reported climbing into their den with a mother and her pups. This was not a reputation they had enjoyed in recent times. For thousands of years, attitudes toward the grey wolf have been mixed. Native American medicine men summoned the wolf who furnished hunting advice and guided travelers in dangerous situations to safety. In eighteenth-century Europe, Little Red Riding Hood's tragic encounter with a wolf served as a warning to all small children of the perils of getting too close to the predator. Pioneers in North America shivered at the howls of wolves and shared tales of the animal's insatiable appetite for cattle.[2]

The New York Times published a favorable review stating, "Mr. Mowat's genial self-mockery is amusing, but his account of the wolves and his wolf information is fascinating."[3] Another review informed the reader that "he will find this reading a delightful experience, as well as a basis for cultivation of a modern point of view toward this much-storied predator." The reviewer further noted, "Since the book is directed to the general reader, it is without documentation. Undoubtedly Mowat has a technical report in the files of the Canadian Wildlife Service in which this documentation has been provided."[4]

This assumption hints at why this seemingly benign tome was met with a great deal of criticism, as well. In *Never Cry Wolf,* Mowat was unsparing in his mockery of the Canadian Wildlife Service, under whose auspices he performed his study of wolves. One of his former supervisors, A. W. F. Banfield, noted that "with a fair share of malice and considerable literary licence with the facts, [Mowat] caricatures us and parodies the Canadian Wildlife Service."[5] Banfield went on to claim that Mowat's book was not particularly original, saying, "During Mowat's 'indoctrination' period in Ottawa, he was given several books to read including Adolph Murie's *The Wolves of Mount McKinley,*

1944. Any resemblance between *Never Cry Wolf* and that book is *not* coincidental. Much is familiar, including first names for the wolves and the crawl into the burrow. [Mowat] disproved no scientific concepts about wolves—only his own misconceptions. Instead he sets up his own straw men to bowl over."[6]

In his book, Mowat said that he was hired by a government "predation control division" to study wolves in order to justify the animal's extermination. Actually, the Wildlife Service asked him to observe wolves as part of the caribou study. There is no evidence that the Canadian government was conducting a "war on wolves" at this time.[7] Contrary to Mowat's assertion in his book that his analysis of wolf behavior conflicted with that of the established scientific community, Douglas Pimlott, of the Department of Zoology at the University of Toronto, argued that "the fact is that scientists of the Wildlife Service have consistently presented the same case that Mowat makes, that is, that killing by humans [not wolves] is the principal problem in the decline of the caribou."[8]

In 1996, a story, which attacked Mowat's credibility, was published in *Saturday Night*, a well-established Canadian general interest magazine. Comparing Mowat's published books (he based at least three of his nonfiction books on his experience with the Canadian Wildlife Service) with archival documents, reporter John Goddard found many discrepancies. In 1948, Mowat was hired by the Canadian Wildlife Service to assist with a study of caribou in the Northwest Territories, about which the government knew little. The agency was concerned that mining activities and an influx of outsiders after the war were having a deleterious effect on the caribou population. Mowat, despite the fact that he apparently had no formal education in science, was to help his friend, who was studying biology, gather as much data on caribou as possible: migration routes, habitats, reproduction rates, etc.[9]

According to Mowat's log book, he completed almost ninety hours of observation in a four-week period. He claimed, in *Never Cry Wolf*, that he spent two years in the tundra, when he actually spent two summers totaling less than six months. His book describes his interactions with the wolves as he engaged in solitary research. In fact, he was never alone with the animals and his wife was with him part of the time.[10]

Mowat was forthcoming about his relationship with facts. He called his writing "subjective nonfiction" because "truth is largely subjective." He asserted that "the primary consideration for a writer is to entertain."[11] Perhaps more telling was Mowat's response to the *Saturday Night* article. He explained that he did not have the time or space to rebut all the accusations, but that they would be dealt with in his forthcoming autobiography. In fact, he did not refute any of the specific allegations in his response. He seemed primarily agitated by the idea that Goddard had access to the private papers Mowat had donated to McMaster University, on which he had imposed an embargo. In fact, Goddard was not given access to those papers (he viewed them somewhere else) and Mowat later apologized to the university for assuming that he had.[12]

Many in the literary community rose to his defense. Naturalist and author Stuart Houston conceded that "anyone who knows Farley knows that he has a difficult time understanding where truth ends and his imagination begins ... and we love him for it."[13]

When he died, his longtime editor, Susan Renouf, asserted that Mowat "was one of the inventors of creative nonfiction. We didn't have a name for it when he wrote it. Nobody knew what to do with what he did, the kind of storytelling he did."[14]

Creative nonfiction, however, does not give the writer permission to misstate the facts. The term does not imply that the author changed the details of events in order to make a book more entertaining. To label a book "nonfiction" creates an implicit contract between the author and the reader, which says, "I will not lie to you." Mowat broke that contract, happily, conceding that he "never let the facts get in the way of the truth!"[15]

Letters from readers written to the Canadian Wildlife Service, however, show that they took this "contract" seriously. One letter writer touted the book as "fabulously well-written, but most important, it is telling the truth." Another cast Mowat as the truth-teller and the scientific community as ill-informed, declaring that "I respectfully suggest that you make it required reading for every member of your Service—and for that reason I have sent you a copy!"[16] Others, however, were more cavalier about the importance of facts. A Carleton University journalism professor admitted that he could forgive Mowat the "venial sin" of embellishment because of the larger good done by "forcing our attention on to the other creatures that inhabit the earth."[17]

Many catalogers may agree with the professor, but when it comes to performing our professional duties we must adhere to a different standard. Our contract is with the catalog user, who deserves to be told what the book is, which is not exactly nonfiction. When an English teacher encourages other educators to use *Never Cry Wolf* in their classrooms because it represents "the best in nonfiction," we have not done our job.[18] The bibliographic record represents the book as nonfiction, and although this book does not warrant a "Fiction" subdivision, there should be a note describing the controversy surrounding it.

In Cold Blood: A True Account of a Multiple Murder and Its Consequences by Truman Capote (1965)

In Cold Blood was a wildly successful book written in a form the world had never seen before, according to its author, Truman Capote. He called it a "nonfiction novel," the artfully written true story of the 1959 murders of four members of the prosperous, respected Kansas Clutter family. Parents, Herbert and Bonnie, along with their children Nancy and Kenyon, were shot and killed in their home during a robbery gone wrong.[1] Capote warned an interviewer not to confuse the nonfiction novel with the documentary novel, which he described as "a popular and interesting but impure genre, which allows all the latitude of the fiction writer, but usually contains neither the persuasiveness of fact nor the poetic attitude fiction is capable of reaching. The author lets his imagination run riot over the facts!"[2] In contrast, Capote asserted that his book was "a narrative form that employed all the techniques of fictional art but was nevertheless immaculately factual."[3]

Capote described a methodical and extensive research process. He recounted that it took about a month for the Kansas locals to become comfortable enough with him to speak candidly. He trained himself to transcribe conversations from memory with 95 percent accuracy because he felt that tape recording or note taking would interfere with communication and make the subject wary. Capote did in-depth research on murders, murderers, and crime, and had filled a small room to the ceiling with letters, newspaper clippings, and court documents.[4]

Reviewers were impressed with the book, but some were unsure of Capote's "nonfiction novel" designation. One noted that "what distinguishes *In Cold Blood* from most run-of-the-mill non-fictional narratives is Capote's use of dialogue and interior monologues based on his characters' actual words…. Though I have reservations about the interior monologues."[5] F. W. Dupee, in *The New York Review of Books*, concluded that despite the lack of documentation, he was persuaded that "*In Cold Blood* is to be read as *fact*."[6] Another reviewer noted, "In his best moments, Capote manages to liberate his images from the events which created them and in those moments *In Cold Blood* seems literally too good to be true."[7]

Less than a year later some journalists aired their own misgivings, questioning if *In Cold Blood* was as "immaculately factual" as Capote claimed. One of the first, Robert Pearman in the *Kansas City Times*, pointed out several minor inaccuracies. Capote had portrayed Bobby Rupp, Nancy Clutter's boyfriend, as an exceptional athletic star, when by Rupp's own admission he "was just an average small-town basketball player."[8] Capote's description of the fate of Nancy's beloved horse, Babe, after Nancy's death was disputed. Capote recounted that a Mennonite farmer bought her for seventy-five dollars and planned to use her for plowing. Actually, the man who bought Babe was not a Mennonite and he paid $182.50 for her, in part because she was in foal. In the summer she was used at the YMCA to train children to ride.[9]

Journalists chronicled more serious discrepancies. While Capote's descriptions of the victims as individuals were superficial, he drew a detailed profile of the murderers, particularly Perry Smith. It is generally recognized in literary circles that in order to make a crime story appealing to the reader he must be led to sympathize with the perpetrator.[10] Capote applied this axiom in several instances through his description of Smith's actions and words. One vignette, allegedly reported by the jailer's wife, Mrs. Meier, who brought Smith his meals, has him reaching out his hands to her and tearfully saying, "I'm embraced by shame."[11] Meier later told a reporter that this incident never happened. She had never heard him cry and that he was actually rather bitter. We cannot rule out the possibility that Smith said these words to Capote, but contrary to the account in the book, Mrs. Meier was not the source of this story.[12]

Capote's account of Smith's last words before he was hanged also do not comport with what witnesses heard. Capote was not present at the execution, but Bill Brown, editor of the Garden City *Telegram* was. He wrote down Smith's last words and verified his notes with other witnesses before he shared them with Capote. According to Brown, Smith said, "Any apology for what I have done would be meaningless at this time. I say this especially because there's a great deal I could have offered society. I certainly think capital punishment is legally and morally wrong. I don't have any animosities toward anyone involved in this matter. I think that is all."[13] Capote recounted, however, Smith said, "It would be meaningless to apologize for what I did. Even inappropriate. But I do. I apologize."[14]

There is also evidence that individuals who provided the greatest research assistance to Capote were portrayed most favorably in the book. None were represented more positively than Kansas Bureau of Investigation agent Alvin Dewey, the lead investigator in the case. The notes that Capote used to write *In Cold Blood* are housed in the New York Public Library, and provide insight into Dewey's role in the book's creation, and possibly Dewey's heroic depiction. Dewey gave Capote and his assistant, novelist Harper Lee, exclusive access to the Clutter files for a week, as well as access to Nancy Clutter's diary. He also granted them private interviews with the two murderers, while denying interviews to other journalists. Capote spent a very short period of time in Kansas doing research, relying on Dewey to send him the information he needed. In addition, Dewey was instrumental in convincing residents of the small Kansas town to cooperate with Capote. In letters Capote penned while writing *In Cold Blood*, he explicitly stated that he intended to make Dewey the hero of the book.[15]

This may account for one small, but telling, distortion of the truth in the book. In 2013, long-lost KBI files were discovered that depict the capture of the killers differently than Capote did in his book. According to Capote, nineteen days after the murders an informant came forward with the names of the suspects and the KBI sent an agent to the home of the parents of one of the killers that same night. In reality, the KBI waited five days before visiting the parents' home because Dewey was convinced that the killers were locals who had a grudge against Herb Clutter. Despite this evidence contradicting Capote's account, Dewey many times vouched for the book's accuracy.[16]

In contrast, Duane West, the prosecutor who won convictions and death sentences against the killers, said that he treated Capote like any other journalist, which apparently did not sit well with Capote. In notes and letters written at the time, he proclaimed contempt for the prosecutor and inaccurately characterized West as subordinate to Logan Green, the more cooperative assistant prosecutor.[17]

Finally, there is the last scene in the book. Dewey runs into Nancy Clutter's best friend while visiting the Clutter graves. She informs Dewey, before she rushes away to a pressing appointment, that Nancy's boyfriend was married and happy, reminding the reader that life goes on, even after tragedy. Capote's biographer, Gerald Clarke, revealed that this fitting last encounter was totally invented. Even Capote admitted that he needed the scene to provide a touching ending to the book.[18]

Perhaps if Capote had not been so adamant that his book was totally truthful and accurate there would not have been much interest in proving his disingenuousness. There is, however, ample evidence that *In Cold Blood* is not simply artful reportage. The degree to which it is fictionalized is not for the cataloger to judge, but when librarians, in good faith, cite *In Cold Blood* as a fine example of narrative nonfiction, one that can be legitimately recommended to patrons as such, catalogers have to acknowledge that our bibliographic record offers no evidence to the contrary.[19] We now have the genre/form heading "Nonfiction novel" for works like this and it should be added to the record, along with, perhaps, a general note alerting the catalog user to the questions surrounding *In Cold Blood*.

Roots by Alex Haley (1976)

It is hard to overstate the impact that the quasi-autobiography *Roots* had on American culture. Published in 1976, Alex Haley's account of the lives of his ancestors captivated the public, who were particularly struck by his claims that he had done extensive genealogical research in order to write a story that was largely fact-based. Haley explained that he had heard stories from his grandmother about a relative that she called "the African," who had been captured in Africa and brought to America as a slave. She told her grandchildren that his name was Kinte, and that he had belonged to "Massa Murray," a tobacco farmer. Armed with this information, Haley spent the next several years researching his ancestry. It was an endeavor that took him to Juffure, a West African village near the Gambian coast, which he claimed was the home of his great-great-great-great grandfather.[1]

When he arrived in Gambia, Haley told some government officials the details of his grandmother's stories, and they in turn referred him to a *griot*, a kind of oral historian, whom he was assured would be able to provide more information. The *griot* spoke for five hours, according to Haley, elaborating on and confirming many of the stories Haley's grandmother had passed down to him. He continued his research at, among other places, the British Museum and the National Archives in Washington. It took him twelve years to research and write *Roots*, but his efforts were well rewarded.[2]

The book's advance print-run of 200,000 sold out immediately, and 1.5 million hardcover copies were sold in the first eighteen months. It amassed several major awards including the Pulitzer Prize. In 1977, the year after the United States' bicentennial celebration, Americans watched the final episodes of a mini-series based on *Roots*. With an estimated 130 million viewers it became the most viewed television series in history. It collected 145 different awards, including nine Emmys.[3] To say that *Roots* was a sensation is an understatement. There was, however, confusion about what exactly it was. It spent months on *The New York Times* nonfiction best seller list, but Haley himself said, "Although it's advertised as nonfiction, perhaps we should call it 'faction.' Every statement in *Roots* is accurate in terms of authenticity—the descriptions of the culture and terrain are based on valid material. The beginning is a re-creation, using novelistic techniques, but as it moves forward more is known and it is more factually based."[4]

Many historians were not satisfied with this equivocation. Although some were happy to call it a historical novel, others argued that factual errors were too numerous to overlook in a book that the publisher claimed was nonfiction and that the author asserted was based on historical research. Historian Willie Lee Rose noted in her review of *Roots* that eighteenth-century Juffure bore little resemblance to the pastoral village depicted in the book. In 1766, the year that Kinte was allegedly captured by slave traders, it was a busy trading center that had a population of around three thousand people. It was tightly controlled by the king of Ñomi who enforced strict slave-trading agreements with the English and French operating on nearby James Island. The king would never have tolerated the abduction of one of his subjects. After Kinte was transported to northern Virginia, according to Haley, he was put to work picking cotton. Rose pointed out that this was a likely scenario in Alabama in 1850, but an impossibility in pre–Revolution Virginia where cotton was not a major crop. She pointed out other anachronisms that spoke to Haley's uncertain grasp of eighteenth-century language, but the missteps regarding Kinte's origin and slave experience called into question the actual existence of Haley's ancestor.[5]

Journalists were soon weighing in. Mark Ottaway, a respected investigative reporter with *The Times of London*, retraced the steps Haley's took in his research. He discovered that the *griot* that Haley consulted was not a true *griot*, a vocation that requires years of apprenticeship, but rather something of a playboy that regaled tourists with his stories. His widow admitted that her husband had been alerted to the information that Haley was seeking in advance. Haley's research had unearthed the existence of a ship carrying slaves that had sailed from Gambia to Annapolis in 1767. Therefore, he needed a Gambian named Kinte who had been captured by slave traders in 1766. When Haley pressed the *griot* to give him the year the abduction he spoke of took place, he responded that it had occurred the year that the king's soldiers came. This hardly narrowed the time period down, since European soldiers were a presence in Africa for hundreds of years, but Haley deducted that it must have been in 1767, the year that British Colonel O'Hara's forces arrived. Although this was a year after Kinte was allegedly captured, it was close to the timeline Haley had developed.[6]

In response to Ottaway's article, Haley protested that his integrity was being attacked and lamented, "Can't we blacks have one case where we are able to go back to our past without someone taking a cheap shot to torpedo it [sic]."[7] After Haley's death in 1992, however, a tape of his interview with the *griot* confirmed that Haley had encouraged him to recount the story that Haley wanted to hear.[8] In the final chapter of *Roots* Haley wrote: "To the best of my knowledge and of my effort, every lineage statement within *Roots* is from either my African or American families' carefully preserved oral history, much of which I have been able conventionally to corroborate with documents. Those documents, along with the myriad textural details of what were contemporary indigenous lifestyles, cultural history, and such that give *Roots* flesh have come from years of intensive research in fifty odd libraries, archives, and other repositories on three continents."[9] Despite this declaration and Haley's protests, the seminal "fact" that propelled this work into the literary stratosphere, that Haley's genealogical detective work had identified a specific African ancestor, was verifiably untrue according to credible evidence presented by historians and journalists.

Haley's troubles were not over. In 1977, Dr. Margaret Walker Alexander filed a lawsuit against him alleging that he had plagiarized portions of her 1966 novel, *Jubilee.* Although this suit was eventually dismissed, another one was filed by Harold Courlander, author of the 1967 novel *The African.* It charged that Haley's book was "copied largely" from Courlander's novel. Haley swore that he was innocent, but eventually settled with Courlander for $650,000.[10]

In one of many contradictory statements, Haley said that he intended to write "a symbolic history of a people."[11] In that, he succeeded and *Roots* remains an important and beloved book. It is not, however, based on exacting genealogical research, nor is it "the true history of Haley's family," as his publisher claimed.[12] Nevertheless, it is cataloged as a collective biography with the subject "African Americans—Biography." It should be cataloged as the historical novel that Haley wrote by assigning the form subdivision "Fiction" and the genre/form heading "Historical fiction."

In His Image: The Cloning of a Man by David M. Rorvik (1978)

Even before David Rorvik's 1978 book *In His Image* was available to reviewers and other readers, it caused a stir. J. B. Lippincott announced that they would soon be marketing a book that they touted as a first-hand account of the first successful cloning of a human being.[1] Rorvik recounted the story of Max, a millionaire, who financed a private laboratory for a brilliant scientist in an East Asian country in order to have himself cloned. The process, facilitated and observed by Rorvik, was successful, resulting in the birth of a baby boy who was Max's genetic twin. Both Max and the scientist who was responsible for this singular achievement wished to remain anonymous.[2]

Other scientists were skeptical. Dr. Robert S. Krooth, a professor of human genetics at Columbia University's College of Physicians and Surgeons, and Dr. Peter Hoppe of Jackson Laboratory in Bar Harbor, Maine, asserted that to their knowledge no mammal species had ever been cloned at this point in time and any reputable researcher would have published details of such a procedure in a scientific journal. Rorvik was not available for interview, but Lippincott avowed that "David Rorvik had assured [the publisher] that it is true. Lippincott does not know."[3]

With this less than robust endorsement by the book's publisher, there was plenty of room for doubt. The city editor of *The Great Falls Tribune* in Great Falls, Montana, revealed that his newspaper had interviewed Rorvik, who was from Ronan, Montana, in 1970. At that time Rorvik told them that "he finds fiction writing more difficult than nonfiction, but is determined to complete his novel, *The Clone*, and perhaps get it made into a movie." Rorvik described his novel as "a pornographic science fiction thriller based on current medical possibilities."[4] Could this novel be the basis of his soon-to-be published nonfiction work on cloning? This certainly looked like a strong possibility.

Lippincott was a well-respected Philadelphia publishing house with both a medical books and a medical journals division. *In His Image*, however, was published by its trade book division, which produced both fiction and nonfiction. The book had been offered to Simon & Schuster prior to landing at Lippincott, but Simon & Schuster were put off by the author's refusal to reveal the facts of the experiment. Lippincott proclaimed that this was simply a case of "sour grapes."[5] Still, the publisher hedged its bets with a disclaimer at the beginning of the book stating that "the account that follows is an astonishing one. The author assures us it is true. We do not know. We believe simply that he has written a book which will stimulate interest and debate on issues of the utmost significance for our immediate future."[6] The author himself stated in the afterword of the book that "I entertain absolutely no expectation that anyone, scientist or layman, will accept this book as proof of the events described herein."[7]

Author Michael Crichton reviewed *In His Image* for *The New York Times*. He wondered if "the book is fact or fiction? The author himself says that he does not expect anyone to accept the book as proof that cloning has occurred. In fact, the criteria of scientific evidence are simply absent." Having concluded that the book was fiction, Crichton evaluated it as such and declared that it was "stupefyingly dull."[8] One scientist did not find that to be the case, however, since his name and research were mentioned in the book without his permission. J. D. Bromhall sued Lippincott and Rorvik alleging that his reputation had been damaged. This resulted in an out-of-court settlement that awarded Bromhall an undisclosed amount.[9] The House Subcommittee on Health and Environment also found the book interesting due to the alarming prospect of human cloning and held a hearing to decide whether cloning research should continue. Rorvik was given two opportunities to speak to the committee, but never appeared.[10]

It seems beyond dispute that both the publisher and the author were telling readers that this book was not to be believed. It was not, however, altogether fiction. Another reviewer, a molecular biologist, was expecting to find "a crude hoax," but found instead a "sophisticated one." In his opinion Rorvik, a former science writer for *Time*, provided a respectable account of the scientific background of genetic cloning with "some technical inaccuracies, but no absurdities."[11]

Despite the presence of some factual information about cloning, *In His Image* is clearly fiction and the bibliographic record should reflect that. Unfortunately, it does not. "Human cloning" is the sole Library of Congress subject entry, without the necessary "Fiction" form subdivision and genre/form heading. A note is also called for in a case like this.

Arming America: The Origins of a National Gun Culture by Michael A. Bellesiles (2000)

Arming America arrived as the country struggled to define the meaning of the right to keep and bear arms, enshrined in the Second Amendment of the Constitution. Historian Michael A. Bellesiles' book had a provocative thesis, arguing that the gun played a relatively insignificant role in eighteenth-century America. This contradicted the common belief that the United States and its people were linked at the country's founding to firearms, and that this relationship is foundational to the American character—self-sufficiency, individualism, and love of freedom. Instead, Bellesiles asserted that the "gun culture," so ingrained in the fabric of the United States, was a product of the rise of the gun industry, not the private ownership of firearms in the colonial period.[1]

Bellesiles relied primarily on probate records, counts of guns at militia musters, and gun censuses to make his argument. He claimed to have studied over eleven thousand probate records of more than twelve hundred counties and found that between 1765 and 1821, not more than 17 percent of estate inventories listed guns. Between 1760 and 1795, the gun ownership rate was even lower, at about 14 percent, and over half of those guns were described as inoperable. Bellesiles pointed out that in the colonial period, guns meant muskets and they were not particularly efficient for hunting or self-defense. They were not accurate, they were hard to reload, and they often misfired. He argued that guns were in short supply in the United States until the Civil War period when large-scale firearms manufacturing began in the North. Because the state was unable to supply enough guns for the militia, the government could, and would, confiscate muskets if their owners were not part of the militia.[2]

Gun rights advocates were outraged by Bellesiles' conclusions, and Charlton Heston, renowned president of the National Rifle Association, was moved to write a letter to the editor of the *New York Times* in response to a favorable review of *Arming America*. Referring to the colonists, Heston argued that "it took them seven years, underfed, frostbitten and underarmed, but in the end they defeated the finest army in the world. They didn't do it with pocket knives."[3] Bellesiles was reviled by the National Rifle Association and other gun rights advocates, and he reported a campaign of harassment against him. The American Historical Association came to his defense, adopting a statement condemning personal attacks on the author.[4]

Most historians were impressed with Bellesiles' research and Columbia University awarded him the prestigious Bancroft Prize for historical excellence. Other scholars, however, were troubled by errors that Bellesiles made in analyzing the data. Chief among his critics was Northwestern University law professor James Lindgren, who noted that in some cases Bellesiles defined a document as a census when, in fact, it was something else. For example, Bellesiles stated that a 1630 gun census conducted in the Massachusetts Bay Colony, which had a population of one thousand people, revealed that only one hundred men had muskets in their possession. Closer inspection of the primary document, however, showed that this was a list of arms for one hundred men that the Massachusetts Bay Company in England wanted to send to America. There was no way to know from this document whether the other nine hundred residents owned guns because this was not a census. Furthermore, surviving probate records from Essex County, Massachusetts, from 1636 to 1650, revealed that 71 percent of male estates and 25 percent of female estates owned guns, a much higher percentage than Bellesiles had claimed.[5]

Bellesiles' analysis of the probate records constituted the most compelling evidence in support of his argument, yet Lindgren asserted that Bellesiles misclassified over 60 percent of the inventories he examined. Bellesiles even included data from San Francisco County probate records that do not exist because they were destroyed in the 1906 San Francisco earthquake and fire. Although Bellesiles later downplayed the importance of the probate records, many historians and book reviewers viewed them as the single most significant piece of evidence that gun ownership was relatively low in the seventeenth and eighteenth centuries.[6]

He also argued that homicide rates, like the rate of gun ownership, were low before the Civil War, suggesting that there is a correlation between gun ownership and homicides. Again, he misrepresented the data. He stated that there were five reported murders in Vermont between 1760 and 1790, citing Vermont Superior Court records. Historian Randolph Roth dissented, noting that the court didn't open until December 1778 and the records from September 1782 to August 1791 are missing. Vermont, indeed all of New England, had high homicide rates during the American Revolution, and 70 percent of adult homicides and probable homicides in Vermont between 1761 and 1790 were committed with guns.[7]

Bellesiles responded to the criticism in an essay in the *Organization of American Historians Newsletter*, strenuously complaining about the hateful e-mails, telephone calls, and faxes he had received, along with calls for his employer, Emory University, to terminate him. He asserted that *Arming America* did not support any particular political position. Bellesiles also emphasized the ten years he spent researching and writing the book, but admitted that a twelve hundred-page manuscript is bound to contain some errors. He argued that the errors were relatively minor. Nevertheless, Bellesiles quietly dropped all of the challenged probate data from Providence, Rhode Island, from the paperback edition of the book.[8]

The Columbia University trustees were not persuaded by Bellesiles' defense and revoked the Bancroft Prize and the $4,000 in prize money, concluding that "he had violated basic norms of scholarship and the high standards expected of Bancroft Prize winners."[9] Bellesiles also resigned from Emory University after an academic panel released a forty-page report that determined that he was "guilty of unprofessional and misleading work."[10] In January 2003, Knopf, the publisher, canceled Bellesiles' contract and stopped selling the book.[11] Bellesiles' went on to teach history part time at Central Connecticut State University. He maintained in 2010 that he still thought "it was a good book, but it ruined my life."[12] He has since written a new nonfiction book, *1877: America's Year of Living Violently*, which was published by the New Press.[13]

The bibliographic record for *Arming America* contains nothing that would alert the catalog user to the myriad problems that exist with the data and the conclusions in *Arming America*. This is a book that should not be mistaken for a reliable account of gun ownership prior to the Civil War, and our users deserve to know that. Lacking an authorized subject heading, subdivision, or genre/form heading for discredited nonfiction, a general note in the bibliographic record would have to suffice.

Honor Lost: Love and Death in Modern-Day Jordan by Norma Khouri (2003) (published in Australia under the title *Forbidden Love* in 2002)

The success of *Honor Lost* was enhanced by the fortuitous timing of its publication. The book by Norma Khouri, a native of Jordan, told the tragic story of the death of her best friend, Dalia, who was the victim of a "crime of honor." Her murderer was

Dalia's own Muslim father who was outraged by her love affair with a Christian and wanted to punish her for bringing dishonor to her family.[1] With the September 11, 2001, attack on New York City still fresh in the world's memory and the accompanying suspicion by many directed toward members of the Islamic faith, Khouri's memoir was of great interest to the reading public.

Khouri went to Athens after her friend's death, having fled Jordan in fear for her life, and wrote *Honor Lost* in internet cafes there. She later moved to Australia where her Australian publisher, Random House, sponsored her for a temporary residence visa. Khouri spent 2003 touring the world and retelling her story. The book was wildly popular in Australia where two hundred thousand copies were sold. An additional fifty thousand copies, published by Atria Books, an imprint of Simon & Schuster, were sold in the United States.[2]

The director of a women's rights lobby group in Jordan, Amal al-Sabbagh, had read the book and was deeply suspicious of its authenticity. First of all, al-Sabbagh had never heard of the killing, which her organization would definitely have known about if it had occurred. In the summer of 2003, al-Sabbagh and a colleague, Rana Husseini, began examining the claims in Khouri's book. They found seventy-three errors and exaggerations, which they submitted to Random House Australia and Simon & Schuster in September 2003. Among those errors, al-Sabbagh and Husseini contested Khouri's claim that she and Dalia ran a unisex hair salon in Jordan in the mid–1990s. That would have been illegal, and none of the hairdressers in Amman, Jordan, nor their union remembered any such place.[3] Husseini also noted that Khouri wrote that the Jordan River was "no longer strong enough to flow down to Amman," but the Jordan River never flowed anywhere near Amman. In addition, Khouri wrote that Dalia's killer was released on bail even though Jordan never releases suspects on bail in capital offenses. Also, nobody in Khouri's alleged Amman neighborhood ever heard of her family or the tragic honor killing.[4] Despite her advocacy for women's rights, Al-Sabbagh felt that Khouri had "ruined the reputation of Jordanian women, saying they were imprisoned in their homes and so on. Jordanian women have excellent education levels that are gradually being translated into participation in the workforce. Her tone is that all Jordanian women live under these traditional practices, which is wrong."[5]

Still, Random House Australia stood behind their author stating that "following our discussions with Norma we are satisfied that, while some names and places have been changed to protect individuals' identities…. *Forbidden Love* is a true and honest account of her experiences."[6] It was not until July 24, 2004, when the *Sydney Morning Herald* reported that its own investigation had revealed that Khouri's memoir was untrue, that Random House Australia and Atria took the claim seriously. The *Sydney Morning Herald's* investigation discovered that Khouri's real name was Norma Majid Khouri Michael Al-Bagain Toliopoulos and that she and her family had left Jordan when she was three years old. She had a United States passport and had lived in Chicago from 1973 until 2000. Khouri was married and had two children, in addition to four American siblings and a mother. Neither her publishers, her agent, nor the Australian Department of Immigration were aware of this.[7]

Ten days after the story appeared Simon & Schuster's Atria imprint, Random House Australia, and Transworld in the United Kingdom ceased shipment of the book and asked that stores withdraw it. Khouri was offered an opportunity to refute the claims in the story and she vowed that she would. She never did.[8]

When asked whether any effort was made to verify Ms. Khouri's account of events, Random House denied any responsibility for doing so. The company said that Ms. Khouri had given them a written warranty prior to the book's publication that "all statements contained in the book purporting to be facts were true," and in any event, the publisher continued, the book was not commissioned or edited in Australia, but was edited by its New York publisher, Simon & Schuster. Random House, however, did not buy the book from Simon & Schuster, but rather from one of its own divisions Transworld UK, which had purchased the rights from Ms. Khouri's agent. Simon & Schuster added that Random House could have done whatever editing or legal work they wished to do.[9] Of course, Simon & Schuster apparently did nothing to verify the book's claims, either.

The three bibliographic records that represent the three publishers of the book, and are the most widely used by libraries, lead catalog users to believe that *Honor Lost* (a.k.a. *Forbidden Love*) is nonfiction because no "Fiction" subdivisions appear in any of them. They should include this form subdivision, and possibly a note spelling out the troubling history of the book. The addition of the genre/form heading "Fiction" is also warranted. The authority record for Norma Khouri does not have any notes that would enlighten the user.

Ananios of Kleitor: Poems & Fragments and Their Reception from Antiquity to the Present collected and translated by George Economou (2009)

Ananios of Kleitor was presented as a scholarly monograph containing fragments of poems written in the fourth century BC by the poet named in the title, with commentary on how his work was received. The first thing the reader saw when she opened the book was a reproduction of a fragment of papyrus. In the introduction, Economou explained, "In translating these poems and fragments of Ananios of Kleitor into the English of our time, I have attempted to convey his sense as accurately and idiomatically as I can." He also included notes on spelling and ended the book with short biographies of each commentator, who ranged from Ananios' contemporaries to twentieth-century classicists.[1]

The back cover included blurbs from well-known poets Marjorie Perloff and Jerome Rothenberg. Perloff declared that "George Economou ... has here produced his magnum opus, a new edition ... of the renowned but long lost fourth century Greek poet Ananios of Kleitor."[2] Rothenberg, equally enthusiastic, wrote, "In his gathering of the poems & fragments of Ananios of Kleitor George Economou has created a major new body of poetry that goes happily beyond the bounds of scholarly/classical translation as we know or think we've known it."[3]

Ananios himself was a bit of a mystery. We only know that he liked wine, ate cabbage for hangovers, and frequently visited the largest brothel in Corinth. Since the poems make up only a small part of the book, this is perhaps a minor point. The bulk of the book consisted of commentaries on Ananios' poems and letters between twentieth-century commentators that revealed as much about the vicissitudes of life in the academy as they did about Ananios.[4]

The publisher described *Ananios of Kleitor* this way: "Ananios and his scholars and commentators perform their work at the edge of the real world and the margins of a thoroughly historicized and critically acute context," suggesting that it was a straightforward scholarly monograph. In retrospect, however, there are intimations that the book was not what it appeared to be. It was rather what one critic described as "equal parts academic parody, postmodern romance and prose poem."[5]

Ananios and the commentators were all Economou's inventions. Economou did not try very hard to prolong the imposture. In an article published shortly after the book came out he was quoted as saying, "I like to write about different subjects. I don't like to repeat myself. I try new things. I find new things a counter movement against aging. My latest book is an example—it's unlike anything I've ever written. It's about an ancient Greek poet I invented."[6]

The critics, for the most part, got it. There were clues throughout the book, such as a reference to a nonexistent college at Cambridge, that alerted savvy readers to the spoof.[7] One reviewer on the *LibraryThing* website, however, was not aware of the book's pretensions, stating that "this is one of the best books I've read this year despite its being a scholarly study of the poetry written by Ananios of Kleitor."[8]

Books like *Ananios of Kleitor* pose a quandary for catalogers. We certainly owe our users an accurate bibliographic record, but a great deal of the appeal of the book is in the discovery of its inventions by an astute reader. We do not want to rob the reader of that experience through our description. Nevertheless, we should follow the dictates of our profession. The record indicates that George Economou is responsible for the contents of the book and there is an added entry for Ananios of Kleitor. There is an authority record (not to be used under *RDA* until it is reviewed) for Ananios of Kleitor, that provides no hint that Ananios of Kleitor is actually George Economou. There should be cross-references in both authority records. The bibliographic record includes four Library of Congress subject headings for Ananios with the subdivisions "Criticism and interpretation," "Translations into English," "Criticism, Textual–History," and "Criticism and Interpretation–History," all of which would be perfectly appropriate if this were a real work of translation. The form subdivision and the genre/form heading used should be "Fiction."

The Last Train from Hiroshima: The Survivors Look Back
by Charles Pellegrino (2010)

On his website, Charles Pellegrino describes himself as a "scientist working in paleobiology, astronomy, and various other areas; designer for projects including rockets and nuclear devices (non-military propulsion systems), composite construction materials, and magnetically levitated transportation systems; writer."[1] This multi-talented man is also a well-published author, with his book *Ghosts of the Titanic* serving as source material for James Cameron's 1997 hit film *Titanic*. In addition, Pellegrino consulted on Cameron's science fiction blockbuster *Avatar*.[2]

When his book about the detonation of the atomic bombs over Hiroshima and Nagasaki, Japan at the end of World War II was published in 2010, there was every reason to believe it would be a best seller. Indeed, *The Last Train from Hiroshima* quickly rose to number twenty-four on *The New York Times*' hardcover nonfiction best seller list.[3] *Publishers Weekly* praised Pellegrino's ability to weave "all of the book's many elements into a wise, informed protest against any further use of these terrible weapons."[4] These elements included the stories of thirty civilian survivors who, after the first atomic bomb was detonated, fled by train from Hiroshima to Nagasaki, a fateful journey that exposed them to the second attack in Nagasaki. Pellegrino's book also contained accounts by American and Japanese pilots who were present at one or both sites. It was an American, who was allegedly on the flight to Hiroshima, who recounted an unreported incident that occurred while the bomb that destroyed Hiroshima, code name Little Boy, was being built.[5]

According to Pellegrino, Joseph Fuoco was the flight engineer on one of two observation planes that escorted the *Enola Gay*, the B-29 bomber that released its payload on Hiroshima. He was a last minute replacement for James R. Corliss, the regular flight engineer, and he had an astonishing tale to tell. He recalled that Little Boy was being readied at an air base on an island in the Western Pacific when an accident occurred. A burst of radiation killed a scientist and damaged the nuclear fuel assembly, reducing the bomb's destructive power by more than half. In *The Last Train from Hiroshima*, Pellegrino repeatedly referred to the weapon as "a dud."[6]

The Los Alamos weapons laboratory in New Mexico, the birthplace of the bomb, fired back that Little Boy had not been damaged and that it had lost none of its deadly power, citing the seventy thousand people killed by the initial blast. Shortly thereafter, the 509th Composite Group, which flew three B-29 bombers over Hiroshima on that cataclysmic day, declared that Fuoco was not aboard any of the planes. In fact, the regular flight engineer, Corliss, had flown that mission as planned. Corliss died in 1999, but his widow was distraught that her husband, who had been so proud of his participation in the operation, had been erased from events in *The Last Train from Hiroshima*. Pellegrino was shocked, but convinced by the incontrovertible evidence that Fuoco had lied to him.[7] By the time the book was published, Fuoco had also died, but his widow maintained that "he couldn't make up such a thing. I always called him a Boy Scout."[8]

There is no way to know if Fuoco made up the tale and duped Pellegrino, or if Pellegrino invented the story himself, but additional questions surrounding the book do not bolster the author's credibility. Henry Holt, the book's publisher, became suspicious about two other individuals mentioned in *The Last Train from Hiroshima*. Pellegrino's narrative referred to a Father Mattias, who lived in Hiroshima and committed suicide. A Jesuit scholar named John MacQuitty presided over Mattias' funeral, according to the author. Pellegrino later claimed that he used pseudonyms for the men to protect their privacy, although there is no mention of that in the book. Henry Holt questioned the existence of both priests and asserted that Pellegrino did not provide sufficient evidence to address their concerns.[9]

Questions about Pellegrino's education proved to be the last straw for the publisher. He stated on his website and in the author's biography in the back of the book that he held a doctorate from Victoria University of Wellington in New Zealand. When the university denied that this was true, Pellegrino explained that he was awarded a Ph.D., but it had been revoked by the university a few years later when his dissertation became fodder in a dispute over evolutionary theory. The university confirmed that Pellegrino had been a Ph.D. student in the 1980s, but that "he submitted a thesis which in the unanimous opinion of the examiners was not of a sufficient standard for a Ph.D. to be awarded."[10]

Henry Holt did not pull the books off the shelves, but it ended its relationship with Pellegrino and stopped shipping and printing any additional copies, stating that "the author of any work of nonfiction must stand behind its content."[11] Filmmaker James Cameron, who planned to produce a movie based on the book, did not back down, however, saying, "All I know is that Charlie would not fabricate, so there must be a reason for the misunderstanding."[12] Nevertheless, no film was made. For his part, Pellegrino claimed he had been deceived by Fuoco and acknowledged that "you can't have the wrong history going out. It's got to be corrected."[13] In 2015 Rowman & Littlefield published his revised version in a book entitled *To Hell and Back: The Last Train from Hiroshima*.

What is a librarian to do with a book with so many troubling issues surrounding it? This question was posed on the website *Swiss Army Librarian*, where one librarian said, "Mainly I want to protect school kids and other unknowing people from taking portions of this book as fact—which is what the library is confirming by shelving it in non-fiction. But so far, neither Charles Pellegrino (author) nor Henry Holt (publisher) has issued an easy-to-print statement to include in the book."[14]

Does this explain why there is no indication in the bibliographic record that this nonfiction book has serious errors in it? If so, it is not a sufficient reason. Over one thousand libraries own *The Last Train from Hiroshima*, which means thousands of catalog users are being misled. We owe it to our patrons to add a note regarding the problems with the book. The authority record for Pellegrino states that he has a Ph.D. from Victoria University of Wellington, New Zealand, which is also inaccurate and should be changed.

Imagine: How Creativity Works by Jonah Lehrer (2012)

Jonah Lehrer has a talent for presenting scientific information in a compelling and accessible manner. He majored in neuroscience at Columbia University, was a Rhodes Scholar, and became a contributing editor at *Wired* and *Scientific American Mind*, and a staff writer for *The New Yorker*. Before he turned thirty-one, the prolific Lehrer had also produced three books about the brain: *Proust Was a Neuroscientist* (2007), *How We Decide* (2009), and *Imagine: How Creativity Works* (2012).[1]

All three books received generally favorable reviews, but Lehrer is a science writer, not a scientist, and the scientific community had criticisms, especially regarding the third book. One particularly scathing review was written by psychology professor Christopher Chabris who cited many elementary errors in the book. Lehrer described one test that required divergent thinking, but Chabris contended that most psychologists agree that the test actually measures convergent thinking. Lehrer's diagram, showing the part of the brain that becomes active when the subject recognizes the solution to a problem, is incorrect, according to Chabris. He also disparaged Lehrer's tendency to support his arguments by citing studies and failing to note that the studies have not been replicated and that the science has not been settled.[2]

The scientific community did not, however, cause Lehrer's downfall. The credit for that went, indirectly, to Bob Dylan. The first chapter of *Imagine* was titled "Bob Dylan's Brain," and Lehrer referenced Dylan's song-writing process to support his arguments about how creativity works. At one point, Lehrer recounted, Dylan was bereft of inspiration after a two-week tour in England. He went to a cabin in upstate New York to be alone and take a break from song writing. After this hiatus, Dylan was rejuvenated and quickly wrote his masterpiece, "Like a Rolling Stone," and in the process created a new type of song. His lyrics were inscrutable, and in Lehrer's words, "he could write vivid lines filled with possibility without knowing exactly what those possibilities were."[3] Dylan even coined a new word, "juiced," in the lyrics, which we now define as "drunk." The problem was, as Isaac Chotiner asserted in his review of *Imagine* for *The New Republic*, that nearly everything in this chapter was "inaccurate, misleading, or simplistic."[4] Dylan did not go upstate right after his English tour and he was only there for a few days, not two weeks. He did not invent the word "juiced." It had, in fact, been in circulation long before that. Also, Dylan had written songs with obscure lyrics, such as those for "Mr. Tambourine Man," before his solitary visit to upstate New York.[5]

These were minor quibbles compared to the problems exposed by journalist Michael C. Moynihan, who described himself as "something of the Dylan obsessive."[6] As he read Lehrer's chapter on Dylan, he was puzzled by some quotations that were unsourced. In one case Lehrer fused together fragments of two quotations on different topics to support his argument. Moynihan contacted Lehrer and inquired about the source of the troublesome quotations. Where had Lehrer found these unknown quotations that could not be found in a searchable database composed of over three hundred Dylan interviews, made freely available online by a Polish fan? Lehrer claimed that Dylan's manager, Jeff Rosen, had given him access to an extended and unreleased interview shot for Martin Scorsese's documentary *No Direction Home*. When Moynihan confronted Lehrer with the fact that Rosen denied ever meeting him, however, Lehrer confessed that he had lied. He had not met or corresponded with Jeff Rosen, and he could not cite sources for the questionable quotations.[7] Although these and other errors were dismissed by some Lehrer supporters as simple missteps by a young journalist,

Moynihan argued that "making up sources, deceiving a fellow journalist, and offering accounts of films you have never seen and emails never exchanged, is, to crib Bob Dylan, on a whole other level."[8]

Houghton Mifflin Harcourt (HMH), the publisher of *Imagine*, as well as Lehrer's two previous books, agreed. The book had debuted at the top of The New York Times best seller list and remained there for sixteen weeks, with over 200,000 copies in hardcover and e-book sold. Nevertheless, HMH took the unusual step of recalling the book, asking booksellers to return it at the publisher's expense, and offering purchasers refunds. *The New Yorker* also solicited and received Lehrer's resignation, and *Wired* severed ties with him.[9] Seven months later, after internal fact-checking, HMH pulled Lehrer's second book, *How We Decide*, from stores and, once again, offered customers refunds. The publisher did not divulge the problems they found.[10]

It appeared to casual observers that Lehrer's writing career was over; however, just three months after *How We Decide* was recalled, he had a new book deal with Simon & Schuster. It was titled *A Book About Love*, and its source material included the author's own experience with love and forgiveness after his fall from grace. While Simon & Schuster said their decision to work with Lehrer was about second chances, the more cynical commentators noted that his previous books had made a great deal of money for the publisher. Might this have motivated Simon & Schuster to take a chance on Lehrer?[11] Lehrer's latest book has received decent reviews, and thus far has not been recalled.

Lehrer's disastrous publishing record is a librarian's nightmare on more than one level. First, the fallout from the recall of *Imagine* meant that he did not speak at the American Libraries Association Midwinter Conference, as he was scheduled to do. *American Libraries* was planning to publish an interview with Lehrer, but at the last minute these plans were scrapped when *Imagine* was pulled from bookstores.[12] Then there is the fact that over two thousand libraries own the book, but there is no indication of its troubled history in the bibliographic record (the same holds true for the record for *How We Decide*). If the publisher took the unusual step of recalling these books, the bibliographic records should reflect that fact in a general note.

The Embassy House: The Explosive Eyewitness Account of the Libyan Embassy Siege by the Soldier Who Was There by Morgan Jones and Damien Lewis (2013)

The violent terrorist attack on the American consulate on September 11, 2012, in Benghazi, Libya, ignited a fierce debate in the United States. Four Americans were killed, including Ambassador to Libya, J. Christopher Stevens, and many conservatives believed that the Obama administration had failed to provide adequate security for the consulate. The critics seemed to be vindicated when a security contractor named Morgan Jones appeared on the television program *60 Minutes* on October 27, 2013, and claimed to be an eyewitness to the attack. He described the consulate's inadequate security measures—no razor wire, no security lights, no watchtowers, no functioning CCTV cameras.[1]

Jones was in a position to make these claims because he was employed during that period by Blue Mountain Group, a private British security company. He asserted that his guard force commander had called and frantically reported that the consulate was under attack. Jones rushed to the compound, discovered that roadblocks had been put up by the Sharia Brigade, and then scaled the back wall of the consulate looking for any Americans. Finding none, he left, but later realized that the Westerners that he was searching for were already dead. Jones was particularly galled by the administration's claim that the attack stemmed from a protest over an anti–Islam video *The Innocence of Muslims*, instead of a well-planned attack by al-Qaeda militants. Jones complained that although he provided "detailed testimony and photographic evidence to an alphabet soup of American agencies—the State Department and FBI among others—and that my evidence was arguably the most detailed the U.S. administration possessed immediately following the attack, I cannot understand how the administration argued that this was a spontaneous demonstration that got out of hand. From my testimony alone it clearly was not."[2]

A few days later, Jones' account was being questioned. Morgan Jones turned out to be a pseudonym for Dylan Davies. Davies had co-written a book with Damien Lewis called *The Embassy House*, which was released two days after the *60 Minutes* interview and contained the same account. It had been published by Threshold Books, an imprint of Simon & Schuster, a subsidiary of CBS, which is the home of *60 Minutes*. The program quickly acknowledged that it had erred in not disclosing this connection, but stood by the story Davies gave in his interview. Davies insisted that "the account in my book is consistent with what I gave the F.B.I. and U.S. authorities about what happened in Benghazi."[3]

The written account of the event that Davies provided to his employer three days after the attack, however, was at odds with the account he gave on *60 Minutes*. He told Blue Mountain that "we could not get anywhere near [the consulate] ... as roadblocks had been set up."[4] This account was also contained in the incident report that Blue Mountain gave to the State Department. Davies acknowledged that the report accurately reflected what he had told his supervisor, but that it was a lie. He claimed that he had not told the truth because he didn't want to admit that he had disobeyed his supervisor's order to stay away from the compound. Davies explained in his book that his supervisor "was my boss, but more important, he was a father figure and a man of unrivaled experience."[5] In addition, Davies insisted that the accounts that he had given U.S. officials from various agencies, including the F.B.I. and the State Department, matched the ones in his book and the *60 Minutes* interview.[6] Administration officials confirmed that the F.B.I. had interviewed him, but the information he gave them did not corroborated the account he had given on television and in his book. Instead it matched the incident report that Blue Mountain had submitted, which had been based on information they received from Davies. CBS confirmed this with their own F.B.I. sources.[7]

Although the political fallout from this controversy may never be sorted out, CBS

Other Nonfiction

quickly acknowledged that their reporting had been inaccurate. Jeff Fager, the top executive at CBS News, called the segment "as big a mistake as there has been."[8] The report was removed from the CBS News website and Lara Logan, the correspondent for the segment, apologized on air for the mistakes in the report.[9] Threshold Books followed suit, stating that "in light of the information that has been brought to our attention since the initial publication … we have withdrawn from publication and sale all formats of this book, and are recommending that booksellers do the same."[10]

Nevertheless, based on the holdings shown on OCLC, at least 287 libraries own *The Embassy House*. Perhaps reflecting the political uproar over the Benghazi attack, the holdings are roughly equally divided between the record that treats the book as nonfiction and the one that treats it as fiction. Strangely, the record that declares the book is fiction, contains this quoted summary note: "The explosive eyewitness account of the Libyan embassy siege, by the soldier who was there." There is no indication what the source of this quotation is, but it seems to contradict the record's fiction designation. Given that the publisher withdrew the book, the assignment of the "Fiction" genre/form heading and form subdivision would be appropriate. A note documenting the troubled history of the book is also called for.

Fiction

> Wanting to put a face on a creative work is a trait so old it is almost genetic.
> —Tony Baker, *Hobart Mercury* (May 31, 1996)

The potential cataloging problems inherent in self-identified fiction and poetry would appear to be minimized by the fact that these are works of the imagination. Veracity is not an issue, thus relieving the cataloger of the task of determining genre. The problems associated with authorship, however, more than make up for that. These challenges are complicated by the evolving views on authorship and authenticity in the world of literature and criticism.

The cataloging code has moved away from the *AACR2* concept of "main entry" as an organizing principle. *RDA* positions authorship not as an attribute of the work, but rather as an entity related to the work.[1] Although this may suggest that identifying the author is of less importance when cataloging under *RDA* as opposed to *AACR2*, the concept of authorship remains central in both standards. Neither standard, however, encourages catalogers to use extreme measures to ferret out the real identity of an author if he chooses to use a pseudonym.

Both *AACR2* and *RDA* can accommodate multiple names and multiple identities. *AACR2* instructs in 22.2B2 that "if a person has established two or more bibliographic identities, as indicated by the fact that works of one type appear under one pseudonym and works of other types appear under other pseudonyms or the person's real name, choose, as the basis for the heading for each group of works, the name by which works in that group are identified."[2] RDA states in 9.2.2.8, "If an individual has more than one identity, choose the name associated with each identity as the preferred name for that identity."[3] The relationship between multiple identities, if we have done our job well, is spelled out in authority records through cross-references, and perhaps notes. These records, however, are invisible to all but the most sophisticated users.

In Western culture, literary attribution is important in that it identifies the "owner" of the intellectual property contained in a work.[4] While this fulfills certain legal and commercial requirements, it does not preclude an author from using a pseudonym. The Brontë sisters wrote as the Bell brothers because, according to Charlotte Brontë, "We had a vague impression that authoresses are liable to be looked on with prejudice."[5] More recently, Christina Lynch and Meg Howrey published their fantasy novel *City of*

Dark Magic under the name Magnus Flyte because they saw studies asserting that while women would buy books written by either men or women, men preferred books written by men.[6]

The concept of authorship in the literary world can be very complex. For example, Roland Barthes' essay "The Death of the Author," which argued that a text should be read independent of the author's identity and intention, and Michel Foucault's theory that the figure of the "author" is an interpretative construct, have made the identification of authors potentially more challenging.[7] Barthes and Foucault posit an ethereal authorial identity. These theoretical currents notwithstanding, literary critics and scholars, as well as other catalog users, remain interested in the more mundane, corporeal identity of authors, regardless of the name under which they choose to write.

This is often because of other considerations that are currently important in the world of literature. One of these is cultural appropriation, defined as "a term used to describe the taking over of creative or artistic forms, themes, or practices by one cultural group from another. It is in general used to describe Western appropriations of non–Western or non-white forms, and carries connotations of exploitation and dominance."[8] For example, when American author Arthur Golden wrote *Memoirs of a Geisha* it was considered by some to be Western appropriation of Eastern culture.

Some have argued that cultural appropriation is not always unacceptable. They assert that "appropriation" suggests that something is being taken away from the affected cultural group, but the readership for fiction or poetry about Native American culture, for example, is not finite. If people read a book about another culture written by someone from outside the culture, it doesn't mean that they will read fewer books written by those who are members of the culture. Others contend that literature set in a particular culture is not authentic if it has been written by someone from outside the culture, suggesting that ethnic equals authentic. However, Tony Hillerman, who was not Native American, wrote a popular series of detective novels that were immersed in Navajo culture, with a Native American protagonist. With a few exceptions, the Navajo did not resent Hillerman, and, in fact, awarded him the Special Friend of the Dineh (Navajo) award. His books are also taught in Navajo schools.[9]

There does seem to be general agreement in the literary world that one kind of cultural appropriation is beyond the pale. Authors should not try to pass themselves off as members of another culture by adopting a culturally-identifiable pseudonym and identity. This is often viewed as fraudulent and some readers feel angry if they are taken in by a false identity the author has created.[10]

Consider the case of poet Yi-Fen Chou. In 2015, Native American writer Sherman Alexie, was the guest editor of *The Best American Poetry* anthology, published annually. After reading through hundreds, or maybe thousands, of poems he selected one written by Chou titled "The Bees, the Flowers, Jesus, Ancient Tigers, Poseidon, Adam and Eve."[11] Later Alexie explained why he chose it and his rationale provides great insight into the intersection of poetry and ethnicity: "I'd been drawn to the poem because of its long list title (check my bibliography and you'll see how much I love long titles) and, yes, because of the poet's Chinese name. Of course, I am no expert on Chinese names so

Fiction

I'd only assumed the name was Chinese. As part of my mission to pay more attention to underrepresented poets and to writers I'd never read, I gave this particular poem a close reading. And I found it to be a compelling work. In rereading the poem, I still found it to be compelling. And most important, it didn't contain any overt or covert Chinese influences or identity."[12]

When Chou submitted his contributor note, however, he honestly stated that Yi-Fen Chou is a pen name he uses. His real name is Michael Derrick Hudson and he lives in Fort Wayne, Indiana. He went on to say that "after a poem of mine has been rejected a multitude of times under my real name, I put Yi-Fen's name on it and send it out again. As a strategy for 'placing' poems this has been quite successful for me."[13] No wonder Alexie did not find any Chinese influences. Although Alexie found out about the false identity before the anthology was published, he decided to include the poem, knowing that he would open himself up to ridicule (and, indeed, there was an explosion of outrage directed both at Alexie and Hudson in the poetry community). He explained, "If I'd pulled the poem then I would have been denying that I was consciously and deliberately seeking to address past racial, cultural, social, and aesthetic injustices in the poetry world.... In the end, I chose each poem in the anthology because I love it. And to deny my love for any of them is to deny my love for all of them."[14]

Sometimes authors present themselves as translators of nonexistent works by someone from a different culture. Such was the case when Kenneth Rexroth wrote a book of poetry that he claimed to have translated from the work of Marichiko, a Japanese woman. He was initially praised for his sensitive interpretation of the poetry of a woman from a foreign culture. Because cultural appropriation was not particularly a concern at the time, when it was discovered that there was no Marichiko and that the poems were actually written by Rexroth, there was little criticism other than from some who argued that his act exploited women.[15] Rexroth had no need to assume an ethnic identity to improve his chances of publication. He was already a revered figure in the poetry world. Perhaps Rexroth would have agreed with Joyce Carol Oates who wrote, "Like the experience of first authorship, writing under a pseudonym, for those of us who have attempted it, gives one the sense of discovering oneself by way of (re-)defining oneself, even if it is only for the space of a single book."[16]

The reactions to some of these cases were fraught in the literary world, but how should we respond in the world of cataloging? If we agree that we have a responsibility to represent works accurately, not merely as they present themselves, in bibliographic and authority records, then we should not mislead the catalog user by omitting well-founded information that more fully provides crucial context. Notes and cross-references for variant names are the tools we currently possess to accomplish this. Our task is to convey this information while avoiding biased or inflammatory language. Because we are dealing with questions of identity, the authority record is the appropriate place to communicate with the catalog user about any authorial misdirection. We will discover, however, that some catalogers have dealt with these complex situations in ways we might not expect.

Fiction

Wild Cat Falling by Mudrooroo (1965)

Mudrooroo's debut novel, *Wild Cat Falling*, was touted as the first published novel by an Australian Aboriginal writer. At the time, however, he wrote under his birth name, Colin Johnson, and it was not until 1988 that he took an Aboriginal name of his own creation, Mudrooroo, which means "paperbark," a native Australian tree. By 1996, he had published seven novels, four books of poetry, and several works of Aboriginal studies. Mudrooroo was arguably Australia's best known writer at the time and was viewed as one of the most prominent Aboriginal public intellectuals.[1] He had the standing to challenge the authenticity of Aboriginal writing, arguing that "just because something is written by a person who identifies as an Aborigine doesn't make it an Aboriginal work."[2]

Born in 1938, Mudrooroo was the son of a woman of English and Irish descent and a man named Thomas Creighton Patrick Johnson, who died two months before his son's birth. Mudrooroo's paternal grandfather's death certificate stated that he was born in North Carolina, making Mudrooroo at least partially African American. This was not the family history that he claimed, however. In one interview he explained his adopted name this way: "'Mudrooroo' means paperbark in the Bibbulmum [*sic*] language which is my mother's people's language; and so I changed my name to Mudrooroo."[3] The Bibbulmun (also called Nyoongah) are Indigenous peoples of southwestern Australia.[4]

Mudrooroo's experiences as a youth followed a pattern of hardships typically endured by Australian Aboriginal people at the time. He was separated from his mother when, at the age of nine, he was caught stealing and sent by a magistrate to the Christian Brothers' orphanage in Perth. After seven years in the institution, he reconnected with his mother. When Mudrooroo was seventeen, he was sentenced to twelve months in Fremantle Gaol. He was released into the care of Mary Durack, a novelist and poet, and he stayed with her for some time. Some critics have speculated that Durack assumed that Mudrooroo was an Aboriginal person and that at this point he adopted this identity himself.[5]

Thus, it appears that his claim of a literary Aboriginal identity drove his personal identity, as well. If Mudrooroo had not been a prominent literary figure, no one would have cared about his racial identity, and it is entirely possible that he would not have identified as an Aborigine. Indeed, he admitted that in the late 1950s he "knocked about in the inner-city pubs" of Melbourne.[6] At that time, Indigenous Australians were denied the right to drink alcohol; therefore, Mudrooroo was not representing himself as an Aboriginal person.[7]

No one questioned Mudrooroo's ethnic assertions until 1996 when the Dumbartung Aboriginal Corporation, an Australian organization that promotes and protects Aboriginal cultural activity, began investigating claims by Mudrooroo's relatives that they were unable to find evidence that they were of Aboriginal descent. Mudrooroo's sister Betty Polgaze had conducted genealogical research, and not only was their paternal grandfather of African American descent, but she found nothing to substantiate

Aboriginal ancestry on their mother's side, although this was his central claim to his Indigenous identity. Soon several Aboriginal groups, including the Nyoongah community, were asking for further investigation. The story became more perplexing when Mudrooroo announced that his half-sister, Joyreen Stamsfield, was really his mother, a claim she vehemently denied. Stamsfield offered to have her DNA tested to prove her credibility. Eventually, Mudrooroo agreed to undergo testing as well, but there is no indication that this ever occurred.[8]

Mudrooroo never acknowledged that there was any basis for doubting his claim to be an Aborigine, but his exile from the literary and scholarly elite was swift and complete. Whether this was a case of mistaken identity or a hoax did not matter. He was stripped of his awards and credentials, and disowned by intellectuals and Aboriginal peoples alike. In 2001 he moved to India, and then to Nepal to study Buddhism.[9]

The authority record for Mudrooroo contains several cross-references, including one for Colin Johnson and four for variations on his Aboriginal name. There is also an authority record for Colin Johnson with a cross-reference for Mudrooroo. The bibliographic record for *Wild Cat Falling* is correctly designated as fiction and there are no general notes addressing the controversy. Although the author continued to deny that his claim of Aboriginal identity was untrue, the conclusion of the Dumbartung Aboriginal Corporation is convincing. The inclusion of cross-references in the authority record provides objective information to the catalog user. The addition of a source note in the authority record citing Dumbartung's investigation would be justified.

Jack Rivers and Me by Paul Radley (1981)

Paul Radley was the darling of the Australian literary world in 1980 when his unpublished manuscript won the inaugural *Australian*/Vogel Literary Prize. The rules stated that entrants must be thirty years old or younger, which was not a problem for Radley who was eighteen at the time. He collected other awards, as well, including the Young Australian of the Year in 1981. In 1983, the Literary Board presented him with a writer-in-fellowship at Stirling University in Scotland. Not bad for a young man who left school at the age of sixteen and admitted that he had only read two books in his life—*The Pearl* and *The Old Man and the Sea*. Radley's manuscript was published in 1981 by Allen & Unwin.[1]

Jack Rivers and Me, the first book in a planned trilogy, was told from the perspective of a five-year-old boy nicknamed Peanut who had an imaginary friend, Jack Rivers. The plot was slight, revolving around Peanut's decision to banish Jack before he starts school. Although Australians were charmed by the book, American reviewers' assessments were more tempered. One review of the first American edition warned that "American readers will find it not so much brilliant as affecting and pretentious by turns; still most will respond warmly to the author's rich descriptions of small-town family life in the Australian outback and to the novel's fine and touching (though often rococo) delineation of the end of a small boy's childhood dreams."[2]

Fiction

The *Australian*/Vogel Award came with a $10,000 prize, which Paul Radley used to travel overseas with his uncle Jack Radley. When Paul was offered the fellowship at Stirling University, he insisted that his uncle accompany him, which the Literary Board found odd. Author Tom Shapcott was the director of the Board at the time and he explained that "the suspicion was that Jack had some sort of particularly close involvement with Paul."[3] This perception was reinforced by comments that Paul made in interviews, such as, "Uncle Jack and I work together. We're like a team. If Uncle Jack were to die or something was to happen to him, I would be lost."[4]

The trilogy was completed with the publication of two more books allegedly written by Paul: *My Blue Checker Corker* and *Me and Good Mates*. Paul continued to make curious statements in interviews. He told *Vanity Fair*, which referred to him as the Down Under Brett Easton Ellis, that "it was very satisfying to be a writer but now I have a job at Majestic Motors [where he was a car washer] I don't have to do it any more."[5] In another, he admitted that he couldn't type, so it did not come as a total surprise when, in 1996, Paul publicly admitted that Jack, not he, had written the three books.[6] True, they were loosely based on stories that Paul recorded in the pubs he frequented with a tape recorder given to him by his uncle, but Jack was the one who typed them up and turned them into novels. By this time, he and his uncle had been estranged for six years because, he explained, "I found out he [Jack] was interfering in my life. He had been backstabbing me, interfering in relationships. He'd been doing it from a very early age."[7] Paul was also extremely embarrassed by the homosexual themes in the last book, lamenting that "I didn't want my name on that book, but by then it was too late."[8]

Paul said that he was riddled with guilt and insisted on returning the *Australian*/Vogel prize. He also volunteered to return half of the $10,000 award (he had given the other half to his uncle), but his offer was rejected. Of course, the manuscript would not have been eligible for the prize if Paul's uncle had submitted it since the rules limited entrants to authors under thirty years of age. After the revelation, however, writer David Malouf argued the *Jack Rivers and Me* was still "a very, very good book, whoever wrote it."[9] Peter Bishop, director of the Varuna writers' center at Katoomba, was more cynical, musing that "perception is everything, and people should not believe publishers read things not knowing who is writing them. They do, and if it is an 18-year-old submitting that is more than taken into account. If these books had been submitted by Jack Radley, aged 62, then they would never be published."[10]

The bibliographic records for both the Australian edition and the American edition name Paul Radley as the author. The authority record for Paul Radley includes no cross-reference. A cross-reference should be added for Jack Radley, with a note in the authority record providing the source of the information.

Famous All Over Town by Danny Santiago (1983)

Famous All Over Town was warmly received as the debut novel by young Mexican-American Danny Santiago. It was a coming-of-age story whose protagonist was a fourteen-year-old Latino boy growing up in a turbulent Eastside Los Angeles barrio. One reviewer observed that "the streetwise but innocent narrator is completely authentic; his story is filled with credible dramatic surprises."[1] It became a staple in high school and college classrooms and won the Richard and Hinda Rosenthal Foundation Award of $5,000 for a work of fiction that is a literary but not commercial success. The publisher, Simon & Schuster, considered submitting the book for a Pulitzer Prize, but the rules called for a photograph of the author and they had none in their possession. Santiago was, in fact, very secretive, and because he did not have a phone, the only way his publisher and agent could contact him was at a post-office box in a nearby community.[2]

It was not long, however, before Santiago's true identity was revealed, with the real author's blessing. Santiago was actually a seventy-three-old white man named Daniel James (Santiago is James in Spanish) and he enjoyed a lively biography in his own right. James was an affluent Ivy Leaguer from the Midwest who had been a screenwriter and playwright. He helped write the screenplay for Charlie Chaplin's *The Great Dictator* and wrote the book upon which the successful musical comedy *Bloomer Girl* was based. In 1951, however, his career was upended when he was consigned to Hollywood's blacklist due to his earlier flirtation with the Communist party. He managed to keep working by adopting a pen name, and he and his wife also became increasingly involved in social work on Los Angeles' east side. They worked there as volunteers for approximately twenty-five years and became immersed in the lives of its residents.[3]

When James was writing *Famous All Over Town* he showed Latino friends in the barrio his manuscript, asking them to check for the accuracy of the street slang and the discussions of graffiti. One of the people he consulted said, "He knew he was going to be writing under a Latino pseudonym and he thought it was pretty important to get our feedback on how we would react to it: Would we feel offended? Would we be taken aback?"[4] Many were touched by the loving portrait of their community and its inhabitants.[5]

Why did James write under a pen name, especially one that suggested an ethnicity that was not his to claim? His close friend, writer John Gregory Dunne, was troubled by James' actions at first, but came to understand that James "felt for nearly twenty years he had been unable to write under his own name both because of the blacklist and because he had lost confidence in his own ability."[6] James wrote to Dunne, "[Santiago] is much freer than I am myself. He seems to know how he feels about everything and none of the ifs, ands and buts that I'm plagued with."[7] When Dunne asked him if he was concerned about being accused of manufacturing a hoax, "he shrugged and said the book itself was the only answer. If the book were good, it was good under whatever identity the author chose to use."[8]

The bibliographic record for *Famous All Over Town* designates Danny Santiago as the author and both the Santiago and the Daniel James authority records cross-reference each other. Both authority records contain notes citing the source of information about his pseudonym. Nothing else is needed.

Fiction

The Hand That Signed the Paper by Helen Demidenko (1994)

The Hand That Signed the Paper was celebrated and denounced in approximately equal measure in the author's home country of Australia. In 1993, it won the *Australian*/Vogel award, which honors unpublished manuscripts written by authors under thirty-five. In addition to a cash award, the prize winner's manuscript is published by Allen & Unwin. The prize money, Demidenko said, would allow her father, an illiterate Ukrainian emigrant and taxi driver, to take his first plane trip. She proudly reported that her Irish mother, who left school at the age of twelve to work as a domestic, read her first book, the one written by her daughter.[1]

Demidenko predicted that her novel would be controversial, and that proved to be correct. Drawing on her Ukrainian heritage, and tales told around the family dinner table, the book recounted the story of the Holocaust from the perspective of the Ukrainians, who had been starved and persecuted under the communists prior to the Nazi invasion in 1941. It followed Ukrainian peasant Vitaly Kovalenko, which Demidenko told her publisher was loosely based on her uncle. Kovalenko, like many Ukrainians, was only too happy to help the Nazis slaughter the Jews, who they believed were the primary force behind the Bolshevik movement, which ultimately became the Communist Party of the Soviet Union. Many in the Australian Jewish community viewed her novel as anti–Semitic, an attempt to justify Ukrainian collaboration with the Nazis.[2]

Robert Manne, one of Australia's most prominent conservatives, pointedly wrote, "The ideological identification of Jews and Bolsheviks was nothing less than the central strand in the Nazi warrant for genocide." He went on to say that he thought "it undeniably true that her novel advances the thesis that the famine in Ukraine was objectively the responsibility of Jewish Bolshevism and that those Ukrainians who became involved in the Jewish genocide had been turned into savages, and were now killing Jews, as acts of ethnic revenge."[3] For her part, Demidenko countered, "I didn't set out to justify the Ukrainian involvement in Jewish atrocities. There's a vast gulf between explaining something and condoning something. I hope I made it clear in the book that that kind of behavior is never excusable regardless of who perpetrates it."[4] Nevertheless, Gerard Henderson, the director of the Sydney Institute fretted that "*The Hand That Signed the Paper* will be read widely in schools and colleges where most students and some teachers will lack the historical understanding to handle it."[5]

Somewhat surprisingly, the Ukrainian community seemed to rally around Demidenko, even threatening to take action against American lawyer Alan Dershowitz under racial vilification laws, for critical comments he made about the book. Despite the negative reaction to the published novel expressed by many outside the Ukrainian community, Demidenko continued to collect awards, including the esteemed Gold Medal of the Association for the Study of Australian Literature and the premiere Australian literary prize, the Miles Franklin.[6]

The controversy did not end there, however. On August 19, 1995, *The Courier-Mail*, a Brisbane, Australia, newspaper, broke the story that Demidenko was not

The Hand That Signed the Paper

who she presented herself to be. In fact, her last name was Darville, not Demidenko, and her parents emigrated from northern England. Her father worked in civil engineering and she had no connection to Ukraine.[7] Her mother tried to put things in perspective, saying, "It's fiction for heaven's sake, she wrote under a pseudonym, lots of authors do that."[8] Her brother defended her creation of a false Ukrainian identity as a "great marketing exercise," and argued that "she did it to protect her family and, let's face it, nobody, not even I, had any idea that the book was going to be as good as it was."[9]

Her publisher was ambivalent about the disclosure, given that book sales were soaring, but after Darville met with representatives from Allen & Unwin she issued an apology saying, in part, that she was sorry that she had referred to her novel as "faction," a mixture of fact and fiction.[10] It later came out that Darville had submitted the book to the University of Queensland Press in early 1993 as a work of nonfiction, claiming that the events in the manuscript really happened, and that it was based on taped interviews with, among others, her uncle Vitaly Demidenko. The manuscript was rejected.[11]

Naturally, many people looked askance at the major awards Darville had collected. Helen Daniel, editor of the *Australian Book Review*, asserted, "I was appalled that Helen Darville won the Miles Franklin. I had always thought it was a mediocre book. And personally, I do think that it is anti–Semitic."[12] Darville's critic Robert Manne said, "Perhaps Demidenko's youth or gender or unfashionable ethnic identity weighed with judges more heavily than they should have."[13] Jill Kitson, one of the Miles Franklin judges maintained, however, that "that isn't how literary prizes work. You're mad if you think we sit around discussing people's surnames."[14] Allen & Unwin republished *The Hand That Signed the Paper* under Darville's real name.

Darville's troubles weren't over yet, however. In September of 1995, she was accused of plagiarizing parts of her novel. Allen & Unwin must have reached their limit, because they froze delivery of the book and launched an investigation. The lawyers representing the publisher concluded, however, that the book was not plagiarized after consulting with Darville's attorneys, who explained that she was merely using an accepted "postmodern" literary technique that draws on previous works in the genre. The executive director of the Australian Society of Authors, Lynne Spender, suggested that using postmodernism as a defense was very clever because most people are totally confused by the term.[15]

The record for the original 1994 edition is bare-bones, with no subject headings and nothing in the fixed field indicating that it is fiction. Enhancing this record would be in order. Darville's authority record contains a cross-reference for Helen Demidenko and a source note referring the user to documentation regarding her adoption of a pseudonym. The record for the edition published under Darville's real name in 1994 contains appropriate subject headings, with the form subdivision "Fiction." Nothing else is needed.

Fiction

My Own Sweet Time by Wanda Koolmatrie (1994)

From the beginning it was difficult to categorize *My Own Sweet Time.* Articles referred to the book as either an autobiography or a novel.[1] The book itself offered no clarity. Nothing on the cover or in the introduction suggested that it was an autobiography, but the plot hewed closely to the author's biography released by the publisher. *My Own Sweet Time* told the story of an Aboriginal woman who was the victim of then existing Australian state policy that gave the government the right to remove Aboriginal children from their families and place them in institutions or with foster families, but it had a lighthearted, comic tone.[2]

What was clear was that it was written by an Aboriginal woman named Wanda Koolmatrie. Published by Magabala Books, which specialized in Indigenous literature, *My Own Sweet Time* was met with resounding acclaim.[3] An early review enthused that it was "a romp, but a romp related by a wise woman. Koolmatrie has the apparently artless style that you find in tales told by your grandfather—if he was gifted."[4] It won the Dobbie Literary Award, which recognizes first time women writers "who have published fiction or non-fiction classified as 'life writing.' This includes novels, autobiographies, biographies, literature and any writing with a strong personal element. The object of the Awards is to encourage Australian women writers to improve and advance Australian literature for the benefit of the community."[5]

Despite the book's enthusiastic reception, it probably would have slipped into obscurity, given the abundance of writing emerging from the Aboriginal community at the time, if not for a surprising revelation about the author. Magabala Books was ready to publish Koolmatrie's second book, but insisted that they must meet the author before its release. It was then that Leon Carmen, a forty-seven-year-old white man, acknowledged that he was the author of *My Own Sweet Time.*[6] He, along with his friend and agent, John Bayley, hatched the deception together, for a very practical reason. In 1997, Carmen told a reporter that "the publishing world seemed to be regulated by academics promoting their various hobby horses…. It's not something that can be proved, but there seemed to be a widespread notion that middle-aged people had nothing to say. Especially blokes. That if they weren't already established authors, they could forget about it and drive trucks or something."[7] Carmen declared, "I created a character and breathed life into her. I can't get published, but Wanda can."[8]

Carmen's second book contract was cancelled by Magabala Books and they stopped distribution of *My Own Sweet Time.* The publisher issued a statement, saying, "Trust is an important part of Aboriginal culture. In this respect Magabala Books has been too trusting, and fallen perhaps into the same trap as the ancestors of Australia's indigenous people have done in the past."[9] It seemed unlikely that *My Own Sweet Time* would find another publisher. In 2004, however, Trafford Publishing reissued the book, acknowledging and dismissing the controversy by stating that "there was an accusation of 'cultural theft' by those who clearly hadn't read the novel."[10]

The bibliographic records for both the 1994 and 2004 editions clearly mark the book as a work of fiction. The fixed field for literary form confirms this and there are no subject entries. The authority record contains a cross-reference for "Carmen, Leon," and a note explaining the deception. This is sufficient.

Sarah by J. T. LeRoy (2000); *The Heart Is Deceitful Above All Things* by J. T. LeRoy (2001); *Harold's End* by J. T. LeRoy (2004)

J. T. LeRoy's debut novella was a coming-of-age story told from the point of view of a twelve-year-old boy whose mother was a truck-stop prostitute. She was a terrible mother who liked to dress him up as a girl, but the boy adored her, even following her into the trade. Critics were surprisingly taken with the book, with one explaining that "his language turns the tawdriness of hustling into a world of lyrical and grotesque beauty, without losing any of its authenticity."[1] The same critic also highlighted another dimension of the book, asking, "Does it matter that [LeRoy] is 20 years old? That he grew up in rural West Virginia and later on the streets of San Francisco? That he started publishing at 16, under the pseudonym Terminator? It does. And yet it shouldn't."[2] Another declared, "Sometimes, very occasionally, the story behind a book is more interesting than the story in the book. J. T. LeRoy's *Sarah* is as extreme an example of this syndrome as one is ever likely to find."[3]

LeRoy's unlikely journey began when he was a young, drug-addicted teenager living in San Francisco and working as a prostitute. While in a state of emotional turmoil, LeRoy called the Child Crisis Center. Using his street name, Terminator, he spoke to psychologist Dr. Terrence Owens, with whom he developed a deep and trusting relationship over many months. Terminator refused to meet the doctor in person, but at Owens' suggestion, began writing about his life on the street. Owens was impressed with Terminator's writing and he showed it to a neighbor who was in the film industry. The neighbor suggested that Terminator should contact an acquaintance of his, poet Sharon Olds. Emboldened by the positive responses he received to his writing, Terminator sent a story he had written to novelist Dennis Cooper who in turn shared it with an editor at Crown Publishing. It was not long before LeRoy had an agent and a book deal. Terminator adopted the name J. T. LeRoy and continued to be reclusive, only communicating with agents and editors in phone conversations and e-mail exchanges. When he finally came out of hiding, albeit wearing a wig and sunglasses, LeRoy revealed himself to be an androgynous young man with the ability to enchant literary and Hollywood luminaries. His admirers included Carrie Fisher, Winona Ryder, Tatum O'Neal, Diane Keaton, Courtney Love, Debbie Harry, Shirley Manson (who wrote a song about him), and Suzanne Vega.[4]

LeRoy still preferred to communicate by e-mail and phone, but when he appeared in person, author Mary Gaitskill said, "He was extraordinarily charismatic.... Talking to him, I suddenly had a feverish fantasy that I must find someone to marry and get a house and adopt him. He aroused those feelings in everyone—but he didn't have that effect with heterosexual males."[5] LeRoy lived with a social worker, who had reached out to him when he was thirteen or fourteen, and her husband. They went by the names of Speedie (or sometimes, Emily) and Astor and were also musicians, performing in a band called Thistle. Outsiders viewed the relationship between the three with suspicion, fearing that Speedie and Astor were exploiting LeRoy emotionally and economically.[6]

LeRoy's first book, *Sarah*, was published in 2000, when he was twenty years old, and marketed as a semiautobiographical novel. Director Gus Van Sant bought the film rights to *Sarah* and commissioned LeRoy to write a screenplay about a school shooting that was the genesis of Van Sant's 2003 film *Elephant*.[7] LeRoy's second book, *The Heart Is Deceitful Above All Things*, was a collection of short stories published in 2001 and described in *Library Journal* as a "picaresque memoir set mainly in the urban underbelly of San Francisco."[8] Actress and director Asia Argento adapted the book to film and screened it on the sidelines of the Cannes Film Festival.[9] In 2002, LeRoy had an early version of a story titled *Harold's End* published in *McSweeney's*, and in 2005 it was published by Last Gasp Books as a novella. Critics noted its small size, one hundred pages, which included an introduction by Dave Eggers, an afterword by LeRoy's editor, a dozen watercolors by Australian artist Cherry Hood, and almost four full pages of acknowledgments. Albert Mobilio of *The New York Times* grumbled that "it's no exaggeration to say it takes more time to read through the press packet than the actual story—a modest, sometimes affecting tale of a boy, his pet and scatological perversion."[10]

That same year, LeRoy's odyssey came to an abrupt end. Stephen Beachy, a creative writing professor at the University of San Francisco, decided to pursue the rumors and gossip that were circulating about LeRoy's identity. LeRoy's reclusiveness and strange behavior made many people suspicious. One of those was author Armistead Maupin, who had been taken in several years earlier by a writer named Anthony Godby Johnson, who claimed to be a child with AIDS and was the author of a heartbreaking memoir (see entry for *A Rock and a Hard Place*). After Beachy's exposé was published Maupin asserted, "The minute I read the *New York* magazine piece, I knew that the situation was almost identical."[11]

Beachy presented a solid circumstantial argument that LeRoy was not who he said he was. His research led him to Speedie and Astor, whose real names were Laura Albert and Geoffrey Knoop. Then, in early 2006, *The New York Times* provided documentary proof that the person who appeared publicly as J. T. LeRoy was Geoffrey Knoop's half-sister, Savannah Knoop. In a later article, they disclosed that Laura Albert, a forty-year-old woman who was Geoffrey Knoop's romantic partner and the mother of his child, was the person who spoke to friends and journalists on the phone, and she was the real author of LeRoy's three books. Geoffrey Knoop soon confirmed the story, acknowledging that he had seen Albert writing the books and that he had helped out on the business side. He explained that after *Sarah* was published, requests for interviews began coming in and Albert and Knoop knew that they needed someone to appear in public as LeRoy. It was then that they recruited Savannah Knoop to play the role of the androgynous young man.[12]

In 2007, Albert herself was compelled to tell her side of the story when she was sued for fraud by a film production company that had signed a contract with J. T. LeRoy to make a feature film of *Sarah.* They contended that the contract was null and void because J. T. LeRoy did not exist. Albert's lawyer told the jury that she was physically and sexually abused as a child and had been institutionalized in psychiatric wards and in a group home where she was a ward of the state.[13] Albert testified that when she moved to San Francisco in 1988 she started calling suicide hot lines from a pay phone and adopted a teenage-boy alter ego as a way to distance herself from the psychological pain that she was experiencing. When asked about recruiting her partner's sister to impersonate LeRoy in public, she said, "She became JT. It's like a trinity. We experienced it. It was as if he would leave me and enter her—I know how it sounds."[14] Albert lost the civil case and was ordered to return the $116,500 the film company had paid her. Later she was ordered by the judge to pay $350,000 in legal fees incurred by the film company, as well.[15]

Albert did not disappear from the national stage, however. In 2015, director Marjorie Sturm released *The Cult of JT LeRoy,* a documentary recounting the literary saga. At the 2016 Sundance Film Festival Albert appeared (as herself) after the premier of the well-received documentary *Author: The JT LeRoy Story*, directed by Jeff Feuerzeig. There she told the audience that she was working on a memoir and insisted that for her J. T. LeRoy remains a very real persona.[16]

The bibliographic records for the three books allegedly written by J. T. LeRoy identify them, appropriately, as fiction in the fixed field and include the "Fiction" form subdivision. There are summary notes in all of the records, with one describing *The Heart Is Deceitful Above All Things* as "a collection of short autobiographical stories." This note should be removed. The authority record for J. T. LeRoy contains two notes. One tells the user that LeRoy was born in 1980 and also wrote under the pseudonym Terminator, and the other informs us that "LeRoy was a hoax; actual author was woman named Laura Albert." There is a cross-reference for Albert. The note stating that LeRoy is a "hoax" suggests that the cataloger understands Albert's motives and is not objective. It should be replaced with a note using more neutral language.

The Honored Society by Michael Gambino (2001)

In 2001, Michael Gambino was riding high. He had just published a book with Pocket Books, a division of Simon & Schuster after receiving a $500,000 advance. In addition, he had been offered a deal for a six-hour miniseries based on his book, *The Honored Society.* Gambino immodestly declared himself "Simon & Schuster's golden boy."[1] Although his book was marketed as a novel about a young man in the Mafia, with the cachet of the Gambino name attached it was widely believed to be a thinly-veiled memoir about the author's own experiences in organized crime.[2] The publisher, accepting Gambino's claim that he was the illegitimate grandson of the Mafia boss Carlo Gambino, promoted it as the creation of "the highest-ranking mob member ever to record the innermost workings" of the Mafia.[3]

In 2002, Simon & Schuster discovered the Michael Gambino was actually Michael

Fiction

Pellegrino and was not associated with the Gambino family in any way when Thomas Gambino, the son of Carlo, dispatched a lawyer to inform the publisher that Pellegrino was a fraud.[4] Simon & Schuster sued the author and took the unusual step of suing the agency that represented him, explaining that "we need to be able to rely on (talent agencies) to bring us authors and literary properties that are authentic and as billed. Without that reliability, the whole relationship of the whole business collapses."[5] The publisher withdrew the book and asserted that they had been the victims of fraud. One of Pellegrino's lawyers contended that Pellegrino himself believed that he was the illegitimate grandson of Carlo Gambino because he had been told that since childhood. In addition, his lawyers questioned why the author's biography should matter at all. He never claimed he had written an autobiography.[6]

The lawsuit was settled in 2004, and while the litigants were not at liberty to reveal the terms, Pellegrino implied that he had been allowed to keep the entire $500,000 advance. He claimed that he was "simply a first-time author caught up in a publisher's publicity campaign."[7]

The Honored Society is cataloged as it was represented, with "Fiction" form subdivisions. There is also no cross-reference in the Michael Gambino authority record for Michael Pellegrino. The catalog user would be served best by a cross-reference and a source note in the authority record.

Poetry

The Darkening Ecliptic: Poems by Ern Malley (1944)

Max Harris, editor of the avant-garde Australian literary journal *Angry Penguins*, was captivated by the poetry manuscript he received in the mail in late 1943. The eighteen poems were sent to him by Ethel Malley, the sister of poet Ern Malley. Ethel found his work, titled *The Darkening Ecliptic*, among his belongings after he died on July 23, 1943, at the age of twenty-five. She knew nothing about poetry, but felt that she owed it to her brother to send the poems to someone who did.[1]

Harris was a perfect choice. Malley's modernist poetry was exactly the type of verse that Harris wanted to showcase in *Angry Penguins*. So enthusiastic was Harris that he published a special issue of the journal devoted to Malley's poetry. Brian Elliot, a lecturer at Adelaide University and Harris' teacher, became suspicious when he read the poems, however. He believed that Harris himself was the author and published a review of the work in the form of a poem in *On Dit*, the journal of Adelaide University. An acrostic that read M-A-X-H-A-R-R-I-S-H-O-A-X was formed by the lines of the poem. This sent the Australian press into a frenzied search for the real poet, and even Harris, knowing that he wasn't the author, began to wonder if he had been duped.[2]

It was not long before the truth emerged. *Fact*, a supplement of Sydney's *Sunday Sun*, had an inside source in reporter Tess van Sommers. She was a friend of the perpetrators, Harold Stewart and James McAuley, and had overheard them discussing it. Stewart and McAuley were poets who had once been enamored of avant-garde poetry, but had lost their enthusiasm for it.[3] They confessed to the newspaper that the creation of Malley (and his sister, Ethel) was a "serious literary experiment" designed to tweak the devotees of modernism.[4] The question that they sought to answer was, "Can those who write, and those who praise so lavishly, this kind of writing tell the real product from consciously and deliberately concocted nonsense?"[5]

Their deception became even more outrageous when they admitted that they had lifted their language from various books they had laying around, such as a *Collected Shakespeare*, a dictionary of quotations, the *Concise Oxford Dictionary*, and even an American report on the breeding grounds of mosquitoes.[6] Stewart and McAuley claimed that they wrote their self-described bad surrealistic poetry in a single afternoon and evening, following these rules of composition:

1. There must be no coherent theme, at most, only confused and inconsistent hints at a meaning held out as a bait to the reader.
2. No care was taken with verse technique, except occasionally to accentuate its general sloppiness by deliberate crudities.
3. In style, the poems were to imitate, not Mr. Harris in particular, but the whole literary fashion as we knew it from the works of Dylan Thomas, Henry Treece and others.[7]

The first poem, "Dürer: Innsbruck, 1495," was a ringer, however. McCauley had previously written it as a serious effort, but judged it to be unsuccessful. McAuley suggested that he and Stewart could draw Harris in by starting the manuscript with a "real" poem.[8]

Harris was interviewed by a journalist working for the *Sunday Sun* who asked him if he had suspected that the poems might be a hoax. Harris told a friend that he responded, "Of course we did. Numbers of people pointed out that possibility, but we consider it not our job to act as a detective agency towards our contributors, but to sincerely evaluate the material sent to us."[9] English poet and literary critic Herbert Read wrote Harris after reading the Malley poems, affirming that "though I find them very uneven, often obscure and sometimes absurd, yet allowing as I would normally do for some adolescent crudity, the general effect is undoubtedly poetic, and poetic on an unusual level of achievement."[10]

How, you may ask, can poems created as McCauley and Stewart described be considered successful? Read argued that "in poetry, in art generally, it is not the originality of the unit that matters, but the genuineness of the total conception. A good poem might conceivably be composed of bits and pieces from a hundred different sources."[11] Thus, Harris hoped that the Malley "experiment" would not be viewed simply as a hoax, but would offer an opportunity to begin a critical conversation about the sources of poetic creativity.[12]

In August 1944, however, the Ern Malley story took an unexpected turn. Harris was charged under an obscure section of the South Australian Police Act with selling "indecent advertisements," which were identified as thirteen passages in the issue of *Angry Penguins* devoted to Malley's poetry.[13] One poem in its entirety was considered obscene. The police officer who had investigated the case, Detective Vogelesang, was called as a witness for the prosecution. He described Harris as uncooperative in his responses to questioning. Harris refused to provide Vogelesang with his interpretations of certain poems and passages, contending that "I don't know what the author intended by that poem. You had better ask him."[14]

Under cross-examination, Vogelesang admitted that he had only read *Angry Penguins* in order to question Harris, and that his claims that some of the language in the poems was immoral represented his own opinions.[15] It was obvious that the detective was not a regular consumer of poetry, but in the prosecutor's eyes this made him the ideal surrogate for the general public. One poem led him to declare, "It offends my decency to suggest that a character means that he wants sexual intercourse. I think that is immoral."[16] In another, he objected to the word "incestuous," but admitted that he didn't know what the word meant. He asserted, "I think there is a suggestion of indecency about it."[17] When the trial ended, Harris was found guilty and fined five pounds in lieu of six weeks in prison.[18]

The bibliographic record for *The Darkening Ecliptic* identifies Ern Malley as the author, but also includes a note citing a publisher's statement that Ern Malley does not exist and that it was apparently written to expose the modern literary movement. This should be removed. The record for the 1961 republication of the work titled *Ern Malley's Poems* includes no such note. The authority records for Ern Malley, James McCauley, and Harold Stewart contain cross-references to each other. The Malley record contains a note that refers to *The Darkening Ecliptic* as a "hoax." More neutral language should be used.

The Love Poems of Marichiko by Marichiko, translated by Kenneth Rexroth (1978)

Kenneth Rexroth, poet and translator, published his first book of poetry, *In What Hour*, in 1940. Rexroth was a conscientious objector during World War II, and he also provided humanitarian aid to Japanese-Americans who were at risk of evacuation and internment. This provided him with an opportunity to explore his interest in East Asian culture with his Japanese-American acquaintances.[1]

In 1955, two of Rexroth's works of translation, *One Hundred Poems from the French* and *One Hundred Poems from the Japanese*, were published. A year later his *Thirty Spanish Poems of Love and Exile* and *One Hundred Poems from the Chinese* appeared and his reputation as a major translator was established. In the 1960s, Rexroth was increasingly disenchanted with the so-called technological revolution, believing that it contributed to the decline of Western civilization. More and more he embraced Asian culture and Buddhism, and in 1967 he visited Japan and other Asian countries.[2]

According to some critics, Rexroth's admiration for Yosano Akiko, a Japanese woman poet, influenced his creation of *The Love Poems of Marichiko*, published in 1978.[3] He and his publisher, Christopher Books, presented it as the work of a young Japanese woman (using a pseudonym), which Rexroth had translated into English. Given his reputation as a translator, no one had any reason to doubt him. When, however, Rexroth was being considered for an award for his translation of Marichiko's work, he admitted that he had actually written the poems himself.[4] Later he claimed that Marichiko was his lover, which did not go over well at the Third Annual Santa Cruz Poetry Festival, where some people in the audience hissed when his reading was over. Some were offended by what they perceived as his objectification of a young woman.[5] They were not placated when he told them, "I was a feminist before most of your mothers were born."[6]

Nevertheless, there is little evidence that anyone was bothered by his initial attempt to fool his readers. In 1979 the work was published with two other collections in a book titled *The Morning Star* and one reviewer was still laboring under the belief that *The Love Poems of Marichiko* was translated by Rexroth, noting that "this translated sequence redeems the book; and while Rexroth's own work is often disappointing, the energy and skill of his translation continue to make him our most influential interpreter of Oriental verse."[7]

The bibliographic record for the small-run book *The Love Poems of Marichiko* cites "Marichiko" as the author, with an added entry for Rexroth as the translator. There is also an authority record for Marichiko, which contains no cross-reference to Kenneth Rexroth. Likewise, the Rexroth record contains no cross-reference to Marichiko. The bibliographic record for *The Morning Star* reflects the title page accurately by recording Kenneth Rexroth as the author of all three works contained in the book, with no added entry for the nonexistent Marichiko. There should be cross-references to each other in both the Rexroth and Marichiko authority records. Rexroth's authority record should also contain a note citing the source of information about his pseudonym.

Doubled Flowering: From the Notebooks of Araki Yasusada by Araki Yasusada (1997)

In 1991, translations of the poetry of Araki Yasusada began appearing in major poetry journals such as *American Poetry Review, Grand Street, Conjunctions*, and the British journal *Stand.* Each poem was accompanied by a harrowing biography that explained that Yasusada was a survivor of the atomic bomb that was dropped on Hiroshima, Japan by the Americans at the end of World War II. Most of his family, including his wife and two daughters, died in the initial blast or of lingering radiation sickness. Yasusada himself died in 1972. Eight years later his surviving son discovered fourteen spiral notebooks belonging to Yasusada, which contained poems, English class assignments, and diary entries. In addition, correspondence and drawings were inserted in the notebooks.[1]

Yasusada's poems, combining Japanese sensibilities with the avant-garde poetics of Western culture, were translated by Tosa Motokiyu, Okura Kyojin, and Ojiu Norinaga, all of whom were either born or lived in Hiroshima. Editors and critics were drawn to the unique voice of a witness to one of the most significant events in the twentieth century.[2]

That wasn't the real story, however. By the time *Doubled Flowering*, a collection of Yasusada's poetry, was published in 1997, the poetry community was beginning to suspect that they had been fooled. The unpublished manuscript had begun appearing in the mailboxes of well-known academics, but was presented to them as the work of an invented persona created by an unknown individual or group of individuals. Many editors who had published Yasusada's poems were furious. The editor of *American Poetry Review*, Arthur Vogelsang, published an apology to his readers in his journal and allegedly said, "This is essentially a criminal act."[3] The response from Bradford Morrow, the editor of *Conjunctions*, was more tempered, asserting that "if it was written by a Hiroshima survivor, as a literary response to that experience, then it's an amazing historical document and certainly a remarkable technical achievement. If it's just someone being emphatic in another culture fifty years later, it's legitimate but not as interesting."[4] Others, assuming that the author was not Japanese, objected to what they viewed as cultural appropriation. Professor of Japanese culture at Amherst College John Solt called it "Japanized crap." Wesleyan Press, on the verge of publishing *Doubled Flowering*, dropped the project.[5]

Roof Books stepped in and published the book, which included commentary explaining that the poems were actually the creation of Tosa Motokiyu. Tosa Motokiyu was the pseudonym of a poet who died in 1996, shortly before *Doubled Flowering* was published. Kent Johnson, a professor at Highland Community College in Freeport, Illinois, and Javier Alvarez, a Mexican folk singer, were former roommates of Motokiyu in college and served as his literary executors. They promised Motokiyu before he died that they would never reveal his true identity.[6] This is probably not true either. While it is now widely believed that the poems attributed to Motokiyu were written by Kent Johnson, he has never acknowledged this. In an interview in 2015, he said, "I have never claimed authorship of the Yasusada writing, and I never will."[7]

Doubled Flowering would appear to be a clear-cut hoax, but is that the right word for it? "Yasusada" and his "translators" left several obvious clues that he could not have been a Japanese man alive when Hiroshima was destroyed by the atomic bomb. Well-known poet Marjorie Perloff noted that Yasusada's biography, which accompanied submissions of his poems, stated that he "attended Hiroshima University sporadically between 1925 and 1928, with the intent of receiving a degree in Western Literature."[8] There were, however, no "Western Literature" courses in 1920s Japan and Hiroshima University was not founded until 1949. Several other anachronisms appeared in his biography and correspondence.[9] In interviews with Johnson, he directed conversations to issues of authorship, creativity, and authenticity. He wondered, "Given the fact that attributional indeterminacy is a part of the fabric of the work, why shouldn't that indeterminacy be welcomed into the very fabric of the reading experience."[10]

"Experiment" rather than "hoax" is perhaps a better description of Yasusada and his poetry, although that is speculation. It seems likely that whoever created Yasusada wished to engage the poetry community rather than achieve fame and fortune under false pretenses. What is a cataloger to do with a work that seems designed to complicate the very notion of authorship?

The answer appears in the bibliographic record in the form of a declared author and general and contents notes. By indicating that Kent Johnson is the author, we presume to present as fact that he is responsible. Despite fevered speculation, no definitive answer has emerged regarding authorship. The summary note states that "Araki Yasusada is a kind of literary hoax" with all the negative connotations that elicits. Johnson's authority record has "see from" references to "Araki, Yasusada" and "Yasusada, Araki," and there is no authority record for Araki Yasusada. There is a note in Johnson's authority record stating that he has admitted the ruse, citing an article in *Stand Magazine*. The portion of the article cited, however, references a quotation from an article in another publication, *The American Poetry Review*. It claims that Johnson admitted that he was the author, but Johnson denies this.[11]

When so many so-called "hoaxes" go unacknowledged in our catalogs, due to ignorance or an abundance of caution, why does the record for this book include unproven conclusions? If we value objectivity, this record does not reflect that. This is a literary dispute that catalogers should avoid becoming engaged in. Araki Yasusada should be named as the author in the bibliographic record. The notes should be removed from the bibliographic record and the source note in the authority record should consist of more neutral language. In addition, an authority record should be established for Yasusada. No cross-references should appear in either authority record.

Saracen Island: The Poems of Andreas Karavis by David Solway (2000)

Greek poet Andreas Karavis emerged on the North American literary scene in 1999 when a few of his poems, translated by Canadian poet David Solway, appeared in the *Atlantic Monthly*, the *Journal of Modern Greek Studies*, and *Matrix*. That same year, *Books in Canada* republished an interview with Karavis, including a photograph, that had originally appeared in the Greek journal *Elladas*.[1] Here, Karavis was described as a solitary fisherman born in Xania, Greece, in 1932. On his fishing excursions he studied Greek literature and philosophy and taught himself Ancient Greek and rudimentary Latin. He was also an established poet with two books of poetry published in Greece, where one of his poems was widely anthologized.[2]

In 2000, Signal Editions published a book of Karavis' poetry that was translated by Solway titled *Saracen Island: The Poetry of Andreas Karavis*. From the beginning there were questions about who actually authored the poems. One critic who reviewed the book was nonchalant about the possibility that Karavis was not the poet, saying that "such controversy is healthy at a time when cultural standards and the customary reading of poetry are at a low ebb."[3] Attendees at a party in a Montreal restaurant to launch *Saracen Island* were curious if Karavis would appear, and indeed a Greek-speaking man in a fisherman's cap showed up, but he kept to himself. Karavis was still a mystery man.[4]

The whispers about Karavis became more widespread when a reporter for *The Globe and Mail* wrote a lighthearted article in 2000 speculating that Karavis and Solway were one and the same. When contacted, Solway vigorously denied the claim, stating, "I couldn't possibly have written them. I have broken into tears at Karavis' work. Karavis is definitely real."[5] Soon after, a more forceful argument for the nonexistence of Karavis appeared. Poet Carmine Starnino wrote an article that was published in the Montreal *Gazette*, in which he declared that Karavis "was a hoax perpetrated by Solway."[6] He noted that "Karavis' existence hassles many of the tenets we put our faith in as readers, and the major tenet this Greek poet has complicated in all sorts of delightful ways is the authenticity of authorship."[7]

Saracen Island

The *Gazette* soon received a letter from Solway disputing Starnino's claim that he was Karavis. Another letter arrived from travel writer Fred Reed asserting that he had met Karavis, who, by the way, was of Turkish descent, not Greek. A third letter from Barabaro Joannides stated that her husband had met Karavis several times.[8]

A few weeks later the *Gazette* published another article that contradicted all the letters that had affirmed Karavis' existence. Solway had confessed to the reporter that *Saracen Island* was indeed a ruse. Solway was the author of all poems attributed to Karavis. He, however, did not perpetrate this deception alone. The publisher of *Saracen Island*, Michael Harris, was part of a close network of poets, along with Solway, writing at the time in Québec. Starnino was also part of the poetry group and had sent Karavis' poems, which he knew were written by Solway, to the editor of *Books in Canada*. Letter-writer Reed was a friend and Joannides was Solway's sister. What about the photograph of Karavis and the mysterious fisherman who appeared at the book-launch party? He was Solway's family dentist, Dr. Heft.[9]

The question, then, is why did they do it? Solway refers to the sheer fun of the practical joke noting that "Canadians are not a very exciting people. Like rubes at a carnival, they need to be poked, challenged, gulled, bedazzled, so that the collective jaw drops in something other than an insufficiently stifled yawn."[10] But he hinted at a more personal motive when he said, "I realized a few years back that as a Canadian who resisted the national drift to sameness and tameness, I would probably never manage to acquire the respect and notice of my countrymen I feel is my due. Unless I set about reinventing myself as someone else, preferably someone exotic and mysterious."[11]

The bibliographic record credits David Solway with authorship of *Saracen Island*, which is a valid interpretation of the title page. The authority records for Solway and Karavis include cross-references to each other. There is a note in Solway's authority record stating that "Andreas Karavis, a Greek Poet born 1932, is in fact Solway's pseudonymous creation." Nothing more needs to be done.

Conclusion

Now that we've reviewed many case studies of deceptive books, we can see the variety of challenges that librarians face when dealing with these kinds of resources. Although catalogers agree that their job is to construct bibliographic records that are accurate, unbiased, and useful to catalog users, we sometimes disagree on how to best accomplish these goals. To return to the questions posed in the introduction: Do we honor the author's and publisher's representation of the book even after it has been established that the work is deceptive, or do we alter the bibliographic record to acknowledge the deception? Should all genres be treated the same? If we change a bibliographic record to reflect a new understanding of the book's genre, how is this best done?

I would argue that catalogers should not continue to misrepresent a work in the catalog once we have strong evidence that it is not what it claims to be. For example, if everything in the bibliographic record for the fictional *Love and Consequences* leads the catalog user to believe that it is nonfiction, then we are misrepresenting it, and to do so makes the information in our catalogs misleading and provides less value to users. Sometimes the potential damage done by a bibliographic record that provides an inaccurate representation of a work by the author and publisher is great. As we have seen, deceptions may spread like a virus through other works that utilize the false information in their own nonfiction books. Works of legitimate historical research were negatively impacted by relying on discredited information in *Illustrated Life of Doc Holliday*, for example.

Less consequential, perhaps, is the effect on the public's perception of a book, which may depend on the name and identity of the person who purportedly wrote it. For example, Robert Galbraith's detective novels attracted much more attention when J. K. Rowling admitted, shortly after her first pseudonymous book was published, that she was the author and that Galbraith was her pen name. Whether one considers this a reasonable response or not does not factor into the actions taken by the cataloger because our concern is accuracy and ethical cataloging. We must do what we can to let catalog users know that Rowling and Galbraith are one and the same, because it is true and it may be useful information.

Catalogers should also alert catalog users to misrepresentation of veracity and/or authorship in all genres. Some may argue that readers of fiction and poetry have few, if any, expectations in this regard, but it is not uncommon for historians and other

Conclusion

scholarly researchers to study works in these genres. For example, Mudrooroo's book *Wild Cat Falling*, which was touted as the first published novel by an Australian Aboriginal writer, could very well be considered a valuable primary resource by someone writing a scholarly book about Aboriginal authors in Australia. The value to the researcher is negated, however, when she discovers that it was really written by someone with no Aboriginal ancestry. Researchers, and all catalog users deserve to have that information, although it should be presented as a fact, not an accusation.

That said, there can also be a downside to accuracy when it comes to fiction and poetry. We have seen examples of books, such as *Ananios of Kleitor*, where deceptions regarding authorship or origin are central to the author's creative vision, and the reading experience is enhanced by the reader's growing awareness of the deception. For works such as this, should catalogers prize accuracy over art? Should cultural appropriation, a growing issue in the literary community, be an abiding concern that guides our cataloging decisions for these genres? There are no perfect answers to these questions, in part because catalog users are a diverse group and may benefit from different information in the record, but catalogers, need to remain committed to the values and ethics that guide our profession.

This requires that we be alert to reliable information that is made public regarding misrepresentation of books by authors and/or publishers. It also requires that catalogers evaluate the information objectively and apply non-biased remedies to the bibliographic record. Answering the questions below might help with this task:

1. Has the publisher acknowledged that the charges of misrepresentation are true?
2. Has the author conceded that the charges of misrepresentation are true?
3. Are the sources that are making the claim that a book has been misrepresented reliable?

If the cataloger can answer the first or second question in the affirmative, then he must edit the record to provide an accurate description of the book. If, however, neither the author nor the publisher acknowledges the deception, should we ignore a growing body of legitimate evidence that they are not presenting the work accurately?

We should not, but we must tread even more carefully as catalogers. In a few of the case studies discussed, such as *Sleepers,* both the publisher and the author maintain that the book is a memoir and not the work of fiction that some journalists have claimed. In cases such as this, the credibility and number of sources making the claim is paramount and the judgment of the cataloger becomes crucial. In my judgment, as a cataloger, the evidence that *Sleepers* is a work of fiction is not conclusive, therefore, I would not add a genre/form heading for "Fiction," but I would add a note describing the questions surrounding it. Contradicting the author and publisher is not something that we should shy away from, but erring on the side of caution is advised.

How can catalogers best convey this needed information to the catalog user? As we become aware that an author is using a pen name, that information should be reflected in the authority record with cross-references. In cases where the author writes

Conclusion

under two or more names, multiple authority records with cross-references will be needed. Of course, more seamless access to authority records in the online catalog would provide catalogers with an additional opportunity to communicate this information to users.[1]

In the bibliographic record, recently authorized genre/form headings may be the most useful tool we have when cataloging deceptive works. Several of the memoirs and autobiographies discussed in this book would benefit from the addition of the genre/form headings "Autobiographical fiction" (fiction that is based on events in the author's life but employs fictional characters intermixed with fictional events) or "Fictional autobiographies" (works that present themselves as autobiographies but whose narrators and events are fictional). *A Million Little Pieces* is an example of the former and the latter would be appropriately applied to *The Education of Little Tree.* In the case of a book such as *Go Ask Alice*, "Diary fiction" (fiction written in diary form) is a genre/form heading that clearly applies. What do you do with an allegedly nonfiction book, such as *In Cold Blood*, which is a mix of nonfiction and fiction? Truman Capote called it a "nonfiction novel," and fortunately we have the recently authorized genre/form heading "Nonfiction novels" (works that intentionally blend verifiably factual journalistic research with fictional elements) at our disposal.[2]

The genre/form headings discussed above provide us with useful tools for cataloging books that straddle genres, but we are lacking accurate form subdivisions in these cases. A bibliographic record for a book that warrants the genre/form heading "Autobiographical fiction," for example, is neither entirely fiction nor entirely nonfiction, so neither the form subdivision "Fiction" nor the form subdivision "Biography" is quite right. Perhaps we should assign both, although this is far from satisfactory.[3] Of course for books such as the fictional autobiography *The Cradle of the Deep*, the genre/form heading and form subdivision "Fiction" is sufficient.

For "nonfiction" books that contain erroneous (or fictional) elements, such as *Imagine* or *The Last Train from Hiroshima*, the use of the genre/form heading and form subdivision "Fiction," is just as misleading and inaccurate as characterizing them as nonfiction. They are neither wholly one nor the other. A form subdivision such as "Disputed nonfiction" would give catalogers a tool for accurately cataloging these works. The creation of a form subdivision and a genre/form heading such as "False translations" would also be useful for works like *Saracen Island* and *The Love Poems of Marichiko.*

Alterations in classification may also be necessary. When it comes to classifying deceptive works, Karen Snow, a professor in the Graduate School of Library and Information Science at Dominican University, points out that cataloger's judgment is vital. She notes that Margaret B. Jones' alleged memoir *Love and Consequences* is a work of fiction and should be classified as such. James Frey's *A Million Little Pieces*, however, is a mixture of fact and fiction and is more appropriately classed in Biography or Drug Addiction than Fiction.[4] Given that we can only place a book in one location, well thought out decisions that may not be totally satisfactory must be made.

Notes in both the bibliographic and authority records are often needed, and I would normally suggest that they be quoted from a reliable source, but media reporting

Conclusion

on deceptive works is sometimes inflammatory and may smack of bias. For example, the record for the American edition of fictional biography *The Life of John William Walshe, F. S. A.* that was presented as nonfiction, includes a quotation from *The Nation* that states that the book "is but the product of Mr. Carmichael's busy brain," which does not sound particularly objective even though it comes from a reliable source. Better to write a less colorful note, such as the general note that is also included stating that it is "an imaginary biography." Even though the note is not a quotation, the cataloger can, and should, provide sources for this conclusion. The use of the terms "hoax" or "fraud" in either record is troublesome. Both imply an intentional act designed to trick readers, which suggests that the cataloger knows what motivated the author. Although it is tempting to describe the false Holocaust memoir *Fragments* as a hoax, some people are convinced that the author actually believes that he is a survivor because of the "memories" he recovered while in therapy. The author's belief is demonstrably untrue, but we do not know that his actions were intended to trick anyone. Determining the author's motivations is well beyond the expertise of catalogers.

The suggestions given above may be useful in the MARC environment, but do not necessarily address challenges catalogers face due to the nature of an evolving online catalog. In truth, our ability to determine what users see in the catalog will diminish, as we encourage non-catalogers to "enhance" records with keyword tags and annotations that are not subject to the same ethical standards that catalogers strive to follow.[5] As we move to linked data, new possibilities and challenges will appear. Linked data enhances contextualization of works for catalog users, in part by connecting users to relevant outside sources whose contents are not under our stewardship. Although our role in crafting the information the user is exposed to in our catalogs will change, grappling with questions of authenticity, identity, and veracity in relation to our profession's responsibilities and ethical standards will remain relevant.

Notes

Preface

1. The term "work(s)" is used as a synonym for book or monograph throughout this book.
2. Jana Brubaker, "Ambiguous Authorship and Uncertain Authenticity: A Cataloger's Dilemma," *Cataloging & Classification Quarterly* 34, no. 2 (2002): 19–30.
3. Joseph P. Kahn, "Fabrications Acknowledged, a Bestseller is Withdrawn," *Boston Globe*, August 1, 2012, http://www.bostonglobe.com/lifestyle/style/2012/08/01/jonah-lehrer-book-pulled-boston-based-publisher-houghton-mifflin-harcourt-after-author-admits-fabrication/R64AXel66XZbh5lOJipV3K/story.html.
4. Theresa Connors, "Three Cups of Tea," Autocat (listserv), November 16, 2011, https://listserv.syr.edu/scripts/wa.exe?A0=AUTOCAT&t=&X=B22A8AFEF6727D13A1.

Introduction

1. American Library Association, "Code of Ethics of the American Library Association," amended January 22, 2008, http://www.ala.org/advocacy/proethics/codeofethics/codeethics.
2. George Plimpton, "The Story Behind a Nonfiction Novel," *New York Times*, January 16, 1966, ProQuest Historical Newspapers: The New York Times (doc. ID: 117466874).
3. "A Million Little Lies: Exposing James Frey's Fiction Addiction," *The Smoking Gun*, January 4, 2006, http://www.thesmokinggun.com/documents/celebrity/million-little-lies.
4. Evgenia Peretz, "James Frey's Morning After," *Vanity Fair*, June 2008, http://www.vanityfair.com/culture/features/2008/06/frey200806.
5. George C. Kohn, "Donation of Constantine," *Dictionary of Historic Documents* (New York: Facts on File, 1991), 78.
6. William Bedford Clark, "Col. Crockett's Exploits and Adventures in Texas: Death and Transfiguration," *Studies in American Humor* 1, no. 1 (June 1982) (new series 2): 66–67, http://www.jstor.org/stable/42573129.
7. Joyce Carol Oates, "Success and the Pseudonymous Writer: Turning over a New Self," *New York Times*, December 6, 1987, ProQuest Historical Newspapers: The New York Times (doc. ID: 110719688).
8. Edwin McDowell, "Being an Author by Any Other Name," *New York Times*, October 14, 1984, ProQuest Historical Newspapers: The New York Times (doc. ID: 122543197).

A Few Words About Cataloging Terms

1. "Bibliographic Formats and Standards," OCLC, accessed September 2, 2017, https://www.oclc.org/bibformats/en.html.
2. "MARC 21 Format for Authority Data," Library of Congress, Network Development and MARC Standards Office, last modified May 17, 2017, https://www.loc.gov/marc/authority/ad670.html.
3. "Library on Congress Genre/Form Terms," Library of Congress, accessed September 2, 2017, http://id.loc.gov/authorities/genreForms.html.

Deceptive Works

1. "The SAS Man Who Never Was Breaks Ranks as Cover Is Blown," *The Scotsman* (Edinburgh), November 15, 2001, http://www.scotsman.com/news/uk/the-sas-man-who-never-was-breaks-ranks-as-cover-is-blown-1-584346.
2. Edwin McDowell, "Being an Author by Any Other Name," *New York Times*, October 14, 1984, ProQuest Historical Newspapers: The New York Times (doc. ID: 122543197).
3. Victor Navasky, "Conspiracy Theory Is a Hoax Gone Wrong," *New York Magazine*, November 17, 2013, http://nymag.com/news/features/conspiracy-theories/iron-mountain-hoax/.

Barriers to Accurate Cataloging

1. Kate Newman, "Book Publishing, Not Fact-Checking," *Atlantic*, September 3, 2014, http://www.theatlantic.com/entertainment/archive/2014/09/why-books-still-arent-fact-checked/378789/.
2. Ibid.
3. Carl Bialik, "An Interview with the Smoking Gun," *Gelf Magazine*, January 17, 2006, http://www.gelfmagazine.com/*archives*/an_interview_with_the_smoking_gun.php.

Notes

Codes and Standards

1. "About the Subject Headings Manual PDF Files," Library of Congress, Cataloging and Acquisitions, accessed August 28, 2017, https://www.loc.gov/aba/publications/FreeSHM/freeshmabout.html.
2. Thompson A. Yee, "Preface," *Classification and Shelflisting Manual*, Library of Congress, accessed August 28, 2017, https://www.loc.gov/aba/publications/FreeCSM/preface.pdf.
3. Charles A. Cutter, *Rules for a Dictionary Catalog*, 4th ed. rewritten (Washington, D.C.: Government Printing Office, 1904), 6.
4. Ibid., 12.
5. International Federation of Library Associations and Institutions, IFLA Cataloguing Section, "Statement of International Cataloguing Principles (ICP)," 2016 edition with minor revisions, 2017, https://www.ifla.org/files/assets/cataloguing/icp/icp_2016-en.pdf.
6. Chris Oliver, *Introducing RDA: A Guide to the Basics* (Chicago: American Library Association, 2010), 15.
7. American Library Association, "Code of Ethics of the American Library Association," amended January 22, 2008, http://www.ala.org/advocacy/proethics/codeofethics/codeethics.
8. "Guidelines for ALCTS Members to Supplement the American Library Association Code of Ethics, 1994," http://www.ala.org/alcts/resources/alaethics.
9. American Library Association, "Labeling and Rating Systems: An Interpretation of the *Library Bill of Rights*," amended July 15, 2009, http://www.ala.org/advocacy/intfreedom/librarybill/interpretations/labelingrating.
10. Sheila A. Bair, "Toward a Code of Ethics for Cataloging," *University Libraries Faculty & Staff Publications*, Paper 11 (2005): 5, http://scholarworks.wmich.edu/library_pubs/11/.
11. Ibid., 16.
12. *Anglo-American Cataloguing Rules*, 2nd ed. (Chicago: American Library Association, 1998), 311.
13. *RDA Toolkit: Resource, Description and Access* 0.4.3.4, accessed May 13, 2014, http://access.rdatoolkit.org/.
14. Ibid., 0.4.3.6.
15. Ibid., 0.4.3.5.
16. Ibid.
17. Michele Seikel, "General Notes in Catalog Records Versus FRBR User Tasks," *Cataloging & Classification Quarterly* 51, no. 4 (January 28, 2013): 421, doi: 10.1080/01639374.2012.749318.
18. Karen Smith-Yoshimura, Catherine Argus, Timothy J. Dickey, Chew Chiat Naun, Lisa Rowlison de Ortiz, Hugh Taylor, *Implications of MARC Tag Usage on Library Metadata Practices* (report produced by OCLC Research in support of the RLG Partnership, 2010), 12, http://www.oclc.org/content/dam/research/publications/library/2010/2010-06.pdf.
19. Barbara B. Tillett, "Keeping Libraries Relevant in the Semantic Web with Resource Description and Access (RDA)," *Serials* 24, no. 3 (November 2011): 267.
20. Ibid., 270.

Memoirs and Autobiographies

1. Ben Yagoda, *Memoir: A History* (New York: Riverhead Books, 2009), 7, 9.
2. Ibid., 240; Ann Rothe, *Popular Trauma Culture: Selling the Pain of Others in the Mass Media* (New Brunswick: Rutgers University Press, 2011), 87; Sanford Pinsker, "The Landscape of Contemporary American Memoir," *Sewanee Review* 111, no. 2 (spring 2003): 313, http://www.jstor.org/stable/27549356.
3. Yagoda, *Memoir*, 246.
4. Evgenia Peretz, "James Frey's Morning After," *Vanity Fair*, June 2008, http://www.vanityfair.com/culture/features/2008/06/frey200806#; Rothe, *Popular Trauma Culture*, 107.
5. Steve Almond, "Liar, Liar, Bestseller on Fire," *Boston Globe*, March 6, 2008, http://archive.boston.com/bostonglobe/editorial_opinion/oped/articles/2008/03/06/liar_liar_bestseller_on_fire/.
6. Gore Vidal, *Palimpsest: A Memoir* (New York: Random House, 1995), 5.
7. Annie Dillard, "Introduction," in *The Best American Essays 1988*, ed. Annie Dillard (New York: Ticknor & Fields, 1988), xvii.
8. Dinty W. Moore, *The Truth of the Matter: Art and Craft in Creative Nonfiction* (New York: Pearson Longman, 2007), 4.
9. Robin Gerster, "War Horrors Merge Reality and Fiction," *Sydney Morning Herald* (Australia), April 22, 1995, LexisNexis Academic.
10. Susan Rubin Suleiman, *Crises of Memory and the Second World War* (Cambridge: Harvard University Press, 2006), 166.
11. Caroline Rosenthal and Stefanie Schäfer, ed., *Faking Identity? The Impostor Narrative in Northern American Culture* (Frankfurt: Campus Verlag, 2014), 19.
12. Daniel Mendelsohn, "But Enough About Me," *New Yorker*, January 25, 2010, http://www.newyorker.com/magazine/2010/01/25/but-enough-about-me-2.
13. Michiko Kakutani, "'Amaze Me,' Mother Said, so That's What She Did," *New York Times*, November 5, 2009, http://www.nytimes.com/2009/11/06/books/06book.html.
14. Esther Addley, "So Bad It's Good," *Guardian*, June 15, 2007, http://www.theguardian.com/society/2007/jun/15/childrensservices.biography.
15. Martin H. Evans and Geoffrey Hooper, "Three Misleading Diaries: John Knyveton MD—from Naval Surgeon's Mate to Man Midwife," *International Journal of Maritime History* 26, no. 4 (2014): 776.
16. Yagoda, *Memoir*, 250.
17. Gary L. Roberts, "Trailing an American Mythmaker: History and Glenn G. Boyer's Tombstone Vendetta," accessed August 28, 2015, http://home.earthlink.net/~knuthco1/IMWEfiles/Mythmaker1source.htm.

Col. Crockett's Exploits and Adventures in Texas

1. James Atkins Schackford, *David Crockett: The Man and the Legend* (Chapel Hill: University of North Carolina Press, 1956), 273–74.

Notes

2. William Bedford Clark, "Col. Crockett's Exploits and Adventures in Texas: Death and Transfiguration," *Studies in American Humor* 1, no. 1 (June 1982) (new series 2): 66, http://www.jstor.org/stable/42573129.

3. W. W. Boyd, review of *The Autobiography of David Crockett*, by Hamlin Garland, *Indiana Magazine of History* 19, no. 4 (December 1923): 383, http://www.jstor.org/stable/27786112.

4. Shackford, *David Crockett*, 274.

Awful Disclosures of Maria Monk

1. William S. Cossen, "Monk in the Middle: The *Awful Disclosures of the Hotel Dieu Nunnery* and the Making of Catholic Identity," *American Catholic Studies* 125, no. 1 (spring 2014): 25, doi: 10.1353/acs.2014.0013.

2. Ray Allen Billington, "Maria Monk and Her Influence," *The Catholic Historical Review* 22, no. 3 (October 1936): 284–287, http://www.jstor.org/stable/25013504; André Pelchat, "Maria Monk's Awful Disclosures…," *Beaver* 88, no. 6 (December 2008), America: History and Life (doc ID: 36006571).

3. "Maria Monk and Her Impostures," *The Catholic Telegraph*, October 5, 1837, ProQuest American Periodicals Series II (doc ID: 89936209).

4. "Profligacy of the Roman Clergy," *The New-England Telegraph, and Eclectic Review* 2, no. 11 (November 1836), ProQuest American Periodicals Series II (doc ID: 136127803).

5. "Awful Disclosures of Maria Monk," *Christian Watchman* (October 21, 1836), ProQuest Periodicals Series II (doc ID: 127205611).

6. William L. Stone, "Maria Monk and the Nunnery of the Hotel Dieu, Being an Account of a Visit to the Convents of Montreal…," (New York: Howe & Bates, 1836), 34, http://books.google.com/books?id=JY2gCW1ea8UC&printsec=frontcover&source=gbs_ge_summary_r&cad=0#v=onepage&q&f=false.

7. "Maria Monk and Her Impostures," *Quarterly Christian Spectator* 9, no. 2 (June 1, 1837), ProQuest American Periodicals Series II (doc ID: 127810372).

8. Pelchat, "Maria Monk's Awful Disclosures."

9. "Character of Maria Monk, With a Likeness," *American Phrenological Journal* 11, no. 9 (October 1, 1849), ProQuest Periodicals Series II (doc ID: 137854781).

10. "Maria Monk Died the Other Day…," *The North Star*, October 13, 1849, African American Newspapers, Accessible Archives.

The Life of John William Walshe, F. S. A.

1. Montgomery Carmichael, *The Life of John William Walshe, F. S. A.* (New York: E. P. Dutton, 1902), vii.

2. Ibid., vii–viii.

3. Ibid., xii.

4. Review of *The Life of John William Walshe*, ed. Montgomery Carmichael, *Literary World: A Monthly Review of Current Literature* 33, no. 8 (August 1, 1902); "The Life of John William Walshe," *New York Times*, August 2, 1902, http://www.nytimes.com/1984/08/10/books/publishing-endowment-gives-4-writers-25000.html; "The Life of John William Walshe, F. S. A.," *Outlook* 71, no. 10 (July 5, 1902): 658–9, http://hdl.handle.net/2027/ucl.b2989337?urlappend=%3Bseq=682

5. "The Life of John William Walshe, F. S. A.," *Spectator* 89 (July 26, 1902): 124–5, http://hdl.handle.net/2027/mdp.39015035604670?urlappend=%3Bseq=138.

6. "The Life of John William Walshe, F. S. A.," *Outlook*.

7. Review of *The Life of John William Walshe*.

8. Harold Hannyngton Child, "A Modern Saint," *Times Literary Supplement*, no. 26 (July 11, 1902): 204, *Times Literary Supplement* Historical Archive (doc. ID EX1200000475).

9. "Books and Men," *New York Times*, September 13, 1902, ProQuest Historical Newspapers: The New York Times (doc. ID: 96160248).

Long Lance

1. Because opinions diverge regarding the acceptable term for American Indians, I have used both "Indian," and "Native American" throughout.

2. Chief Buffalo Child Long Lance, *Long Lance* (New York: Cosmopolitan Book Corp., 1928), xiii.

3. Donald B. Smith, *Chief Buffalo Child Long Lance: the Glorious Imposter* (Red Deer, Alberta: Red Deer Press, 1999), 204–207.

4. Ibid., 23–27.

5. Tyee Bridge, "The Many Larger-Than-Life Lives of Long Lance (Part 1)," *The Calgary Herald (Alberta)*, October 19, 2007, Final edition, LexisNexis Academic.

6. Ibid.

7. Tyee Bridge, "The Many Larger-Than-Life Lives of Long Lance (Part 2)," *The Calgary Herald (Alberta)*, October 19, 2007, Final edition, LexisNexis Academic.

8. Tyee Bridge, "The Many Larger-Than-Life Lives of Long Lance (Part 3)," *The Calgary Herald (Alberta)*, October 19, 2007, Final edition, LexisNexis Academic; The website for Kainai First Nation, accessed February 7, 2014, http://www.bloodtribe.org.

9. Smith, *Chief Buffalo Child*, 167–68.

10. Ibid., 195, 203–204.

11. Karina Vernon, "The First Black Prairie Novel: Chief Buffalo Child Long Lance's *Autobiography* and the Repression of Prairie Blackness," *Journal of Canadian Studies/Revue d'études canadiennes* 45, no. 2 (spring 2011): 44, Project Muse.

12. Smith, *Chief Buffalo Child*, 213–14, 226.

13. Ibid., 228.

14. Mordaunt Hall, "The Screen," *New York Times*, May 20, 1930, ProQuest Historical Newspapers: The New York Times (doc ID: 98972359).

15. Smith, *Chief Buffalo Child*, 268, 312.

16. "Chief Long Lance Ends His Life in California," *New York Times*, March 22, 1932, ProQuest Historical Newspapers: The New York Times (doc ID: 99741514).

17. Barbara Aitken, "Studies in the Process of Change among the American Indians," *Man* 36 (September 1936): 163, http://www.jstor.org/stable/2791118.

18. Barbara Aitken, "Civilization of the American Indian," *Man* 38 (July 1938): 116, http://www.jstor.org/stable/2792911.

The Cradle of the Deep

1. Anne Colby, "Meet the Grandmother of Memoir Fabricators," *Los Angeles Times*, March 14, 2008, http://articles.latimes.com/print/2008/mar/14/entertainment/et-cradle14.

2. Fanny Butcher, "Sea's Girl Child Tells Story of Windjammer," *Chicago Daily Tribune*, March 2, 1929, ProQuest Historical Newspapers: Chicago Tribune (doc. ID: 181035478).

3. Arthur Warner, "Joan of another Ark," *Nation* 128, no. 3326 (April 3, 1929): 401, EBSCOhost, The Nation Archive (doc. ID: 13593212)

4. "A Sea-Going Lass Whose Nurse Was a Sailmaker," *New York Times*, March 10, 1929, ProQuest Historical Newspapers: The New York Times (doc. ID: 105036619).

5. Warner, "Joan of Another Ark," 401.

6. Colby, "Meet the Grandmother."

7. *Ibid.*

8. "In the Driftway," *Nation* 128, no. 3329 (April 24, 1929): 506, EBSCOhost, The Nation Archive (doc. ID: 13593304).

9. Geoffrey T. Hellman, "Profiles: How to Win Profits and Influence Literature—III," *New Yorker* 15, no. 35 (October 14, 1939): 26.

10. *Ibid.*

11. Colby, "Meet the Grandmother."

12. Hellman, "Profiles," 26.

Pilgrims of the Wild

1. Brower, Kenneth, "Grey Owl," *The Atlantic*, January 1990: 2. https://www.theatlantic.com/past/docs/issues/90jan/greyowl.htm.

2. David Howes and Constance Classen, "Grey Owl, White Indian," *Canadian Icon*, 2014, http://canadianicon.org/table-of-contents/grey-owl-white-indian/.

3. *Ibid.*

4. Brower, "Grey Owl," 9.

5. Donald B. Smith, *From the Land of Shadows* (Saskatoon, Saskatchewan: Western Producer Prairie Books, 1990), 11–12.

6. Brower, "Grey Owl," 10; Smith, *From the Land of Shadows*, 36, 71–73.

7. Howes and Classen, "Grey Owl, White Indian."

8. Albert Braz, "The Modern Hiawatha: Grey Owl's Construction of His Aboriginal Self," in *Autobiography in Canada: Critical Directions*, ed. Julie Rak (Waterloo, Ontario: Wilfrid Laurier University Press, 2005), 60–62. E-brary.

The Diary of a Surgeon in the Year 1751–1752; Surgeon's Mate; Man Midwife

1. Martin H. Evans and Geoffrey Hooper, "Three Misleading Diaries: John Knyveton MD–from Navel Surgeon's Mate to Man Midwife," *International Journal of Maritime History* 26, no. 4 (2014): 763.

2. "An 18th Century Surgeon: Puzzles of a 'Reconstructed Diary,'" review of *The Diary of a Surgeon in the Year 1751–1752*, by John Knyveton, *Times Literary Supplement*, Issue 1880 (February 12, 1938): 103, Times Literary Supplement Historical Archive (Doc. ID EX1200259818).

3. *Ibid.*

4. M. F. Ashley-Montagu, review of *The Diary of a Surgeon in the Year 1751–1752*, by John Knyveton, *Isis* 28, no. 2 (May 1938): 479, http://www.jstor.org/stable/225709.

5. Saul Jarcho, M. D., "Two Years in an Eighteenth-Century Surgeon's Life," review of *The Diary of a Surgeon in the Year 1751–1752*, by John Knyveton, *New York Times*, December 12, 1937, ProQuest Historical Newspapers: The New York Times (doc. ID: 101986977).

6. Review of *The Diary of a Surgeon in the Year 1751–1752*, by John Knyveton, *Journal of the American Medical Association* 110, no. 25 (June 18, 1938): 2109.

7. Iolo Aneurin Williams, "John Knyveton," review of *The Diary of a Surgeon in the Year 1751–1752*, by John Knyveton, *Times Literary Supplement*, Issue 2326 (August 31, 1946): 411, Times Literary Supplement Historical Archive (Doc. ID EX1200280004).

8. J. B. Whitmore, "Letter to the Editor," *Times Literary Supplement*, Issue 2327 (September 7, 1946): 427, Times Literary Supplement Historical Archive (Doc. ID EX120068731).

9. Ernest Gray, "Letter to the Editor," *Times Literary Supplement*, Issue 2330 (September 28, 1946): 465, Times Literary Supplement Historical Archive (Doc. ID EX120068456).

10. Evans and Hooper, "Three Misleading Diaries," 775–76.

My Sister and I

1. R.J. Hollingdale, review of *My Sister and I*, by Friedrich Nietzsche, *Journal of Nietzsche Studies*, no. 2 (Autumn 1991): 97, http://www.jstor.org/stable/20717554.

2. Oscar Levy, introduction to *My Sister and I*, by Friedrich Nietzsche (Los Angeles: Amok, 1990), xi.

3. A.K. Placzek, review of *My Sister and I*, by Friedrich Nietzsche, *Saturday Review of Literature*, February 2, 1952, 19.

4. Walter Kaufmann, "Nietzsche and the Seven Sirens," *Partisan Review*, v. 19, no. 3 (May-June 1952), 365.

5. Placzek, review, 19–20; Henricus Antonius "Han" van Meegeren made a fortune in the 1930s selling what he claimed were Johannes Vermeer paint-

ings. They were, however, forgeries painted by van Meegeren.

6. Kaufmann, "Nietzsche and the Seven Sirens," 372–74.

7. *Ibid.*

8. Hollingdale, review, 98.

9. Walter Kaufmann, *Nietzsche: Philosopher, Psychologist, Antichrist* (Princeton: Princeton University Press, 1968), 496; Kaufmann erroneously recorded the man's name as David George Plotkin.

10. Walter K. Stewart, "*My Sister and I*: the Disputed Nietzsche," in *My Sister and I*, by Friedrich Nietzsche (Los Angeles: Amok, 1990), lx

11. Heward Wilkinson, "Retrieving a Posthumous Text-Message; Nietzsche's Fall: The Significance of the Disputed Asylum Writing," *International Journal of Psychotherapy* 7, no. 1 (2002): 67, EBSCOhost Academic Search Complete (doc. ID: 9708013583).

The Long Walk

1. Nash K. Burger, "Books of The Times: Power Generated by Restraint Deaths and Then the Monsters," *New York Times*, April 28, 1956: 30, ProQuest Historical Newspapers: The New York Times (doc. ID: 113879540).

2. Linda Willis, *Looking for Mr. Smith* (New York: Skyhorse Publishing, 2010), 17.

3. R. D. Charques, "Enduring to the End," *Times Literary Supplement*, Issue 2826 (April 27, 1956): 249, Times Literary Supplement Historical Archive (doc. ID: EX1200103893).

4. Eric Shipton, "Fact–Or Fantasy," *Geographical Journal* 122, no. 3 (September 1956): 370–72, doi: 10.2307/1791022.

5. Richard Brooks, "Epic Fantasy: Long Walk Dismissed as Tall Story," *Sunday Times*, December 19, 2010, EBSCOhost Newspaper Source (accession no.: 7EH42782957).

6. Willis, *Looking for Mr. Smith*, 141.

7. *Ibid.*, 135, 148.

8. Hugh Levinson, "Walking the Talk?" *BBC News*, BBC, October 30, 2006, last updated October 30, 2006, http://news.bbc.co.uk/2/hi/uk_news/magazine/6098218.stm;

9. Willis, *Looking for Mr. Smith*, 261–64; "Witold Glinski," *Telegraph*, July 3, 2013. http://www.telegraph.co.uk/news/obituaries/10158049/Witold-Glinski.html.

Travels with Charley

1. Edward Weeks, review of *Travels with Charley*, by John Steinbeck, *The Atlantic* 210, no. 2 (August 1992): 136; "Books–Authors," *New York Times*, May 4, 1962, ProQuest Historical Newspapers: The New York Times (doc. ID: 116086223).

2. Charles McGrath, "A Reality Check for Steinbeck and Charley," *New York Times*, April 4, 2011, ProQuest Historical Newspapers: The New York Times (doc. ID: 1620477547); Robert Gottlieb, "The Rescue of John Steinbeck," *New York Review of Books* 55, no. 6 (April 17, 2008), http://www.nybooks.com/articles/archives/2008/apr/17/the-rescue-of-john-steinbeck/.

3. Orville Prescott, "Books of the Times," *New York Times*, July 27, 1962, ProQuest Historical Newspapers: The New York Times (doc. ID: 116223848).

4. Steigerwald, Bill, "Sorry, Charley." *Reason* 42, no. 11 (April 2011): 58–62, EBSCOhost, Academic Search Complete (doc. ID 59284712).

5. "The Truth About Charley," *New York Times*, April 10, 2011, ProQuest Historical Newspapers: The New York Times (doc. ID: 1634232956); McGrath, "Reality Check."

6. Gottlieb, "Rescue of John Steinbeck."

7. Steigerwald, "Sorry, Charley."

8. "Truth About Charley."

9. *Ibid.*

10. McGrath, "Reality Check."

11. *Ibid.*

Go Ask Alice

1. Anonymous, *Go Ask Alice* (Englewood Cliffs, NJ: Prentice-Hall, 1971), n. pag.

2. *Ibid.*, 159.

3. *Ibid.*

4. William Cole, "About Alice, a Rabbit, a Tree…," *New York Times*, September 9, 1973, ProQuest Historical Newspapers: The New York Times (doc. ID: 119821051).

5. John W. Conner, review of *Go Ask Alice*, by Anonymous, *English Journal* 62, no. 1 (January 1973): 146–47, doi: 10.2307/814105

6. Jack Forman, review of *Go Ask Alice*, by Anonymous, *Library Journal* 97, no. 6 (March 15, 1972): 1174.

7. Review of *Go Ask Alice*, by Anonymous, *Publishers Weekly* 201, no. 14 (March 27, 1972): 80.

8. John J. O'Connor, "Diary of a Schoolgirl En Route to Death," *New York Times*, February 11, 1973, ProQuest Historical Newspapers: The New York Times (doc. ID: 119681094).

9. Alleen Pace Nilsen, "The House That Alice Built," *School Library Journal* 26, no. 2 (October 1979), EBSCOhost Academic Search Complete (doc. ID: 6064477).

10. *Ibid.*; *Contemporary Authors*, New Revision Series, s.v. "Sparks, Beatrice (Mathews) 1918-."

11. "Beatrice Ruby Sparks," *Salt Lake City Tribune*, May 30, 2012, http://www.legacy.com/obituaries/saltlaketribune/obituary.aspx?pid=157846946.

12. Nilson, "The House that Alice Built."

13. *Ibid.*

14. Beatrice Sparks, *Voices* (New York: Dell, 1980), cover.

15. Alleen Pace Nilsen, "Reminiscing: One Perspective on ALAN's Beginnings," *ALAN Review* 40, no. 3 (summer 2013), http://scholar.lib.vt.edu/ejournals/ALAN/v40n3/nilsen.html.

16. "100 Most Frequently Challenged Books by Decade," accessed January 17, 2015, http://www.ala.org/bbooks/frequentlychallengedbooks/top100.

17. Nilsen, "Reminiscing."

18. *The National Union Catalog: A Cumulative Author List Representing Library of Congress Printed Cards and Titles Reported by Other American Libraries, 1968–1972*, s.v. "Anonymous."

Notes

I Married Wyatt Earp; Illustrated Life of Doc Holliday

1. Larry D. Ball, review of *I Married Wyatt Earp: The Recollections of Josephine Sarah Marcus Earp*, collected and edited by Glenn G. Boyer, *Journal of the Southwest* 19, no. 4 (winter 1977): 364–5; Jeff Sharlet, "Author's Methods Lead to Showdown Over Much-Admired Book on Old West," *Chronicle of Higher Education* 45, no. 40 (June 11, 1999): 19.
2. Sharlet, "Author's Methods Lead to Showdown."
3. Josephine Sarah Marcus Earp, *I Married Wyatt Earp: The Recollections of Josephine Sarah Marcus Earp*, ed. Glenn G. Boyer (Tucson: University of Arizona Press, 1976), 255.
4. Tony Ortega, "I Varied Wyatt Earp," *Phoenix New Times*, March 4, 1999, http://www.phoenixnewtimes.com/news/i-varied-wyatt-earp-6421331; Sharlet, "Author's Methods Lead to Showdown."
5. Ibid.
6. Ibid.
7. Glenn Boyer, *Illustrated Life of Doc Holliday* (Glenwood Springs, CO: Reminder Publishing, 1966), cover.
8. Ibid., 58.
9. Gary L. Roberts, "Trailing an American Mythmaker: History and Glenn G. Boyer's Tombstone Vendetta," accessed August 28, 2015, http://home.earthlink.net/~knuthco1/IMWEfiles/Mythmaker1source.htm.
10. Ibid.
11. Ortega, "I Varied Wyatt Earp."
12. Ibid.
13. Ibid.
14. Andrew Richard Albanese, "Bogus Bride," *Salon*, February 8, 2000, http://www.salon.com/2000/02/08/earp/.
15. Ortega, "I Varied Wyatt Earp."
16. Sharlet, "Author's Methods Lead to Showdown."
17. Ibid.
18. Jefferson Decker, "History Expose: The Facade Behind the Front," *Tombstone Tumbleweed*, March 16, 2000, http://home.earthlink.net/~knuthco1/IMWEfiles2/articles-IMWEsource.htm.

The Education of Little Tree

1. Angeline Goreau, review of *The Education of Little Tree*, by Forrest Carter, *Entertainment Weekly*, September 13, 1991, http://www.ew.com/article/1991/09/13/education-little-tree.
2. Mary M. Moynihan, review of *The Education of Little Tree*, by Forrest Carter, *Teaching Sociology* 19, no. 1 (January 1991): 110–112, http://www.jstor.org/stable/1317589.
3. "Is Forrest Carter Really Asa Carter? Only Josey Wales May Know for Sure," *New York Times*, August 26, 1976, ProQuest Historical Newspapers: The New York Times (doc. ID: 122874747).
4. Felicia R. Lee, "Best Seller Is a Fake, Professor Asserts," *New York Times*, October 4, 1991, ProQuest Historical Newspapers: The New York Times (doc. ID: 108670841).
5. Ibid.
6. Dana Rubin, "The Real Education of Little Tree," *Texas Monthly*, February 1992, http://www.texasmonthly.com/content/real-education-little-tree; Lee, "Best Seller Is a Fake"; Bernard Weinraub, "Movie With a Murky Background: The Man Who Wrote the Book," *New York Times*, December 17, 1997, ProQuest Historical Newspapers: The New York Times (doc. ID: 109758170).
7. Dan T. Carter, "The Transformation of a Klansman," *New York Times*, October 4, 1991, ProQuest Historical Newspapers: The New York Times (doc. ID: 108667740).
8. Allen Barra, "The Education of Little Fraud," *Salon*, December 20, 2001, http://www.salon.com/2001/12/20/carter_6/.
9. Clint Eastwood, "Happy Transformation," *New York Times*, October 16, 1991, ProQuest Historical Newspapers: The New York Times (doc. ID: 108659065).
10. Esther B. Fein, "Book Notes," *New York Times*, October 30, 1991, ProQuest Historical Newspapers: The New York Times (doc. ID: 108715081).
11. Weinraub, "Movie with a Murky Background."
12. Rubin, "The Real Education."

Michelle Remembers

1. Herbert Mitgang, "Congdon Publishers Sold to Frenchman," *New York Times*, November 18, 1979, ProQuest Historical Newspapers: The New York Times (doc ID: 123909184).
2. Jeffrey S. Victor, "Moral Panics and the Social Construction of Deviant Behavior: A Theory and Application to the Case of Ritual Child Abuse," *Sociological Perspectives* 41, no. 3 (1998): 545, http://www.jstor.org/stable/1389563.
3. Kerwin Lee Klein, "Remembrance and the Christian Right," in *From History to Theory* (Berkley: University of California Press, 2011), 142, http://www.jstor.org/stable/10.1525/j.ctt1ppb2k.
4. Kristin McMurran, "A Canadian Woman's Bizarre Childhood Memories of Satan Shock Shrinks and Priests," *People*, September 1, 1980, http://www.people.com/people/archive/article/0,,20077308,00.html.
5. Ibid.
6. Ibid.
7. Klein, "Remembrance and the Christian Right," 141–143.
8. Jay Sharbutt, "Cauldron Boils Over Geraldo's 'Devil Worship': 'Satan' Wins Ratings, Loses Advertisers," *Los Angeles Times*, October 27, 1988, http://articles.latimes.com/1988-10-27/entertainment/ca-449_1_devil-worship.
9. Bette L. Bottoms, Phillip R. Shaver, and Gail S. Goodman, "An Analysis of Ritualistic and Religion-Related Child Abuse Allegations," *Law and Human Behavior* 20, no. 1 (February 1996): 4–6, http://www.jstor.org/stable/1394040; Klein, "Remembrance and the Christian Right," 143.
10. Victor, "Moral Panics," 356.

Notes

11. "Michelle Remembers: The Debunking of a Myth," *The Mail on Sunday*, September 30, 1990, 41, https://xeper.org/pub/pub_wh_michelle.html.

Satan's Underground

1. Bob and Gretchen Passantino and Jon Trott, "Satan's Sideshow: The True Lauren Stratford Story," *Cornerstone*, accessed February 9, 2015, http://www.answers.org/satan/stratford.html.
2. *Ibid.*
3. *Ibid.*
4. *Ibid.*
5. *Ibid.*
6. Diane E. Taub and Lawrence D. Nelson, "Satanism in Contemporary America: Establishment or Underground," *The Sociological Quarterly* 34, no. 3 (August 1993): 531, http://www.jstor.org/stable/4121110; Bob and Gretchen Passantino and Jon Trott, "Lauren Stratford: From Satanic Ritual Abuse to Jewish Holocaust Survivor," *Cornerstone*, accessed February 9, 2015, http://www.answers.org/satan/laura.html.
7. Blake Eskin, A Life in Pieces: *The Making and Unmaking of Binjamin Wilkomirski* (New York: W. W. Norton, 2002), 97–98.

Mutant Message Downunder

1. Robert Milliken, "Truth Goes Walkabout in Outback? Aborigines Outraged as U.S. Author Makes a Million with 'New Age Fantasy' of Lost Tribe in the Bush," *The Independent*, December 11, 1994, http://www.independent.co.uk/news/world/truth-goes-walkabout-in-outback-aborigines-outraged-as-us-author-makes-a-million-with-new-age-fantasy-of-lost-tribe-in-the-bush-1389189.html.
2. Cath Ellis, "Helping Yourself: Marlo Morgan and the Fabrication of Indigenous Wisdom," *Australian Literary Studies* 21, no. 4 (October 2004): 151, EBSCOhost Academic Search Complete (doc. ID: 16370295); Milliken, "Truth Goes Walkabout."
3. Ellis, "Helping Yourself," 151–52.
4. *Ibid.*, 152–53.
5. *Ibid.*, 155–56.
6. *Ibid.*, 156.
7. John E. Stanton, "Marlo Morgan's Mutant Message Downunder: An Anthropological Perspective," accessed March 23, 2015, http://dumbartung.org.au/stanton2.html.
8. Ellis, "Helping Yourself," 156–57; Joel Friedlander, "The Incredible Self-Publishing Journey of Marlo Morgan and the Mutant Message Down Under," *The Book Designer* website, last modified January 4, 2011, http://www.thebookdesigner.com/2011/01/the-incredible-self-publishing-journey-of-marlo-morgan-and-the-mutant-message-down-under/.

A Rock and a Hard Place

1. Tad Friend, "Virtual Love," *The New Yorker*, November 26, 2001, 88.
2. *Ibid.*, 89–90.
3. *Ibid.*, 90.
4. Richard Miller, "Anthony Godby Johnson, the Invisible Boy, Part I," *A Man I Dreamt Up* (blog), August 3, 2006, http://armisteadmaupin.com/blog/?p=341.
5. Friend, "Virtual Love," 90.
6. Michele Ingrassia, "The Author Nobody's Met," *Newsweek*, May 30, 1993, http://www.newsweek.com/author-nobodys-met-193220.
7. *Ibid.*
8. Meg Cox, "Crown Publishers Denies Boy's Book on Aids is Hoax," *Wall Street Journal*, May 25, 1993, LexisNexis Academic.
9. Friend, "Virtual Love," 92.
10. *Ibid.*
11. *Ibid.*, 92–94.
12. *Ibid.*, 93–94.
13. Miller, "Anthony Godby Johnson."
14. Elizabeth Vargas, Richard Gerdau, Susan Miller, Michael Mendelson, "Believing in Tony's Existence," *ABC News*, http://abcnews.go.com/2020/story?id=2221860.
15. Friend, "Virtual Love," 96–98.

Sleepers

1. Review of *Sleepers*, by Lorenzo Carcaterra, *Publishers Weekly* 242, no. 23 (June 5, 1995): 45.
2. Tom De Haven, review of *Sleepers*, by Lorenzo Carcaterra, *Entertainment Weekly*, July 14, 1995, http://www.ew.com/article/1995/07/14/sleepers.
3. Jonathan Kirsch, review of *Sleepers*, by Lorenzo Carcaterra, *Los Angeles Times*, August 23, 1995, http://articles.latimes.com/1995-08-23/news/ls-38142_1_lorenzo-carcaterra.
4. De Haven, review of *Sleepers*.
5. *Ibid.*
6. Barbara Wickens, "Truth or Fiction?" *Mcclean's* 108, no. 35 (August 28, 1995): 48, EBSCOhost Academic Search Complete (doc. ID: 9509144882).
7. David Stout, "A Hell's Kitchen Tale Is Doubted and Defended," *New York Times*, July 7, 1995, ProQuest Historical Newspapers: The New York Times (doc. ID: 109527377).
8. *Ibid.*
9. *Ibid.*
10. Mary B. W. Tabor, "Book Notes," *New York Times*, July 26, 1995, ProQuest Historical Newspapers: The New York Times (doc. ID: 109525091).
11. *Ibid.*
12. Paul Gray and Elizabeth L. Bland, "Tiny Pieces of Flesh," *Time*, July 31, 1995, EBSCOhost Academic Search Complete (doc. ID: 9508017563).
13. Bernard Weinraub, "'Sleepers' Debate Renewed: How True Is a 'True Story'?" *New York Times*, October 22, 1996, ProQuest Historical Newspapers: The New York Times (doc. ID: 109565358); Bill Donohue, "Hoax Movie, Sleepers, Defames Catholic School and Priest," *Catalyst Online*, November 11, 1996, http://www.catholicleague.org/hoax-movie-sleepers-defames-catholic-school-and-priest.
14. Weinraub, "'Sleepers' Debate Renewed."

Notes

Stoker

1. Konrad Kwiet, "Anzac and Auschwitz: The Unbelievable Story of Donald Watt," *Patterns of Prejudice* 31, no. 4 (1997): 54.
2. Rochelle Tubb, "I Stoked Furnaces at Auschwitz," *Sun Herald* (Sydney, Australia), April 2, 1995, LexisNexis Academic.
3. Ibid.
4. Brian Woodley, "Shadow of a Doubt," *Weekend Australian*, March 29, 1997, LexisNexis Academic; Catherine Lambert, "A Soldier's Tale Comes to Light," *Sunday Herald Sun* (Melbourne, Australia), February 4, 2001, EBSCOhost Newspaper Source (accession no.: 200102041083885143).
5. Woodley, "Shadow of a Doubt"; Kweit, "Anzac and Auschwitz," 56, 58.
6. Woodley, "Shadow of a Doubt."
7. Ibid.
8. Muller, Filip, "Filip Muller's Testimony: Auschwitz," on remember.org: A People's History of the Holocaust & Genocide, accessed March 7, 2015, http://remember.org/witness/wit-sur-mul; Darren O'Brien, "Donald Watt's 'Stoker': The Perils of Testimony," *Genocide Studies Newsletter* 3, no. 3 (March-April 1997): 7.
9. Kweit, "Anzac and Auschwitz," 55.

Fragments

1. Anne Whitehead, "Telling Tales: Trauma and Testimony in Binjamin Wilkomirski's 'Fragments,'" *Discourse* 25, no. 1/2 (winter and spring 2003): 120, http://www.jstor.org/stable/41389667.
2. Jonathan Kozol, "Children of the Camps," *Nation* 263, no. 13 (October 28, 1996): 24, EBSCOhost Academic Search Complete (doc. ID: 9610177847).
3. Julie Salamon, "Childhood's End," *New York Times*, January 12, 1997, ProQuest Historical Newspapers: The New York Times (doc. ID: 109664127).
4. Paul Maliszewski, "A Holocaust Fantasy," *The Wilson Quarterly (1976-)*, 26, no. 3 (summer 2002): 110, http://www.jstor.org/stable/40260644.
5. Blake Eskin, *A Life in Pieces* (New York: W. W. Norton, 2002), 30–31, 108.
6. Ibid., 70–72.
7. Doreen Carvajal, "A Holocaust Memoir in Doubt: Swiss Records Contradict a Book on Childhood Horror," *New York Times*, November 3, 1998, ProQuest Historical Newspapers: The New York Times (doc. ID: 109886743).
8. Cynthia Cotts, "True or Faux?" *Village Voice*, June 15, 1999, http://www.villagevoice.com/1999-06-15/news/true-or-faux/.
9. Carvajal, "A Holocaust Memoir."
10. Ibid.;
11. Cotts, "True or Faux?"
12. Ibid.
13. Martin Arnold, "Making Books: In Fact, It's Fiction," *New York Times*, November 12, 1998, ProQuest Historical Newspapers: The New York Times (doc. ID: 109967598).
14. Cynthia Cotts, "'Fragments' of the Imagination," *Village Voice*, May 9, 2000, http://www.villagevoice.com/2000-05-09/news/fragments-of-the-imagination/.
15. Cotts, "True or Faux?"

Misha

1. David Mehegan, "Incredible Journey," *Boston Globe*, October 31, 2001, http://www.boston.com/ae/books/articles/2001/10/31/incredible_journey/?page=full.
2. P.C., review of *Misha: A Memoire of the Holocaust Years*, by Misha Defonseca, *People*, August 11, 1997, EBSCOhost Academic Search Complete (doc. ID: 9708060208).
3. Carolyn Kellogg, "Woman Who Invented Her Holocaust Memoir Must Return $22.5 Million," Jacket Copy, *Los Angeles Times*, May 12, 2014, http://www.latimes.com/books/jacketcopy/la-et-jc-invented-holocaust-memoir-20140512-story.html.
4. P. C., *Misha*.
5. David Mehegan, "Author Admits Making Up Memoir of Surviving Holocaust," *Boston Globe*, February 29, 2008, http://www.boston.com/ae/books/articles/2008/02/29/author_admits_making_up_memoir_of_surviving_holocaust/.
6. Blake Eskin, "The Girl Who Cried Wolf: A Holocaust Fairy Tale," *Boston Magazine*, September 2008, http://www.bostonmagazine.com/2008/08/the-girl-who-cried-wolf-a-holocaust-fairy-tale/5/.
7. Kellogg, "Woman Who Invented Her Holocaust Memoir."
8. Eskin, "The Girl Who Cried Wolf. '
9. "Author of Hoax Holocaust Memoir to Pay $22.5 Million," *Times of Israel*, May 11, 2014, http://www.timesofisrael.com/author-of-hoax-holocaust-memoir-to-pay-22500000/.
10. Mehegan. "Author Admits Making Up Memoir."

The Autobiography of Howard Hughes

1. Stephen Fay, Lewis Chester, and Magnus Linklater, *Hoax: The Inside Story of the Howard Hughes—Clifford Irving Affair* (New York: Viking Press, 1972), 5, 35.
2. Ibid., 32.
3. Ibid., 36–39.
4. Ibid., 45–46.
5. Henry Raymont, "Howard Hughes' Memoirs Are Bought For Book and Serial in Life Magazine," *New York Times*, December 8, 1971, ProQuest Historical Newspapers: The New York Times (doc. ID: 119130421).
6. Ibid.
7. "Statements by Hughes and Two Publishers in Autobiography Controversy," *New York Times*, January 10, 1972, ProQuest Historical Newspapers: The New York Times (doc. ID: 119441381).
8. Ibid.
9. Wallace Turner, "Hughes Book: Plight of the Publishers," *New York Times*, January 29, 1972, ProQuest Historical Newspapers: The New York Times

Notes

(doc. ID: 119415027); Wallace Turner, "Tales of Hughes Proving Elusive," *New York Times*, February 6, 1972, ProQuest Historical Newspapers: The New York Times (doc. ID: 119395109).

10. Wallace Turner, "More Writings on Hughes Like Irving's Are Revealed," *New York Times*, February 14, 1972, ProQuest Historical Newspapers: The New York Times (doc. ID: 119405259).

11. "Text of Statements from Time Inc. and McGraw-Hill," *New York Times*, February 12, 1972, ProQuest Historical Newspapers: The New York Times (doc. ID: 119435471).

12. Mick Brown, "You Couldn't Make It Up," *Telegraph* (United Kingdom), July 28, 2007, http://www.telegraph.co.uk/culture/3666824/You-couldnt-make-it-up.html; David Wallace-Wells, "Howard Hughes," *New York Magazine*, April 1, 2012, http://nymag.com/news/features/scandals/howard-hughes-2012-4/.

13. Doreen Carvajal, "Media Talk: Finally in Hardcover, the Hughes Hoax," *New York Times*, May 31, 1999. http://nymag.com/news/features/scandals/howard-hughes-2012-4/.

Jihad!

1. "SAS Transcript," *BBC News Newsnight*. BBC, November 14, 2001, accessed August 11, 2014, http://news.bbc.co.uk/2/hi/events/newsnight/1660604.stm.

2. *Ibid*.

3. *Ibid*.

4. Vandana Malone, "Death of an SAS fantasist: Was Tom Carew Murdered—or Did he Fake His Own Death?" *Mail Online*. Daily Mail, December 26, 2009. Web, December 31, 2012.

5. *Ibid*.

6. William Underhill, "Ultimate Fighters," *Newsweek*, September 28, 2001, web exclusive, LexisNexis Academic.

7. Audrey Gillan, "The Fantasy Life and Lonely Death of the SAS Veteran Who Never Was," *Guardian*, January 23, 2009, Web. December 31, 2012.

8. Jim Gilchrist, "AWOL in His Own Phoney War?" *The Scotsman*, November 16, 2001, LexisNexis Academic.

The Blood Runs Like a River Through My Dreams; The Boy and the Dog Are Sleeping; Geronimo's Bones

1. Nasdijj, "The Blood Runs like a River through My Dreams," *Esquire* 131, no. 6 (June 1999): 115, EBSCOhost Academic Search Complete (doc. ID: 3765433).

2. Andrew Chaikivsky, "Nasdijj," *Esquire* 145, no. 5 (May 2006), EBSCOhost Academic Search Complete (doc. ID: 20582137).

3. *Ibid*.; Matthew Fleischer, "Navahoax," *LA Weekly*, January 23, 2006, http://www.laweekly.com/news/navahoax-2141610.

4. MariJo Moore, review of *The Blood Runs Like a River Through My Dreams*, by Nasdijj, *Studies in American Indian Literatures*, series 2, 12, no. 4 (winter 2000), http://www.jstor.org/stable/20736992.

5. Ted Conover, "A Soul That Won't Heal," review of *The Blood Runs Like a River Through My Dreams*, by Nasdijj, *New York Times*, October 15, 2000, ProQuest Historical Newspapers: The New York Times (doc. ID: 91443034).

6. Maria Russo, review of *The Blood Runs Like a River Through My Dreams*, by Nasdijj, *Salon*, October 26, 2000, http://www.salon.com/2000/10/26/nasdijj/#.

7. Fleischer, "Navahoax."

8. Sarah F Gold., Emily Chernoweth, Jeff Zaleski, review of *The Boy and Dog Are Sleeping*, by Nasdijj, *Publishers Weekly* 249, issue 48 (December 2, 2002): 42, EBSCOhost Academic Search Complete (doc. ID: 8585844).

9. Fleischer, "Navahoax."

10. Kay Brodie, review of *Geronimo's Bones: A Memoir of My Brother and Me*, by Nasdijj, *Library Journal* 129, no. 3 (February 15, 2004), EBSCOhost Academic Search Complete (doc. ID: 12229904).

11. Review of *Geronimo's Bones: A Memoir of My Brother and Me*, by Nasdijj, *Kirkus Reviews* 72, issue 2 (April 1, 2004): 73, EBSCOhost Academic Search Complete (doc. ID: 12028789).

12. Fleischer, "Navahoax."

13. Sherman Alexie, "When the Story Stolen Is Your Own," *Time* 167, no. 6 (February 6, 2006): 72, EBSCOhost Academic Search Complete (doc. ID: 19551314).

14. *Ibid*.

15. Fleischer, "Navahoax."

16. Chaikivsky, "Nasdijj."

The Cage

1. Jonathan Sale, Tania Branigan, and Andrew Clennell, "U.S. Claims Briton's Vietnam Tale a Fraud," *Guardian*, November 20, 2002. http://www.theguardian.com/uk/2002/nov/20/books.booksnews.

2. Adrian Weale, Guy Walters, and Ian Cobain, "Englishman's Vietnam War Story 'Is Just Fiction,'" *Times of London*, November 20, 2002.

3. Patrick Barnes, review of *The Cage*, by Tom Abraham, *BBC*, accessed May 10, 2015, http://www.bbc.co.uk/shropshire/culture/writestuff/2002/10/the_cage_review.shtml.

4. Sale, "U.S. Claims Briton's Vietnam Tale a Fraud."

5. Weale, "Englishman's Vietnam War Story."

6. *Ibid*.

7. *Ibid*.

8. *Ibid*.

9. Adam Luck, "Briton Who Served as U.S. Officer in Vietnam Hits Out at Former Comrades Who Said He Made Up 'Deer Hunter' POW Ordeal in Tiny Submerged Bamboo Cage," *Daily Mail Online*, April 20, 2015, http://www.dailymail.co.uk/news/article-3060645/Briton-served-officer-Vietnam-hits-former-comrades-said-Deer-Hunter-PoW-ordeal-tiny-submerged-bamboo-cage.html.

Notes

A Million Little Pieces; My Friend Leonard

1. David Kemp, "Step 13: Write a Book," review of *A Million Little Pieces*, by James Frey, *New York Times*, June 8, 2013, ProQuest Historical Newspapers: The New York Times (doc. ID: 92594461).
2. Jeff Turrentine, "A Rough Road to Sobriety," review of *A Million Little Pieces*, by James Frey, *Los Angeles Times*, May 18, 2003, http://articles.latimes.com/2003/may/18/books/bk-turrentine18.
3. Jennifer Reese, "Straight Story," review of *A Million Little Pieces*, by James Frey, *Entertainment Weekly* no. 706/707 (April 25, 2003): 152, EBSCOhost Academic Search Complete (doc. ID: 9867754).
4. Sarah F Gold., Emily Chernoweth, Jeff Zaleski, review of *A Million Little Pieces*, by James Frey, *Publishers Weekly* 250, issue 10 (March 10, 2003): 67, EBSCOhost Academic Search Complete (doc. ID: 9257453).
5. Turrentine, "A Rough Road to Sobriety."
6. Janet Maslin, "Cry and You Cry Alone? Not if You Write About It," review of *A Million Little Pieces*, by James Frey, *New York Times*, April 21, 2003, ProQuest Historical Newspapers: The New York Times (doc. ID: 92699933).
7. Tom Zeller, "Before the Fame, a Million Little Skeptics," *New York Times*, January 23, 2006, ProQuest Historical Newspapers: The New York Times (doc. ID: 93283436).
8. Steven Barrie-Anthony, "A Nod from Winfrey Lifts Author," *Los Angeles Times*, September 30, 2005, http://articles.latimes.com/print/2005/sep/30/entertainment/et-frey30.
9. Edward Wyatt, "Best-Selling Memoir Draws Scrutiny," *New York Times*, January 10, 2006, ProQuest Historical Newspapers: The New York Times (doc. ID: 93250677).
10. "A Million Little Lies: Exposing James Frey's Fiction Addiction," *The Smoking Gun*, January 4, 2006, http://www.thesmokinggun.com/documents/celebrity/million-little-lies; Gold, Chernowith, Zaleski, review of *A Million Little Pieces*.
11. "A Million Little Lies."
12. Interview with James Frey *on Larry King Live*, CNN.com, January 11, 2006, http://www.cnn.com/TRANSCRIPTS/0601/11/lkl.01.html.
13. *Ibid.*
14. *Ibid.*
15. Edward Wyatt, "Live on 'Oprah,' a Memoirist is Kicked Out of the Book Club," *New York Times*, January 27, 2006, ProQuest Historical Newspapers: The New York Times (doc. ID: 93278658).
16. *Ibid.*
17. *Ibid.*
18. *Ibid.*
19. Edward Wyatt, "Frey Says Falsehoods Improved His Tale," *New York Times*, February 2, 2006, ProQuest Historical Newspapers: The New York Times (doc. ID: 93266277); Laura Barton, "The Man Who Rewrote His Life," *Guardian*, September 15, 2006, http://www.theguardian.com/books/2006/sep/15/usa.world; Rich Motoko, "Publisher and Author Settle Suit Over Lies," *New York Times*, September 7, 2006, ProQuest Historical Newspapers: The New York Times (doc. ID: 93156225).
20. Troy Patterson, "The Godfather: James Frey's Tribute to His Surrogate Dad, an Ex-Cokehead Mafioso," *New York Times*, August 21, 2005, ProQuest Historical Newspapers: The New York Times (doc. ID: 92979936); Associated Press, "Frey Admits Lying; Oprah Apologizes to Viewers," Today.com, January 27, 2006, http://www.today.com/popculture/frey-admits-lying-oprah-apologizes-viewers-2D80556017.

Kathy's Story

1. J. S., "BookNews," *Independent.ie*, June 29, 2006, http://www.independent.ie/opinion/analysis/booknews-26376823.html.
2. Patsy McGarry, "'Magdalen' Author Challenged," *Irish Times*, September 20, 2006, EBSCOhost Newspaper Source (accession no.: 9FY2557694544).
3. Carol Ryan, "Seeking Redress for a Mother's Life in a Workhouse," *New York Times*, February 6, 2003, http://www.nytimes.com/2013/02/07/world/europe/seeking-redress-in-ireland-over-magdalene-laundry.html; Fintan O'Toole, "The Sisters of No Mercy," *Guardian*, February 15, 2003, http://www.theguardian.com/film/2003/feb/16/features.review1; Anna Carey, "Depressing but Not Surprising: How the Magdalene Laundries Got Away with It," *New Statesman*, July 17, 2016, http://www.newstatesman.com/religion/2013/07/depressing-not-surprising-how-magdalene-laundries-got-away-it.
4. O'Toole, "The Sisters of No Mercy"; Natalie Clarke, "Brutal Abuse of the Truth?" *Daily Mail* (London), September 23, 2006, LexisNexis Academic.
5. Clarke, "Brutal Abuse of the Truth?"
6. Esther Addley, "Author Accused of Literary Fraud Says: 'I Am Not a Liar. And I Am Not Running Any More,'" *Guardian*, September 22, 2006, http://www.theguardian.com/uk/2006/sep/23/books.booksnews.
7. Clarke, "Brutal Abuse of the Truth?"; Jan Battles, "Kathy Refuses to Put Story to Lie Test," *Sunday Times*, June 10, 2007, EBSCOhost Newspaper Source (accession no.: 7EH1184334974).
8. Hermann Kelly, "Lies of Little Miss Misery—Memoir of Abused Girl Is a Fake, Says New Investigation," *Daily Mail* (London), October 31, 2007, http://www.dailymail.co.uk/femail/article-490977/Lies-Little-Miss-Misery—memoir-abused-girl-fake-says-new-investigation.html.
9. Dearbhail McDonald, "Author Finally Agrees to Sell Home of Her 'Abuser,'" *Independent.ie*, February 2, 2008, http://www.independent.ie/irish-news/author-finally-agrees-to-sell-home-of-her-abuser-26424673.html.
10. Kelly, "Lies of Little Miss Misery,"; Clarke, "Brutal Abuse of the Truth?"
11. David Sharrock, "Author's Family Say Abuse Memoir Is a Cruel Hoax," *Times* (United Kingdom), September 19, 2006, EBSCOhost Newspaper Source (accession no.: 7EH1880843106).

Notes

Three Cups of Tea; Stones into Schools

1. Jon Krakauer, *Three Cups of Deceit* (New York: Anchor Books, 2011), 2–6.
2. Peter Bergen, "⊠Three Cups of Tea' Served with a Grain of Salt?" CNN Entertainment, April 18, 2011, http://www.cnn.com/2011/SHOWBIZ/04/17/three.cups.of.tea.controversy/; Krakauer, *Three Cups of Deceit*, 36–37.
3. "CharityWatch Calls for Resignation of Central Asia Institute's Founder Greg Mortenson," updated April 2012, accessed May 15, 2014, http://www.charitywatch.org/articles/MortensonResignCentralAsiaInstitute.html; Carly Flandro, "Greg Mortenson, Central Asia Institute Mismanaged Money, Reach $1M Settlement With Attorney General's Office," *Bozeman Daily Chronicle*, April 5, 2012, http://www.bozemandailychronicle.com/news/article_77e76d9e-7f3c-11e1-beee-0019bb2963f4.html.
4. "Questions over Greg Mortenson's Stories," CBS News, April 19, 2011, http://www.cbsnews.com/news/questions-over-greg-mortensons-stories-19–04-2011/4/.
5. Krakauer, *Three Cups of Deceit*, 7.
6. Ibid., 7–8.
7. Ibid., 15–19; "Questions over Greg Mortenson's Stories," http://www.cbsnews.com/news/questions-over-greg-mortensons-stories-19–04–2011/.
8. Krakauer, *Three Cups of Deceit*, 44; Greg Jaffe, "How the U.S. Military Fell in Love with 'Three Cups of Tea,'" *Washington Post*, April 21, 2011, http://www.washingtonpost.com/opinions/how-the-us-military-fell-in-love-with-three-cups-of-tea/2011/04/20/AFWqYaJE_story.html.
9. Nosheen Ali, "Books vs Bombs? Humanitarian Development and the Narrative of Terror in Northern Pakistan," *Third World Quarterly* 31, no. 4 (2010), http://ipl.edu.pk/document/Ali-Narratives%20of%20Terror.pdf.
10. Julie Bosman, "Publisher of 'Three Cups of Tea' to Conduct Review," *Media Decoder* (blog), *New York Times*, April 18, 2011, http://mediadecoder.blogs.nytimes.com/2011/04/18/publisher-of-three-cups-of-tea-to-conduct-review/.
11. Gail Schontzler, "Mortenson under Fire From '60 Minutes'—Bozeman Philanthropist Denies Allegations," *Bozeman Daily Chronicle*, April 15, 2011, http://www.bozemandailychronicle.com/news/article_4d3125cc-67d7–11e0-b861–001cc4c002e0.html.

Child P.O.W.

1. "Child P.O.W.," last modified January 6, 2010, https://childpowmovie.wordpress.com/2010/01/06/child-p-o-w-movie-december-7–2011/#more-13.
2. John Leggett, "POW Shares Memories at Street Fair," *Bonney Lake-Sumner Courier-Herald*, July 25, 2007, http://www.blscourierherald.com/news/35974879.html#.
3. "Child P.O.W. (2012)," accessed March 9, 2015, http://nxfilm.com/movies/child-pow-2012–32857.html.
4. J. Michael Houlahan, review of *Child P.O.W.—A Memoir of Survival*, by A. L. Finch, *Ex-POW Bulletin* 68, no. 1/2 (January/February 2011): 17, http://www.axpow.org/files/bulletins/jan-feb11.pdf.
5. J. Michael Houlahan, "Fiction as Fact: False Memories of WWII in the Philippines," *Asia-Pacific Social Science Review* 10, no. 2 (2010): 84–85.
6. A. L. Finch, *Child P.O.W.: A Memoir of Survival* (Enumclaw, WA: Annotation Press, 2007), 126–27.
7. Houlahan, "Fiction as Fact," 84.
8. A. L Finch, *Child P.O.W.*, 163.
9. Houlahan, "Fiction as Fact," 84–85.
10. Sascha Weinzheimer Jansen, review of *Child P.O.W.—A Memoir of Survival*, by A. L. Finch, *Philippine Scouts Heritage Society* (message board), April 14, 2010, http://www.philippine-scouts.org/cgi-bin/yabb2/YaBB.pl?num=1271251020.
11. Ibid.

The Road of Lost Innocence

1. Simon Marks, "Somaly Mam: The Holy Saint (and Sinner) of Sex Trafficking," *Newsweek* 162, no. 21 (May 30, 2014), EBSCOhost Academic Search Complete (doc. ID: 96152659); Abigail Pesta, "Somaly's Story," *Marie Claire* (U.S. edition) 21, no. 10 (October 2014) EBSCOhost MasterFILE Premier (doc. ID: 97993672).
2. Marks, "Somaly Mam."
3. Emily Cook, Review of *Road of Lost Innocence*, by Somaly Mam, *Booklist* 104, no. 22 (August 2008): 17, EBSCOhost Academic Search Complete (doc. ID: 33649062).
4. Pesta, "Somaly's Story."
5. Pat Joseph, "Victims Can Lie as Much as Other People," *Atlantic*, June 5, 2014, http://www.theatlantic.com/international/archive/2014/06/somaly-mam-scandal-victims-can-lie/372188/.
6. Lindsay Murdoch, "Dark Truths or Fiction," *Sydney Morning Herald* (Australia), November 3, 2013, http://www.smh.com.au/world/dark-truths-or-fiction-20131102–2wtwg.html.
7. Marks, "Somaly Mam."
8. Murdoch, Dark Truths or Fiction."
9. Marks, "Somaly Mam."
10. Ibid.
11. Clothilde Le Coz, "Cambodia: Somaly Mam's Ex-Husband Speaks Out," *GlobalPost*, October 8, 2014, http://www.globalpost.com/dispatch/news/regions/asia-pacific/cambodia/140926/cambodia-somaly-mam-Pierre-legros.
12. Pesta, "Somaly's Story."
13. Adam Taylor, "Why Would Somaly Mam Quit Her Own Sex-Trafficking Foundation?" *Washington Post*, May 29, 2014, https://www.washingtonpost.com/news/worldviews/wp/2014/05/29/why-would-somaly-mam-quit-her-own-sex-trafficking-foundation/.
14. Nicholas Kristof, "When Sources May Have Lied," *New York Times*, June 7, 2014, http://kristof.blogs.nytimes.com/2014/06/07/when-sources-may-have-lied/.
15. Ibid.
16. Harriet Fitch Little, "A Year After Her Fall,"

Phnom Penh Post, May 30, 2015, http://www.phnompenhpost.com/post-weekend/year-after-her-fall.

Angel at the Fence

1. "A Survivor's Memoir of the Shoah," review of *Angel at the Fence: The True Story of a Love That Survived*, by Herman Rosenblat, *Kirkus Reviews* 76, no. 23 (December 2008), EBSCOhost, Academic Search Complete (doc. ID: 35778978).
2. Motoko Rich and Joseph Berger, "False Memoir of Holocaust Canceled," *New York Times*, December 29, 2008, http://www.nytimes.com/2008/12/31/books/31opra.html.
3. *Ibid.*
4. Motoko Rich, "Children's Book Based on False Holocaust Account Is Canceled," *New York Times*, December 30, 2008, http://artsbeat.blogs.nytimes.com/2008/12/30/childrens-book-based-on-false-holocaust-account-is-canceled/.
5. Rich and Berger, "False Memoir."
6. *Ibid.*; Gabriel Sherman, "Wartime Lies," *New Republic*, December 26, 2008, http://www.newrepublic.com/article/books/wartime-lies.
7. Dave Itzkoff, "Arts, Briefly: Author Defends Disputed Memoir," *New York Times*, December 27, 2008, http://www.nytimes.com/2008/12/27/books/27arts-AUTHORDEFEND_BRF.html?ref=arts.
8. Motoko Rich, "Publisher Cancels Holocaust Memoir," *New York Times*, December 28, 2008, http://artsbeat.blogs.nytimes.com/2008/12/28/publisher-cancels-holocaust-memoir/.
9. *Ibid.*
10. Motoko Rich, "Children's Book."
11. Motoko Rich, "Publisher Cancels Holocaust Memoir."
12. Anna Horner, "Penelope Holt Addresses Herman Rosenblat Holocaust Hoax in 'The Apple,'" Examiner.com, September 25, 2009, http://www.examiner.com/article/penelope-holt-addresses-herman-rosenblat-holocaust-hoax-the-apple

Love and Consequences

1. Michiko Kakutani, "However Mean the Streets, Have an Exit Strategy," *New York Times*, February 26, 2008, ProQuest Historical Newspapers: The New York Times (doc. ID: 897107593).
2. Motoko Rich, "Gang Memoir, Turning Page, Is Pure Fiction," *New York Times*, March 4, 2008, ProQuest Historical Newspapers: The New York Times (doc. ID: 897104850).
3. Elizabeth Brinkley, review of *Love and Consequences: A Memoir of Hope and Survival*, by Margaret B. Jones, *Library Journal* 133, no. 1 (January 1, 2008), EBSCOhost Academic Search Complete (doc. ID: 28351563).
4. Kakutani, "However Mean the Streets."
5. Mimi Read, "A Refugee from Gangland," *New York Times*, February 28, 2008, ProQuest Historical Newspapers: The New York Times (doc. ID: 897103093).
6. Rich, "Gang Memoir."
7. Motoko Rich, "Lies and Consequences: Tracking the Fallout of (Another) Literary Fraud," *New York Times*, March 5, 2008, ProQuest Historical Newspapers: The New York Times (doc. ID: 897740998).
8. Rich, "Gang Memoir."
9. Motoko Rich, "Foundation Is Questioned After Memoir Is Exposed," *New York Times*, March 6, 2008, ProQuest Historical Newspapers: The New York Times (doc. ID: 897128114).
10. Rich, "Gang Memoir."
11. Rich, "Lies and Consequences."
12. *Ibid.*

The Boy Who Came Back from Heaven

1. Michelle Dean, "The Boy Who Didn't Come Back from Heaven: Inside a Bestseller's 'Deception,'" *Guardian*, January 21, 2015, http://www.theguardian.com/books/2015/jan/21/boy-who-came-back-from-heaven-alex-malarkey.
2. *Ibid.*
3. "'The Boy Who Came Back from Heaven' Recants Story, Rebukes Christian Retailers," *Pulpit & Pen*, January 13, 2013, http://pulpitandpen.org/2015/01/13/the-boy-who-came-back-from-heaven-recants-story-rebukes-christian-retailers/.
4. Dean, "The Boy Who Didn't Come Back."
5. "The Boy Who Came Back."
6. Dean, "The Boy Who Didn't Come Back."
7. *Ibid.*
8. Ron Charles, "'Boy Who Came Back from Heaven' Actually Didn't; Books Recalled," *Washington Post*, January 16, 2016, https://www.washingtonpost.com/news/arts-and-entertainment/wp/2015/01/15/boy-who-came-back-from-heaven-going-back-to-publisher/.
9. Sarah Eekhoff Zylstra, "The 'Boy Who Came Back from Heaven' Retracts Story," *Christianity Today*, January 15, 2015, http://www.christianitytoday.com/gleanings/2015/january/boy-who-came-back-from-heaven-retraction.html.
10. *Ibid.*
11. *Ibid.*
12. Jason Smathers, "The Bible is Sufficient to Know Heaven is Real," *Witnesses Unto the Sun*, June 10, 2014, http://www.witnessesuntome.com/2014/06/the-bible-is-sufficient-to-know-heaven-is-real/.

The Man Who Broke into Auschwitz

1. "Denis Avey, Auschwitz Witness—Obituary," *Telegraph*, August 27, 2015, http://www.telegraph.co.uk/news/obituaries/11828297/Denis-Avey-Auschwitz-witness-obituary.html; "Auschwitz," on United States Holocaust Museum website, last modified August 18, 2015, http://www.ushmm.org/wlc/en/article.php?ModuleId=10005189.
2. Maureen Callahan, "Holocaust Hero ... or Hoax?" *New York Post*, April 24, 2011, http://nypost.

com/2011/04/24/holocaust-hero-or-hoax/; Guy Walters, "Did This British POW Really Smuggle Himself into Auschwitz to Expose the Holocaust…or Is His Account Pure Fantasy and an Insult to Millions Who Died There?" *Daily Mail*, April 8, 2011, http://www.dailymail.co.uk/news/article-1375018/Denis-Avey-broke-Auschwitz-expose-Holocaust-account-insult.html.

3. Walters, "Did This British POW"; "Avey, Denis George (IWM interview)," reel 8, recorded July 16, 2001, on Imperial War Museums website, accessed December 30, 2015, http://www.iwm.org.uk/collections/item/object/80020527; Guy Walters, "The Curious Case of the 'Break into Auschwitz,'" *New Statesman*, November 17, 2011, http://www.newstatesman.com/blogs/guy-walters/2011/11/avey-book-holocaust-auschwitz.

4. Walters, "Did This British POW."
5. Ibid.
6. Ibid.
7. Ibid.
8. Callahan, "Holocaust Hero … or Hoax?"
9. Ibid.
10. Ibid.
11. Mike Collett-White, "Veteran Defends Disputed Story of Auschwitz Heroics," Reuters.com, April 26, 2011, http://www.reuters.com/article/arts-auschwitz-book-idUSLDE73P12520110426.
12. Ibid.
13. Callahan, "Holocaust Hero … or Hoax?"

Other Nonfiction

1. Kate Newman, "Book Publishing, Not Fact-Checking," *Atlantic*, September 3, 2014, LexisNexis Academic.
2. Nora Krug, "The Corrections," *New York Times*, September 25, 2005, ProQuest Historical Newspapers: The New York Times (doc. ID: 92959373).
3. Boris Kachka, "Will Book Publishers Ever Start Fact-Checking? They're Already Starting," *Browbeat* (blog), *Slate*, June 24, 2015, http://www.slate.com/blogs/browbeat/2015/06/24/primates_of_park_avenue_david_brooks_and_alice_goffman_have_all_faced_fact.html; Martin Arnold, "Making Books: Does Nonfiction Mean Factual," *New York Times*, July 20, 2000, ProQuest Historical Newspapers: The New York Times (doc. ID: 91346894); Andrew Richard Albanese, "Loaded Questions," *Publishers Weekly* 257, no. 34 (August 30, 2010), EBSCOhost Academic Search Complete (doc. ID: 53425523).
4. Krug, "The Corrections."
5. Albanese, "Loaded Questions."
6. Ibid.
7. Kachka, "Will Book Publishers Ever Start Fact-Checking?"; Krug, "The Corrections."
8. Krug, "The Corrections."
9. Shannon Palus, "Why Doesn't Anyone Fact-Check Science Books?" *Slate*, August 12, 2016, http://www.slate.com/articles/health_and_science/science/2016/08/why_doesn_t_anyone_fact_check_science_books.html.
10. Krug, "The Corrections."
11. Ibid.
12. Ibid.

13. Don Williams, "Could Bellesiles's Problems Undermine Gun Control?" *History News Network*, July 9, 2002, http://historynewsnetwork.org/article/741.
14. Amy B. Wang, "'Post-Truth' Named 2016 Word of the Year by Oxford Dictionaries," *Washington Post*, November 16, 2016, https://www.washingtonpost.com/news/the-fix/wp/2016/11/16/post-truth-named-2016-word-of-the-year-by-oxford-dictionaries/.
15. Will Manley, "Catalogers, Cast Off Your Shackles," *American Libraries* 31, no. 2 (February 2000): 104.
16. Anne, March 3, 2010 (12:54 a.m.), response on Brian Herzog, "What to Do with 'Last Train from Hiroshima?'" *Swiss Army Librarian* (blog), http://www.swissarmylibrarian.net/2010/03/02/what-to-do-with-last-train-from-hiroshima/.
17. Jeff Scott, March 2, 2010 (5:31 p.m.), response on Brian Herzog, "What to Do with 'Last Train from Hiroshima?'" *Swiss Army Librarian* (blog), http://www.swissarmylibrarian.net/2010/03/02/what-to-do-with-last-train-from-hiroshima/.

Never Cry Wolf

1. Mark Medley, "'He Left a Very Deep Mark on This Country': Farley Mowat Changed the Way Canadians See Their Country and How the World Sees Canada," *National Post* (Canada), May 7, 2014, http://news.nationalpost.com/afterword/farley-mowat-dead-at-92-an-appreciation.
2. Karen Jones, "*Never Cry Wolf*: Science, Sentiment, and the Literary Rehabilitation of *Canis Lupus*," *Canadian Historical Review* 84, no. 1 (March 2003): 66–67, 72, EBSCOhost Academic Search Complete (doc. ID: 9372172).
3. Orville Prescott, "Books of the Times: The Lupine Project and the Ideal Father," *New York Times*, October 11, 1963, ProQuest Historical Newspapers: The New York Times (doc. ID: 116392628).
4. A. M. Stebler, review of *Never Cry Wolf*, by Farley Mowat, *Journal of Wildlife Management* 29, no. 4 (October 1965): 906.
5. A. W. F. Banfield, review of *Never Cry Wolf*, by Farley Mowat, *Canadian Field-Naturalist* 78, no. 1 (January–March 1964): 52, http://www.biodiversitylibrary.org/item/89058#page/62/mode/1up.
6. Ibid., 53–54.
7. John Goddard, "A Real Whopper," *Saturday Night* 111, issue 4 (May 1996), MasterFILE Premier, EBSCOhost (doc. ID: 9605132404).
8. Douglas Pimlott, review of *Never Cry Wolf* by Farley Mowat, *Journal of Wildlife Management* 30, no. 1 (January 1966): 236.
9. Goddard, "A Real Whopper."
10. Ibid.; Banfield, review of *Never Cry Wolf*, 53.
11. Goddard, "A Real Whopper."
12. Farley Mowat, "Mowat Replies to *Saturday Night* Piece," *Globe and Mail* (Canada), May 6, 1996, LexisNexis Academic; Adrian Humphreys, "Mowat Apologizes for Swipe at University," *Calgary Herald* (Canada), May 7, 1996, LexisNexis Academic.
13. Steve Burgess, "Northern Exposure," *Salon*, May 11, 1999, http://www.salon.com/1999/05/11/mowat/.
14. Medley, "'He Left a Very Deep Mark on This Country.'"

15. Goddard, "A Real Whopper."
16. Jones, "*Never Cry Wolf.*"
17. Andrew Duffy, "Mowat Reputation Intact, Even If He Did Tell Tall Tales," *Ottawa Citizen* (Canada), May 14, 1996, LexisNexis Academic.
18. Richard F. Abrahamson and Betty Carter, "Of Survival, School, Wars, and Dreams: Nonfiction That Belongs in English Classes," *English Journal* 76, no. 2 (February 1987): 104, doi:10.2307/818185.

In Cold Blood

1. Eliot Fremont-Smith, "The Killed, the Killers," review of *In Cold Blood*, by Truman Capote, *New York Times*, January 10, 1966, ProQuest Historical Newspapers: The New York Times (doc. ID: 117140209).
2. George Plimpton, "The Story Behind a Nonfiction Novel," *New York Times*, January 16, 1966, ProQuest Historical Newspapers: The New York Times (doc. ID: 117466874).
3. Ibid.
4. Ibid.
5. Robert Ryley, " BR-R-R-R-R-," review of *In Cold Blood*, by Truman Capote, *North American Review* 251, no. 2 (March 1966): 32, http://www.jstor.org/stable/25116356.
6. F. W. Dupee, "Truman Capote's Score," review of *In Cold Blood*, by Truman Capote, *New York Review of Books* 6, no. 1 (February 3, 1966), http://www.nybooks.com/articles/1966/02/03//truman-capotes-score/.
7. Paul Levine, "Reality and Fiction," review of *In Cold Blood*, by Truman Capote, *Hudson Review* 19, no. 1 (spring 1966): 138, http://www.jstor.org/stable/3849353.
8. Phillip K. Tompkins, "In Cold Fact," in *Truman Capote's In Cold Blood: A Critical Handbook*, ed. Irving Malin (Belmont, CA: Wadsworth Publishing, 1968), 45.
9. Ibid., 45–6.
10. Robert Langbaum, "Capote's Nonfiction Novel," review of *In Cold Blood*, by Truman Capote, *American Scholar* 35, no. 3 (summer 1966): 573, http://www.jstor.org/stable/41209405.
11. Tompkins, "In Cold Fact," 53.
12. Ibid.
13. Ibid., 53–4.
14. Truman Capote, *In Cold Blood: A True Account of a Multiple Murder and Its Consequences* (New York: Random House, 1965), 340.
15. Kevin Helliker, "Capote Classic 'In Cold Blood' Tainted by Long-Lost Files," *Wall Street Journal*, February 8, 2013, http://www.wsj.com/articles/SB10001424127887323951904le578290341604113984.
16. Ibid.
17. Ibid.
18. Ralph F. Voss, *Truman Capote and the Legacy of In Cold Blood* (Tuscaloosa: University of Alabama Press, 2011), 92.
19. Abby Alpert, "Incorporating Nonfiction into Readers' Advisory Services," *Reference & User Services Quarterly* 46, no. 1 (fall 2006): 27, http://www.jstor.org/stable/20864596.

Roots

1. Mel Watkins, "A Talk with Alex Haley," *New York Times*, September 26, 1976, ProQuest Historical Newspapers: The New York Times (doc. ID: 122894335); Thomas Lask, "Success of Search for 'Roots' Leaves Alex Haley Surprised," *New York Times*, November 23, 1976, ProQuest Historical Newspapers: The New York Times (doc. ID: 122986127).
2. Donald R. Wright, "Uprooting Kunta Kinte: On the Perils of Relying on Encyclopedic Informants," *History in Africa* 8 (1981): 206–7, http://www.jstor.org/stable/3171516.; Lask, "Success of Search."
3. Helen Taylor, "'The Griot from Tennessee': The Saga of Alex Haley's Roots," *Critical Quarterly* 37, no. 2 (summer 1995): 48, EBSCOhost Academic Search Complete (doc. ID: 9508162401).
4. Watkins, "A Talk with Alex Haley."
5. Willie Lee Rose, "An American Family," *New York Review of Books* 23, no. 18 (November 11, 1976), http://www.nybooks.com/articles/1976/11/11/an-american-family/.
6. Mark Ottaway, "Tangled Roots," *Sunday Times* (London), April 10, 1977, sec. 1, p. 17.
7. John Darnton, "Haley, Assailing Critic, Says 'Roots' Is Sound," *New York Times*, April 19, 1977, ProQuest Historical Newspapers: The New York Times (doc. ID: 123375185).
8. Philip Nobile, "Uncovering *Roots*," *Village Voice* 38, no. 8 (February 23, 1993): 34.
9. Alex Haley, *Roots* (Garden City, NY: Doubleday, 1976), 584.
10. Robert D. McFadden, "Alex Haley Denies Allegation that Parts of 'Roots' Were Copied from Novel Written by Mississippi Teacher," *New York Times*, April 24, 1977, ProQuest Historical Newspapers: The New York Times (doc. ID: 123170398); "'Roots' Grew Out of His 'African,' Courlander Charges in Haley Suit," *New York Times*, May 24, 1977, ProQuest Historical Newspapers: The New York Times (doc. ID: 123314979); Nobile, "Uncovering Roots," 33.
11. McFadden, "Alex Haley Denies Allegation."
12. Ottaway, "Tangled Roots," sec. 1, p. 21.

In His Image

1. Boyce Rensberger, "Scientists Skeptical about Book on Baby Created in Laboratory," *New York Times*, March 4, 1978, ProQuest Historical Newspapers: The New York Times (doc. ID: 123803647).
2. Leonard Isaacs, "The Once and Future Clone," *The Hastings Center Report* 8, no. 3 (June 1978): 45, http://www.jstor.org/stable/3560431.
3. Rensberger, "Scientists Skeptical."
4. Herbert Mitgang, "Cloning Becomes a Publishers' Experiment," *New York Times*, March 11, 1978, ProQuest Historical Newspapers: The New York Times (doc. ID: 123785245).
5. Mitgang, "Cloning Becomes."
6. Harold Schmeck, Jr., "Author of Book on Cloning Offers No Direct Proof Test Succeeded," *New York Times*, March 23, 1978, ProQuest Historical Newspapers: The New York Times (doc. ID: 123776159).
7. Ibid.

8. Michael Crichton, "Cloning Around," *New York Times*, April 23, 1978, ProQuest Historical Newspapers: The New York Times (doc. ID: 123739247).

9. "Cloning-Book Suit Is Settled," *New York Times*, April 8, 1982, ProQuest Historical Newspapers: The New York Times (doc. ID: 121925459).

10. Christopher Earl, "The Press vs. Cloning," *Boston Review*, April 1981, http://bostonreview.net/archives/BR06.2/earl.html.

11. Isaacs, "The Once and Future Clone."

Arming America

1. Garry Wills, "Spiking the Gun Myth," review of *Arming America*, by Michael A. Bellesiles, *New York Times*, September 10, 2000, ProQuest Historical Newspapers: The New York Times (doc. ID: 91474255).

2. *Ibid.*; David Mehegan, "New Doubts about Emory University Gun Historian," *Boston Globe Archives*, September 11, 2001, http://pqasb.pqarchiver.com/boston/doc/405404384.html?FMT=FT&FMTS=ABS:FT&type=current&date=Sep+11%2C+2001&author=Mehegan.

3. Charlton Heston, letter to the editor, *New York Times*, October 1, 2000, ProQuest Historical Newspapers: The New York Times (doc. ID: 91461809).

4. Mehegan, "New Doubts."

5. *Ibid.*; James Lindgren, "Fall from Grace: *Arming America* and Bellesiles Scandal," review of *Arming America*, by Michael A. Bellesiles, *Yale Law Journal* 111, no 8 (April 26, 2002): 2204, http://www.jstor.org/stable/797645 doi:1.

6. Lindgren, "Fall from Grace," 2209–2210, 2212–2214.

7. Randolph Roth, "Guns, Gun Culture, and Homicide: The Relationship between Firearms, the Uses of Firearms, and Interpersonal Violence," *William and Mary Quarterly* 59, no. 1 (January 2002): 236, http://www.jstor.org/stable/3491655.

8. *Ibid.*, 2210; Michael A. Bellesiles, "Disarming the Critics," *OAH Newsletter* 29, no. 4 (November 2001): 3.

9. Robert R. Worth, "Prize for Book Is Taken Back from Historian," *New York Times*, December 14, 2002, ProQuest Historical Newspapers: The New York Times (doc. ID: 92340318).

10. "Author of Gun History Quits after Panel Faults Research," *New York Times*, October 26, 2002, ProQuest Historical Newspapers: The New York Times (doc. ID: 92227200).

11. Andrew Richard Albanese, "Loaded Questions," *Publishers Weekly* 257, no. 34 (August 30, 2010, EBSCOhost Academic Search Complete (doc. ID: 53425523).

12. Patricia Cohen, "Scholar Emerges from Doghouse," *New York Times*, August 4, 2010, ProQuest Historical Newspapers: The New York Times (doc. ID: 1461130167).

13. *Ibid.*

Honor Lost

1. Review of *Honor Lost: Love and Death in Modern-Day Jordan*, by Norma Khouri, *Kirkus Reviews*, accessed October 12, 2016, https://www.kirkusreviews.com/book-reviews/norma-khouri/honor-lost/.

2. Malcolm Knox, "Bestseller's Lies Exposed," *Sydney Morning Herald* (Australia), July 24, 2004, http://www.smh.com.au/articles/2004/07/23/1090464854793.html; Edward Wyatt, "Publisher Says Memoir Is Probably Fiction," *New York Times*, August 14, 2004, ProQuest Historical Newspapers: The New York Times (doc. ID: 92857015).

3. Malcolm Knox, "The Lies Stripped Bare," *Sydney Morning Herald* (Australia), July 24, 2004, http://www.smh.com.au/articles/2004/07/23/1090464851887.html.

4. Ali Abunimah, "A Hoax and Honor Lost for Norma Khouri," *The Daily Star*, August 10, 2004, http://www.dailystar.com.lb/Opinion/Commentary/2004/Aug-10/93029-a-hoax-and-honor-lost-for-norma-khouri.ashx.

5. Knox, "The Lies Stripped Bare."

6. *Ibid.*

7. Knox, "Bestseller's Lies Exposed."

8. Steven Zeitchik, "Atria Withdraws Controversial Memoir," August 2, 2004, http://www.publishersweekly.com/pw/print/20040802/34032-atria-withdraws-controversial-memoir.html.

9. Wyatt, "Publisher Says Memoir Is Probably Fiction."

Ananios of Kleitor

1. George Economou, *Ananios of Kleitor: Poems & Fragments and Their Reception from Antiquity to the Present* (Exeter: Shearsman Books, 2009): 9.

2. *Ibid.*, back cover.

3. *Ibid.*

4. John-Ivan Palmer, review of *Ananios of Kleitor*, by George Economou, *Rain Taxi* 14, no. 4 (winter 2009/2010): 22.

5. Tim Whitmarsh, "Objects of Greek Desire," review of *Ananios of Kleitor*, by George Economou, *Times Literary Supplement* (London, England), July 24, 2009, p. 9.

6. Marga Lincoln, "Poet George Economou: Return of a Native Son." *Independent Record* (Helena, Montana), September 17, 2009, http://helenair.com/entertainment/yourtime/poet-george-economou-return-of-a-native-son/article_50e64ef4-a357-11de-83c6-001cc4c002e0.html.

7. Whitmarsh, "Objects of Greek Desire," p. 9.

8. Bluepiano, "Ananios of Kleitor," *LibraryThing*, accessed October 17, 2016, http://www.librarything.com/work/8751485.

The Last Train from Hiroshima

1. Charles Pellegrino's website, accessed September 2, 2016, http://www.charlespellegrino.com/cp_biography.htm.

2. Gabriel Schoenfeld, "A Career Too Good to Be True," *Weekly Standard*, March 1, 2010, http://www.weeklystandard.com/a-career-too-good-to-be-true/article/422157.

3. William J. Broad, "Doubts Raised on Book's Tale

of Atom Bomb," *New York Times*, February 21, 2010, http://www.nytimes.com/2010/02/21/science/21hiroshima.html.

4. Review of *The Last Train from Hiroshima*, by Charles Pellegrino, *Publishers Weekly* 256, no. 2 (November 23, 2009): 49, EBSCOhost Academic Search Complete (doc. ID: 46740266).

5. *Ibid.*; Dwight Garner, "After Atom Bombs' Shock, the Real Horrors Began to Unfolding," review of *The Last Train from Hiroshima*, by Charles Pellegrino, *New York Times*, January 19, 2010, http://www.nytimes.com/2010/01/20/books/20garner.html; Broad, "Doubts Raised."

6. Broad, "Doubts Raised."

7. *Ibid.*; "Atomic Veterans Incensed Over False Claims in New Book," Veterans of the 509th Composite Group press release, February 21, 2019, http://www.usjapandialogueonpows.org/essays/509pressrelease.pdf.

8. Broad, "Doubts Raised."

9. Steven Levingston, "Henry Holt Drops Publication of 'Last Train from Hiroshima,'" *Washington Post*, March 2, 2010, http://www.washingtonpost.com/wp-dyn/content/article/2010/03/01/AR2010030103325.html.

10. Motoko Rich, "University Rejects Pellegrino Claim in Degree Dispute," *Media Decoder* (blog), *New York Times*, March 5, 2010, http://mediadecoder.blogs.nytimes.com/2010/03/05/university-rejects-pellegrino-claim-in-degree-dispute/.

11. Levingston, "Henry Holt Drops Publication."

12. Dave Itzkoff, "James Cameron Defends Author of Disputed Hiroshima Book," *Arts Beat* (blog) *New York Times*, March 4, 2010, http://artsbeat.blogs.nytimes.com/2010/03/04/cameron-defends-author-of-disputed-hiroshima-book/.

13. Broad, "Doubts Raised."

14. Brian Herzog, "What to Do with 'Last Train from Hiroshima?" *Swiss Army Librarian* (blog), March 2, 2010, accessed September 5, 2016, http://www.swissarmylibrarian.net/2010/03/02/what-to-do-with-last-train-from-hiroshima/.

Imagine

1. Julie Bosman, "Media Decoder: Young Writer with a Following Admits Fabricating Dylan Quotes in a Book," *New York Times*, July 31, 2012, http://query.nytimes.com/gst/fullpage.html?res=9405E7D71730F932A05754C0A9649D8B63; Joseph P. Kahn, "Fabrications Acknowledged, a Bestseller is Withdrawn," *Boston Globe*, August 1, 2012, https://www.bostonglobe.com/lifestyle/style/2012/08/01/jonah-lehrer-book-pulled-boston-based-publisher-houghton-mifflin-harcourt-after-author-admits-fabrication/R64AXel66XZbh5lOJipV3K/story.html.

2. Christopher F. Chabris, "Boggle the Mind," review of *Imagine: How Creativity Works*, by Jonah Lehrer, *New York Times*, May 11, 2012, https://www.bostonglobe.com/lifestyle/style/2012/08/01/jonah-lehrer-book-pulled-boston-based-publisher-houghton-mifflin-harcourt-after-author-admits-fabrication/R64AXel66XZbh5lOJipV3K/story.html.

3. Jonah Lehrer, *Imagine: How Creativity Works* (Boston: Houghton Mifflin Harcourt, 2012), 20.

4. Isaac Chotiner, "The Curse of Knowledge," review of *Imagine: How Creativity Works*, by Jonah Lehrer, *New Republic* 243, no. 10 (June 28, 2012): 32–33.

5. *Ibid.*, 33.

6. Michael C. Moynihan, "Jonah Lehrer's Deceptions," *Tablet*, July 30, 2015, http://www.tabletmag.com/jewish-news-and-politics/107779/jonah-lehrers-deceptions.

7. David Kinney, "Freewheelin': Bob Dylan, Jonah Lehrer and the Truth," *New York Times*, August 2, 2012, http://www.nytimes.com/2012/08/03/opinion/freewheelin-bob-dylan-jonah-lehrer-and-the-truth.html; Moynihan, "Jonah Lehrer's Deceptions."

8. Moynihan, "Jonah Lehrer's Deceptions."

9. Kahn, "Fabrications Acknowledged."; Bosman, "Media Decoder."

10. Michael Moynihan, "Publisher Pulls Jonah Lehrer's 'How We Decide' From Stores," *Daily Beast*, March 1, 2013, http://www.thedailybeast.com/articles/2013/03/01/publisher-pulls-jonah-lehrer-s-how-we-decide-from-stores.html.

11. Jeff Bercovici, "Jonah Lehrer's Sick, Cynical Quest for Forgiveness Gets a Book Deal," *Forbes*, June 7, 2013, http://www.forbes.com/sites/jeffbercovici/2013/06/07/jonah-lehrers-sick-cynical-quest-for-forgiveness/#6e6ac9d49be9.

12. Laurie D. Borman, "Our Roller-Coaster Summer," *American Libraries* 43, no. 9/10 (September 2012): 2.

The Embassy House

1. Karen DeYoung, "'60 Minutes' Broadcast Helps Propel New Round of Back-and-Forth on Benghazi," *Washington Post*, October 31, 2013, http://www.washingtonpost.com/world/national-security/60-minutes-broadcast-helps-propel-new-round-of-back-and-forth-on-benghazi/2013/10/31/fbfcad66–4258–11e3-a751-f032898f2dbc_story.html; Marcus Baram, "Benghazi Eyewitness Book," *International Business Times*, October 29, 2013, http://www.ibtimes.com/benghazi-eyewitness-book-morgan-jones-claims-obama-administration-ignored-his-account-attack-1445938.

2. Baram, "Benghazi Eyewitness Book."

3. Bill Carter, "CBS News Defends Its '60 Minutes'" Benghazi Report," New York Times, November 5, 2013, http://www.nytimes.com/2013/11/06/business/media/cbs-news-defends-its-60-minutes-benghazi-report.html.

4. DeYoung, "'60 Minutes' Broadcast."

5. Eli Lake and Josh Rogin, "Exclusive: Benghazi Whistleblower Says He Was Smeared," *Daily Beast*, November 2, 2013, http://www.thedailybeast.com/articles/2013/11/02/exclusive-benghazi-whistleblower-says-he-was-smeared.html.

6. *Ibid.*

7. DeYoung, "'60 Minutes' Broadcast"; Bill Carter and Michael S. Schmidt, "CBS to Correct Erroneous Report on Benghazi," *New York Times*, November 8, 2013, http://www.nytimes.com/2013/11/09/business/media/cbs-correspondent-apologizes-for-report-on-benghazi-attack.html.

Notes

8. Carter and Schmidt, "CBS to Correct Erroneous Report."
9. Ibid.
10. Rebecca Shabad, "Publisher Halts Book by Benghazi Witness," Briefing Room (blog), *The Hill*, November 8, 2013, http://thehill.com/blogs/blog-briefing-room/news/189736-publisher-of-benghazi-witness-dylan-davies-halts-his-book.

Fiction

1. Richard P. Smiraglia, Hur-Li Lee, and Hope A. Olson, "The Flimsy Fabric of Authorship," *Proceedings of the Annual Conference of CAIS*, 2015, http://www.cais-acsi.ca/ojs/index.php/cais/article/view/452/136.
2. *Anglo-American Cataloguing Rules*, 2nd ed. (Chicago: American Library Association, http://access.rdatoolkit.org/
3. *RDA Toolkit: Resource, Description and Access* 0.4.3.4, accessed May 13, 2014, http://access.rdatoolkit.org/.
4. Smiraglia, Lee, and Olson, "The Flimsy Fabric of Authorship."
5. Stefanie Cohen, "Why Women Writers Still Take Men's Names," *Wall Street Journal*, December 6, 2012, http://www.wsj.com/articles/SB10001424127887324355904578159453918443978.
6. Ibid.
7. Christine Haynes, "Reassessing 'Genius' in Studies of Authorship: The State of the Discipline," *Book History* 8 (2005): 289–90, http://www.jstor.org/stable/30227379.
8. *The Oxford Companion to English Literature*, ed. Margaret Drabble 6th ed., s.v. "cultural appropriation."
9. James O. Young and Susan Haley, "'Nothing Comes from Nowhere': Reflections on Cultural Appropriation as the Representation of Other Cultures," in *The Ethics of Cultural Appropriation*, ed. James O. Young and Conrad G. Brunk (Hoboken: Wiley-Blackwell, 2009), 270–71; Sander L. Gilman, "Introduction: Ethnicity-Ethnicities-Literature-Literatures," *PMLA* 113, no. 1 (January 1998): 23, http://www.jstor.org/stable/463406.
10. Young and Haley, "'Nothing Comes from Nowhere.'" 285.
11. Yi-Fen Chou, "The Bees, the Flowers, Jesus, Ancient Tigers, Poseidon, Adam and Eve," in *Best American Poetry 2015*, ed. Sherman Alexie, series ed. David Lehman (New York: Scribner Poetry, 2015), 25.
12. Sherman Alexie, "Sherman Alexie Speaks Out on The Best American Poetry 2015," *Best American Poetry* (blog), September 7, 2015, http://blog.bestamericanpoetry.com/the_best_american_poetry/2015/09/like-most-every-poet-i-have-viewed-the-publication-of-each-years-best-american-poetry-with-happiness-i-love-that-poem-je-1.html.
13. Yi-Fen Chou, "Yi-Fen Chou," in *Best American Poetry 2015*, ed. Sherman Alexie, series ed. David Lehman (New York: Scribner Poetry, 2015), 167.
14. Alexie, "Sherman Alexie Speaks Out."
15. Linda Hamalian, *A Life of Kenneth Rexroth* (New York: Norton, 1991): 352–3.
16. Joyce Carol Oates, "Success and the Pseudonymous Writer: Turning Over a New Self," *New York Times*, December 6, 1987, ProQuest Historical Newspapers: The New York Times (doc. ID: 110719688).

Wild Cat Falling

1. Peter Monaghan, "Australian Writer Embodies Pressures Facing Aborigines," *Chronicle of Higher Education*, v. 43, no. 17 (December 20, 1996): B2; Eva Rask Knudsen, "Aboriginal Affair(s): Reflections on Mudrooroo's Life and Work," *LiNQ*, v. 39 (December 2012): 107.
2. Victoria Laurie, "Blacks Question 'Aboriginal' Writer / Blacks Question Author's Past," *Weekend Australian*, July 20, 1996, LexisNexis Academic.
3. Maureen Clark, "Mudrooroo: Crafty Imposter or Rebel with a Cause?" in *Who's Who? Hoaxes, Imposture and Identity Crises in Australian Literature*, ed. Maggie Nolan and Carrie Dawson (Queensland: University of Queensland Press, 2004): 104, 106.
4. Rosemary Van Den Berg, *Nyoongar People of Australia: Perspectives on Racism and Multiculturalism* (Leiden: Brill, 2002): xiv.
5. Clark, "Mudrooroo: Crafty Imposter," 104–6.
6. Maureen Clark, *Mudrooroo: A Likely Story, Identity and Belonging in Postcolonial Australia* (Brussels: P.I.E. Peter Lang, 2007): 52.
7. Ibid.
8. Laurie, "Blacks Question"; T. O'Connor, "Author's Heritage Claims Split Family," *Courier Mail* (Queensland, Australia), March 28, 1998, LexisNexis Academic; Andrew Williams, "Mudrooroo to Undergo DNA Test," *Courier Mail* (Queensland, Australia), March 30, 1988, LexisNexis Academic.
9. Knudsen, "Aboriginal Affair(s)" 108; Clark, *Mudrooroo: Likely Story*, 35.

Jack Rivers and Me

1. Andrew Byrne and Susan Wyndham, "The Story Tellers: News Review," *Sydney Morning Herald* (Australia), March 9, 1996, LexisNexis Academic.
2. Review of *Jack Rivers and Me*, by Paul John Radley, *Kirkus Reviews*, accessed April 18, 2016, https://www.kirkusreviews.com/book-reviews/paul-john-radley/jack-rivers-and-me/.
3. Byrne and Wyndham, "The Story Tellers."
4. Ibid.
5. Andrew Byrne, "Loneliness of a Literary Fraud," *The Age* (Melbourne, Australia), March 9, 1996, Late edition, LexisNexis Academic.
6. Ibid.
7. Amanda Meade, "A Sorry Tale," *Australian*, March 7, 1996, LexisNexis Academic.
8. Ibid.
9. Byrne and Wyndham, "The Story Tellers."
10. Byrne, "Loneliness of a Literary Fraud."

Famous All Over Town

1. Cathy Clancy, review of *Famous All Over Town*, by Danny Santiago, *School Library Journal* 30,

no. 2 (October 1983): 180, EBSCOhost Library, Information Science & Technology Abstracts (doc. ID: 5623229).
2. Edwin McDowell, "Publishing: Endowment Gives 4 Writers $25,000," *New York Times*, August 10, 1984, ProQuest Historical Newspapers: The New York Times (doc. ID: 122467648).
3. Garry Abrams, "The Three Lives of Dan James: In a Los Angeles Barrio, the Elderly Screenwriter Found an Alter Ego and a Pen Name; Now His Literary Voice is Finding a Wider Audience," *Los Angeles Times*, June 19, 1998, http://articles.latimes.com/1988-06-19/news/vw-7993_1_dan-james; John Gregory Dunne, "The Secret of Danny Santiago," *New York Review of Books* 31, no. 13 (August 16, 1984), http://www.nybooks.com/articles/1984/08/16/the-secret-of-danny-santiago/.
4. Abrams, "The Three Lives of Dan James."
5. *Ibid.*
6. Dunne, "The Secret of Danny Santiago."
7. *Ibid.*
8. *Ibid.*

The Hand That Signed the Paper

1. In 1982 the *Australian*/Vogel's Literary Award maximum age limit was raised to 35; Malcolm Knox, "The Darville Made Me Do It," *Sydney Morning Herald* (Australia), July 9, 2005, http://www.smh.com.au/news/books/the-darville-made-me-do-it/2005/07/08/1120704550613.html; Sally Loane, "Let's Be Honest, Money Is Everything," *Sydney Morning Herald* (Australia), January 24, 1995, Late edition, LexisNexis Academic.
2. Marjory Bennett, "Awaiting the Storm: Sunday Profile," *Sun Herald* (Sydney, Australia), August 7, 1994, Late edition, LexisNexis Academic; Knox, "The Darville Made Me Do It."
3. Robert Manne, "Forum on the Demidenko Controversy," *Australian Book Review*, no. 173 (August 1995): 15.
4. Bennet, "Awaiting the Storm."
5. Gerard Henderson, "A Fraction Too Much 'Faction,'" *The Age* (Melbourne, Australia), June 27, 1995, Late edition, LexisNexis Academic.
6. Ian Hicks, "Controversial Novel Wins Another Award," *The Age* (Melbourne, Australia), July 4, 1995, Late edition, LexisNexis Academic.
7. Leisa Scott, "Demidenko Invented Life Story, Mother Admits," *Australian*, August 21, 1995, LexisNexis Academic.
8. Jane Freeman, "A Fraction Too Much Faction: How Helen Took Us for a Ride," *Sydney Morning Herald* (Australia), August 21, 1995, LexisNexis Academic.
9. M. Horan, "Author Sorry for Fantasy," *Courier Mail* (Queensland, Australia), August 26, 1995, LexisNexis Academic.
10. Knox, "The Darville Made Me Do It."
11. Philip Shenon, "Sydney Journal: For Fiction, and Fibbing, She Takes the Prize," *New York Times*, September 26, 1995, http://www.nytimes.com/1995/09/26/world/sydney-journal-for-fiction-and-fibbing-she-takes-the-prize.html.
12. Freeman, "A Fraction Too Much Faction."
13. *Ibid.*
14. Debra Jobson, "Publishers Clear Author Darville of Plagiarism," *Sydney Morning Herald* (Australia), Late edition, September 8, 1995, LexisNexis Academic.
15. "Darville Not a Plagiarist, Just Post-Modern," *Daily Telegraph Mirror* (Sydney, Australia), September 8, 1995, LexisNexis Academic.

My Own Sweet Time

1. Philip Morrissey, "Stalking Aboriginal Culture: The Wanda Koolmatrie Affair," *Australian Feminist Studies* 18, no. 42 (November 2003): 299, EBSCOhost Academic Search Complete (doc. ID: 11984851); Maggie Nolan, "In His Own Sweet Time: Carmen's Coming Out," Australian Literary Studies 21, no. 4 (October 2004): 134, EBSCOhost Academic Search Complete (doc. ID: 15410318).
2. Morrissey, "Stalking Aboriginal Culture." 299–300.
3. "Magabala Books," accessed May 18, 2015, https://www.magabala.com/home.
4. Morag Fraser, "A Picaresque Ride with a Shrewd Innocent," *Sydney Morning Herald* (Australia), April 8, 1995, LexisNexis Academic.
5. "Kibble Literary Awards," accessed May 18, 2015, http://www.perpetual.com.au/kibble/awards.htm.
6. Morrissey, "Stalking Aboriginal Culture," 300.
7. Leon Carmen, "Wanda and I," *Courier Mail* (Queensland, Australia), March 15, 1997, LexisNexis Academic.
8. Peter James Spielmann, "New Australian Aboriginal Hoax Uncovered—Award-Winning Author `Wanda Koolmatrie' Isn't Native; and `She' Actually Is a `He'," *Seattle Times*, March 13, 1997, http://community.seattletimes.nwsource.com/archive/?date=19970313&slug=2528563.
9. Debra Jopson and Susan Wyndham, "Hoax Novel Withdrawn from Sale by Publishers," *Sydney Morning Herald* (Australia), March 15, 1997, LexisNexis Academic.
10. "Trafford Publishing," accessed May 18, 2015, http://bookstore.trafford.com/Products/SKU-000150261/My-Own-Sweet-Time.aspx

Sarah; The Heart Is Deceitful Above All Things; Harold's End

1. Catherine Texier, "Lot Lizards," review of *Sarah*, by J.T. LeRoy, *New York Times*, May 7, 2000, ProQuest Historical Newspapers: The New York Times (doc. ID: 91382077).
2. *Ibid.*
3. Elizabeth Young, "Novel of the Week," review of *Sarah*, by J.T. LeRoy, *New Statesman* 129, no. 4501 (August 28, 2000): 43, EBSCOhost Academic Search Complete (doc. ID: 3524272).
4. Guy Lawson, "The Artful Dodger," *Rolling Stone*, no. 1040 (November 29, 2007), EBSCOhost Academic Search Complete (doc. ID: 27658430); Bettijane Levine, "J.T. LeRoy Was Like a Child Raised by

Notes

Wolves," *Chicago Tribune*, February 10, 2005, ProQuest (doc. ID: 420174274).

5. Lawson, "The Artful Dodger."

6. Bruce Handy, "The Boy Who Cried Author," *Vanity Fair*, April 2006, http://www.vanityfair.com/style/2006/04/jtleroy200604.

7. Ibid.

8. Philip Santo, review of *The Heart Is Deceitful Above All Things*, by J.T. LeRoy, *Library Journal* 126, no. 16 (October 2001): 145, EBSCOhost Academic Search Complete (doc. ID: 5313591).

9. Joelle Diderich, "LeRoy's Happy Ending," *Gold Coast Bulletin*, May 22, 2004, EBSCOhost Newspaper Source (accession no.: 20040522WW20097490).

10. Albert Mobilio, "*Harold's End:* Shell Shock," *New York Times*, February 27, 2005, ProQuest Historical Newspapers: The New York Times (doc. ID: 92898947).

11. Heidi Benson, "Soul-Baring Fiction Author J.T. LeRoy Plays with Gender—and Identity. Does It Really Matter Who He Is?" *SFGate*, December 17, 2005, http://www.sfgate.com/entertainment/article/Soul-baring-fiction-author-J-T-LeRoy-plays-with-2556606.php.

12. Stephen Beachy, "Who Is the Real JT LeRoy?" *New York*, October 17, 2005, http://nymag.com/nymetro/news/people/features/14718/; Warren St. John, "The Unmasking of JT Leroy: In Public, He's a She," *New York Times*, January 9, 2006, ProQuest Historical Newspapers: The New York Times (doc. ID: 93311880); Warren St. John, "Figure in JT Leroy Case Says Partner Is Culprit," *New York Times*, February 7, 2006, ProQuest Historical Newspapers: The New York Times (doc. ID: 93269831).

13. Alan Feuer, "Going to Court Over Fiction by a Fictitious Writer," *New York Times*, June 15, 2007, ProQuest Historical Newspapers: The New York Times (doc. ID: 848105477).

14. Alan Feuer, "At Trial, Writer Recalls an Alter Ego That Took Over," *New York Times*, June 21, 2007, ProQuest Historical Newspapers: The New York Times (doc. ID: 848115094).

15. Alan Feuer, "Jury Finds 'JT LeRoy' Was Fraud," *New York Times*, June 23, 2007, ProQuest Historical Newspapers: The New York Times (doc. ID: 848095785); Alan Feuer, "Judge Orders Author to Pay Film Company $350,000 in Legal Fees," *New York Times*, August 1, 2007, LexisNexis Academic.

16. Bilge Ebiri, "The Documentary *Author: The JT LeRoy Story* Is as Riveting as the Events That Inspired It," *Vulture*, January 22, 2016, http://www.vulture.com/2016/01/sundance-review-author-the-jt-leroy-story.html; Dennis Harvey, "Film Review: 'The Cult of JT LeRoy,'" *Variety*, March 7, 2015, http://variety.com/2015/film/reviews/film-review-the-cult-of-jt-leroy-120.

The Honored Society

1. Paige Smoron, "Inside the World of a Wiseguy," *Chicago Sun-Times*. November 27, 2001.

2. Jeff Zaleski, review of *The Honored Society*, by Michael Gambino, *Publishers Weekly* 248, no. 46 (November 12, 2001): 38, EBSCOhost, Academic Search Complete (doc. ID 5528495).

3. "Publisher Sues Over Mafia Credentials," CNN Money.com, August 29, 2002, http://money.cnn.com/2002/08/29/news/mafia/.

4. Charles Lawrence, "How I Was Duped by the Don Who Was a Con," *The Telegraph*, September 1, 2002, http://www.telegraph.co.uk/news/worldnews/northamerica/usa/1405966/How-I-was-duped-by-the-don-who-was-a-con.html.

5. Felicity Barringer, "Simon & Schuster Sues Author Over His Lineage," *New York Times*, August 29, 2002, http://www.nytimes.com/2002/08/29/business/simon-schuster-sues-author-over-his-lineage.html.

6. Ibid.

7. Steven Zeitchik, "S&S, Mob Novelist Settle Lawsuit," *Publishers Weekly* 251, no. 6 (February 9, 2004), EBSCOhost, Academic Search Complete (doc. ID: 12195843).

The Darkening Ecliptic

1. Christine Wertheim, "The Fall and Rise of Ernest Lalor Malley," *Cabinet*, issue 33 (spring 2009), http://www.cabinetmagazine.org/issues/33/wertheim.php; Bill Ashcroft, "Reading Carey Reading Malley," in *Who's Who? Hoaxes, Imposture and Identity Crises in Australian Literature*, ed. Maggie Nolan and Carrie Dawson (Queensland: University of Queensland Press, 2004): 30.

2. Wertheim, "The Fall and Rise of Ernest Lalor Malley."

3. *Ibid.*

4. James McAuley and Harold Stewart, quoted in Max Harris, introduction to *The Poems of Ern Malley*, by Ern Malley (Sydney: Allen & Unwin, 1988), 6.

5. Ibid.

6. Ashcroft, "Reading Carey Reading Malley," 30.

7. McAuley and Stewart, quoted in Malley, *The Poems of Ern Malley*, 7.

8. Cameron Lowe, "Text and Paratext: Ern Malley and the Function of the Author," *Cordite Poetry Review*, December 1, 2010, https://cordite.org.au/scholarly/text-and-paratext-ern-malley-and-the-function-of-the-author/.

9. Max Harris, quoted in Michael Heyward, *The Ern Malley Affair* (London: Faber and Faber, 1993), 126–127.

10. Herbert Read, quoted in Heyward, *The Ern Malley Affair*, 156–157.

11. Herbert Read, quoted in Malley, *The Poems of Ern Malley*, 9.

12. Ern Malley, *The Poems of Ern Malley* (Sydney: Allen & Unwin, 1988), 10.

13. Heyward, *The Ern Malley Affair*, 184.

14. Jacobus Vogelsang, quoted in Heyward, *The Ern Malley Affair*, 186.

15. Heyward, *The Ern Malley Affair*, 189.

16. Vogelsang, quoted in Heyward, *The Ern Malley Affair*, 190.

17. Ibid., 191.

18. Heyward, *The Ern Malley Affair*, 210.

Notes

The Love Poems of Marichiko

1. Morgan Gibson, *Revolutionary Rexroth, Poet of East-West Wisdom* (Hamden, Conn.: Archon Books, 1986): 17, 21.
2. Ibid., 21, 23–24.
3. Ibid., 83.
4. Kevin Gallagher, review of *The Complete Poems of Kenneth Rexroth*, ed. Sam Hamill and Bradford Morrow, *Boston Review*, April 1, 2003, https://bostonreview.net/poetry/microreviews-0.
5. Linda Hamalian, *A Life of Kenneth Rexroth* (New York: Norton, 1991): 352.
6. Ibid., 353.
7. Review of *The Morning Star*, by Kenneth Rexroth, *Kirkus Reviews*, accessed October 11, 2016, https://www.kirkusreviews.com/book-reviews/kenneth-rexroth-4/the-morning-star-2/.

Doubled Flowering from the Notebooks of Araki Yasusada

1. *Doubled Flowering: From the Notebooks of Araki Yasusada*, ed. and trans. Tosa Motokiyu, Ojiu Norinaga, and Okura Kyojin (New York: Roof Books, 1997), 10; Marjorie Perloff, "In Search of the Authentic Other: The Poetry of Araki Yasusada," in *Doubled Flowering*, 149.
2. Emily Nussbaum, "Turning Japanese: The Hiroshima Poetry Hoax," *Lingua Franca: The Review of Academic Life*, November 1996, 82; "Special Supplement," *American Poetry Review* 25, no. 4 (July/August 1996): 23, www.jstor.org/stable/27782161; Perloff, "In Search of the Authentic Other," 149.
3. Nussbaum, "Turning Japanese."
4. Ibid.
5. Ibid.
6. Full disclosure: the author is acquainted with Kent Johnson; Nussbaum, "Turning Japanese; *Double Flowering*," 139.
7. Kent Johnson, "The Hole of Hypocrisy: A Conversation with Kent Johnson on the U.S. 'Avant-Garde' and Other Fictions," interview by Michael Boughn, *Rain Taxi*, fall 2015, online edition, http://www.raintaxi.com/the-hole-of-hypocrisy-a-conversation-with-kent-johnson-on-the-u-s-avant-garde-and-other-fictions/.
8. Perloff, "In Search of the Authentic Other," 150.
9. Perloff, "In Search of the Authentic Other," 150–52.
10. *Doubled Flowering*, 132.
11. "The Yasusada Saga," *Stand Magazine* 38, no. 1 (1996): 37–8.

Saracen Island

1. Julie Frédette, "Rare Poems Ask Rare Friends: Literary Circles and Cultural Capital. The Case of Montreal's Jubilate Circle" (Ph.D. diss., Université de Sherbrooke, 2014), 103, http://savoirs.usherbrooke.ca/bitstream/handle/11143/94/Fredette_Julie_PhD_2014.pdf, accessed October 24, 2016.
2. Andreas Karavis, "Chorus of Voices We Hear in Wine," interview by Anna Zoumi, *Books in Canada*, October 1999, http://www.booksincanada.com/article_view.asp?id=1260; Diana Kuprel, "Great Authors of Our Time—Andreas Karavis," *Books in Canada*, October 1999, http://www.booksincanada.com/article_view.asp?id=1258.
3. W. J. Keith, review of *Saracen Island: The Poetry of Andreas Karavis*, by David Solway, *University of Toronto Quarterly* 71, no. 1 (winter 2001/02): 370, Project Muse.
4. Ben Downing, "Modern Homer Unmasked as a Mythical Figure," *Guardian*, March 23, 2001, https://www.theguardian.com/books/2001/mar/24/society1.
5. Matthew Hays, "Karavis: Greek God of Poetry or Literary Hoax?" *Globe and Mail* (Canada), October 10, 2000, LexisNexis Academic.
6. Carmine Starnino, "Beware of Greeks Bearing Poems: Who Is Karavis and Why Do We Suddenly Care?" *Gazette* (Montreal, Quebec), October 28, 2000, LexisNexis Academic.
7. Ibid.
8. Joel Yanofsky, "Poetic License Revoked," *Gazette* (Montreal, Quebec), November 18, 2000, LexisNexis Academic.
9. Yanofsky, "Poetic License Revoked"; Frédette, "Rare Poems Ask Rare Friends," i.
10. Downing, "Modern Homer Unmasked."
11. Yanofsky, "Poetic License Revoked."

Conclusion

1. Demian Katz, Ralph Le Van, Ya'aqov Ziso, "Using Authority Data in VuFind," *Code4Lib Journal*, issue 14 (July 23, 2011), http://journal.code4lib.org/articles/5354.
2. Another recent addition to genre/form terms "Creative nonfiction" is not useful for cataloging deceptive works because the scope note in the authority record explains that it is to be applied to "prose works that use literary styles and techniques to present factually accurate narratives in a compelling manner." If a work is truly creative nonfiction, then it is not deceptive.
3. Karen Snow, "An Examination of the Practical and Ethical Issues Surrounding False Memoirs in Cataloging Practice," *Cataloging & Classification Quarterly* 53, no. 8 (2015): 943, doi: 10.1080/01639374.2015.1056571.
4. Ibid., 944.
5. Philip A. Homan, "Library Catalog Notes for 'Bad Books': Ethics vs. Responsibilities," *Knowledge Organization: KO* 39, no. 5 (September 2012): 353.

Bibliography for Case Studies

Abraham, Tom. *The Cage.* London: Bantam Press, 2002.
Avey, Denis, with Rob Broomby. *The Man Who Broke into Auschwitz: A True Story of World War II.* Cambridge: Da Capo Press, 2011.
Bellesiles, Michael A. *Arming America: The Origins of a National Gun Culture.* New York: Alfred A. Knopf, 2000.
Boyer, Glenn G. *Illustrated Life of Doc Holliday.* Glenwood Springs, CO: Reminder Publishing, 1966.
Buffalo Child Long Lance. *Long Lance.* New York: Cosmopolitan Book Corp., 1928.
Capote, Truman. *In Cold Blood: A True Account of a Multiple Murder and Its Consequences.* New York: Random House, 1965.
Carcaterra, Lorenzo. *Sleepers.* New York: Ballantine Books, 1995.
Carew, Tom. *Jihad!: The Secret War in Afghanistan.* Edinburgh: Mainstream, 2000.
Carmichael, Montgomery. *The Life of John William Walshe, F.S.A.* Edited by Montgomery Carmichael. New York: E.P. Dutton, 1902.
Carter, Forrest. *The Education of Little Tree.* New York: Delacorte Press/Eleanor Friede, 1976.
Crockett, Davy. Col. *Crockett's Exploits and Adventures in Texas: Wherein Is Contained a Full Account of His Journey from Tennessee to the Red River and Nathchitoches, and Thence across Texas to San Antonio; Including Many Hair-Breadth Escapes; Together with a Topographical, Historical, and Political View of Texas.* Philadelphia: T. K. and P. G. Collins, 1836.
Darville, Helen. *The Hand That Signed the Paper.* St. Leonards, N.S.W.: Allen & Unwin, 1994.
Defonseca, Misha. *Misha: A Memoire of the Holocaust Years.* Bluebell, PA: Mt. Ivy Press, 1997.
Earp, Josephine Sarah Marcus. *I Married Wyatt Earp: The Recollections of Josephine Sarah Marcus Earp.* Edited by Glenn G. Boyer. Tucson: University of Arizona Press, 1976.
Economou, George. *Ananios of Kleiter: Poems & Fragments and Their Reception from Antiquity to the Present.* Translated by George Economou. Exeter: Shearsman Books, 2009.
Finch, A. L. *Child P.O.W.: A Memoir of Survival.* Enumclaw, WA: Annotation Press, 2007.
Frey, James. *A Million Little Pieces.* New York: N.A. Talese/Doubleday, 2003.
_____. *My Friend Leonard.* New York: Riverhead Books, 2005.
Gambino, Michael. *The Honored Society.* New York: Pocket Books, 2001.
Gray, Ernest. *The Diary of a Surgeon in the Year 1751–1752.* Edited by Ernest Gray. New York: D. Appleton-Century, 1937.
_____. *Man Midwife: The Further Experiences of John Knyveton, M.D., Late Surgeon in the British Fleet, during the Years 1763–1809.* Edited by Ernest Gray. London: Hale, 1946.
_____. *Surgeon's Mate: The Diary of John Knyveton, Surgeon in the British Fleet during the Seven Years War, 1756–1762.* Edited by Ernest Gray. London: R. Hale Ltd., 1942.
Grey Owl. *Pilgrims of the Wild.* London: L. Dickson, 1934.
Haley, Alex. *Roots.* Garden City, NY: Doubleday, 1976.
Irving, Clifford. *The Autobiography of Howard Hughes.* Santa Fe: Terrificbooks.com, 1999.
Johnson, Anthony Godby. *A Rock and a Hard Place: One Boy's Triumphant Story.* New York: Crown Publishers, 1993.
Jones, Margaret B. *Love and Consequences: A Memoir of Hope and Survival.* New York: Riverhead Books, 2008.
Jones, Morgan and Damien Lewis. *The Embassy House.* New York: Threshold Books, 2013.
Khouri, Norma. *Honor Lost: Love and Death in Modern-Day Jordan.* New York: Atria Books, 2003.

Bibliography for Case Studies

Koolmatrie, Wanda. *My Own Sweet Time.* Broome, Western Australia: Magabala Books, 1994.
Lehrer, Jonah. *Imagine: How Creativity Works.* Boston: Houghton Mifflin Harcourt, 2012.
LeRoy, J. T. *Harold's End.* San Francisco: Last Gasp, 2004.
———. *The Heart Is Deceitful above All Things.* New York: Bloomsbury, 2001.
———. *Sarah.* New York: Bloomsbury, 2000.
Lowell, Joan. *The Cradle of the Deep.* New York: Simon & Schuster, 1929.
Malarkey, Kevin and Alex Malarkey. *The Boy Who Came Back from Heaven: A Remarkable Account of Miracles, Angels, and Life beyond This World.* Carol Stream, IL: Tyndale House Publishers, 2010.
Malley, Ern. *The Darkening Ecliptic.* Melbourne: Reed & Harris, 1944.
Mam, Somaly. *The Road of Lost Innocence: The True Story of a Cambodian Childhood.* London: Virago, 2007.
Marichiko. *The Love Poems of Marichiko.* Santa Barbara: Christopher's Books, 1978.
Monk, Maria. *Awful Disclosures of Maria Monk: As Exhibited in a Narrative of Her Sufferings during a Residence of Five Years as a Novice, and Two Years as a Black Nun, in the Hotel Dieu Nunnery at Montreal.* New York: Howe & Bates, 1836.
Morgan, Marlo. *Mutant Message Downunder.* Lees Summit, MO: ǂb MM Co., 1991.
Mortenson, Greg. *Stones into Schools: Promoting Peace with Books, Not Bombs, in Afghanistan and Pakistan.* New York: Viking, 2009.
Mortenson, Greg, and David Oliver Relin. *Three Cups of Tea: One Man's Mission to Fight Terrorism and Build Nations—One School at a Time.* New York: Viking, 2006.
Mowat, Farley. *Never Cry Wolf.* Boston: Little, Brown, 1963.
Mudrooroo. *Wild Cat Falling.* Sydney: Angus and Robertson, 1965.
Nasdijj. *Geronimo's Bones: A Memoir of My Brother and Me.* New York: Ballantine Books, 2004.
———. *The Blood Runs Like a River through My Dreams: A Memoir.* Boston: Houghton Mifflin, 2000.
———. *The Boy and the Dog Are Sleeping.* New York: Ballantine Books, 2003.
Nietzsche, Friedrich. *My Sister and I.* Translated by Oscar Levy. New York: Boar's Head Books, 1951.
O'Beirne, Kathy. *Kathy's Story: A Childhood Hell inside the Magdalen Laundries.* Edinburgh: Mainstream, 2005.
Pellegrino, Charles. *The Last Train from Hiroshima: The Survivors Look Back.* New York: Henry Holt, 2010.
Radley, Paul. *Jack Rivers and Me.* Sydney: Allen & Unwin, 1981.
Rawicz, Slavomir. *The Long Walk: A Gamble for Life.* New York: Harper, 1956.
Rorvik, David M. *In His Image: The Cloning of a Man.* Philadelphia: Lippincott, 1978.
Rosenblat, Herman. *Angel at the Fence: The True Story of a Love That Survived.* New York: Berkley Books, 2008.
Santiago, Danny. *Famous All Over Town.* New York: Simon & Schuster, 1983.
Smith, Michelle and Lawrence Pazder. *Michelle Remembers.* New York: Congdon & Lattes, 1980.
Solway, David. *Saracen Island: The Poems of Andreas Karavis.* Montreal: Signal Editions, 2000.
Sparks, Beatrice. *Go Ask Alice.* Englewood Cliffs, NJ: Prentice-Hall, 1971.
Steinbeck, John. *Travels with Charley: In Search of America.* New York: Viking Press, 1962.
Stratford, Lauren. *Satan's Underground.* Eugene, OR: Harvest House Publishers, 1988.
Watt, Donald. *Stoker: The Story of an Australian Soldier Who Survived Auschwitz-Birkenau.* East Roseville, N.S.W.: Simon & Schuster, 1995.
Wilkomirski, Binjamin. *Fragments: Memories of a Wartime Childhood.* New York: Schocken Books, 1996.
Yasusada, Araki. *Doubled Flowering from the Notebooks of Araki Yasusada.* Edited by Tosa Motokiyu, Ojiu Noringa, and Okura Kyojin. New York: Roof Books, 1997.

Selected Bibliography of Secondary Sources

Adams, Timothy Dow. *Telling Lies in Modern American Autobiography.* Chapel Hill: University of North Carolina Press, 1990.

American Library Association. "Code of Ethics of the American Library Association," amended January 22, 2008, http://www.ala.org/advoscacy/proethics/codeofethics/codeethics.

American Library Association. "Labeling and Rating Systems: An Interpretation of the *Library Bill of Rights*," amended July 15, 2009. http://www.ala.org/advocacy/intfreedom/librarybill/interpretations/labelingrating.

Anglo-American Cataloguing Rules, 2nd ed. Chicago: American Library Association, 1998.

Bair, Sheila A. "Toward a Code of Ethics for Cataloging." *University Libraries Faculty & Staff Publications*, Paper 11 (2005). http://scholarworks.wmich.edu/library_pubs/11/.

Cutter, Charles A. *Rules for a Dictionary Catalog*, 4th ed. rewritten. Washington, D.C.: Government Printing Office, 1904.

D'Agata, John, and Jim Fingal. *The Lifespan of a Fact.* New York: W.W. Norton, 2012.

Gerard, Philip. *Creative Nonfiction: Researching and Crafting Stories of Real Life.* Cincinnati: Story Press, 1996.

Homan, Philip A. "Library Catalog Notes for 'Bad Books': Ethics vs. Responsibilities." *Knowledge Organization: KO* 39, no. 5 (September 2012).

Manley, Will. "Catalogers, Cast Off Your Shackles." *American Libraries* 31, no. 2 (February 2000).

Moore, Dinty W. *The Truth of the Matter: Art and Craft in Creative Nonfiction.* New York: Pearson Longman, 2007.

Newman, Kate. "Book Publishing, Not Fact-Checking." *Atlantic*, September 3, 2014. LexisNexis Academic.

RDA Toolkit: Resource, Description and Access, 0.4.3.4, accessed May 13, 2014, http://access.rdatoolkit.org/.

Rothe, Ann. *Popular Trauma Culture: Selling the Pain of Others in the Mass Media.* New Brunswick: Rutgers University Press, 2011.

Ruthven, K. K. *Faking Literature.* Cambridge: Cambridge University Press, 2001.

Smiraglia, Richard P., Hur-Li Lee, and Hope A. Olson. "The Flimsy Fabric of Authorship." *Proceedings of the Annual Conference of CAIS*, 2015. http://www.cais-acsi.ca/ojs/index.php/cais/article/view/452/136.

Snow, Karen. "An Examination of the Practical and Ethical Issues Surrounding False Memoirs in Cataloging Practice." *Cataloging & Classification Quarterly* 53, no. 8 (2015). doi: 10.1080/01639374.2015.1056571.

Taub, Diane E. and Lawrence D. Nelson. "Satanism in Contemporary America: Establishment or Underground." *The Sociological Quarterly* 34, no. 3 (August 1993). http://www.jstor.org/stable/4121110.

Yagoda, Ben. *Memoir: A History.* New York: Riverhead Books, 2009.

Young, James O. and Susan Haley. "'Nothing Comes from Nowhere': Reflections on Cultural Appropriation as the Representation of Other Cultures." In *The Ethics of Cultural Appropriation*, edited by James O. Young and Conrad G. Brunk. Hoboken: Wiley-Blackwell, 2009.

Index

AACR2 see *Anglo-American Cataloging Rules*
Aboriginal Australians *see* Indigenous Australians
About Us: The Dignity of Children 49
Abraham, Tom 64–65
access points 13, 15
Acting for Women in Distressing Circumstances *see* Agir pour les Femmes en Situation Précaire
added entry 6, 7
AFESIP *see* Agir pour les Femmes en Situation Précaire
The African 91
Agir pour les Femmes en Situation Précaire 74, 75
Akiko, Yosano 121
ALA *see* American Library Association
Albert, Laura *see* LeRoy, J.T.
Alexander, Margaret Walker 91
Alexie, Sherman 63, 106–107
Alvarez, Javier 123
Always Dancing 69
American Library Association 15
American National Jewish Book Award 54
Ananios of Kleitor 97–98, 127
And Die in the West 39
Angel at the Fence 76–77
Angel Girl 77
Anglo-American Cataloguing Rules 3, 4, 13, 15, 16, 105
Angry Penguins 119, 120
The Apple: Based on the Herman Rosenblat Holocaust Love Story 77
Arming America: The Origins of a National Gun Culture 84, 93–95
Astor *see* Knoop, Geoffrey
Auschwitz 45, 52, 53, 54, 81, 82
Australian/Vogel Literary Prize 110, 112, 148; *The Hand That Signed the Paper* 1
authenticity 2, 3, 4, 9–10, 11, 19, 106

Author: The JT LeRoy Story 117
authority records 6–10, 16, 105, 107, 127–128
authorized heading *see* controlled vocabulary
authorship 3, 4, 11, 105–107, 123, 126–127
autobiography 18
The Autobiography of Howard Hughes 57–60
Autocat 2
Avatar (film) 99, 122, 123
Avey, Denis 80–82
Awful Disclosures of Maria Monk 21–23

Bair, Sheila 15
Barrus, Tim *see* Nasdijj
Barthes, Roland 106
Bay View Hotel (Manila, Philippines) 72, 73
Beachy, Stephen 116
The Beautiful Side of Evil 44
Beauty Queen 37
Belaney, Archibald *see* Grey Owl
Bellesiles, Michael A. 84, 93–95
Belmont, Vera 56
Bergen-Belsen 52
Bibbulmun 108
bibliographic record 6, 7
Birkenau *see* Auschwitz
The Blood Runs Like a River Through My Dreams: A Memoir 62, 63
Blue Mountain Group 103
A Book About Love 102
Book of the Month Club 27, 50
Borrowed Time: An AIDS Memoir 47
Box, Edgar *see* Vidal, Gore
The Boy and the Dog Are Sleeping 62, 63
The Boy Who Came Back from Heaven 79–80
Boyer, Glenn G. 38–40
British Special Air Service 9, 60, 61
Bromhall, J.D. 93

Brontë sisters 105
Broomby, Rob 80, 82
Buchenwald 76–77
Buffalo Child Long Lance 19, 24–26
Burden, Douglas 25
Burke, Charles 26

The Cage 64–65
Cameron, James 99, 153
Canadian Wildlife Service 85, 86, 87
Capote, Truman 3, 87–89
Carcaterra, Lorenzo 50–52
Carew, Tom 9, 60–61; and Mujahideen 9, 60
Carlisle Indian Industrial School 25
Carmen, Leon *see* Koolmatrie, Wanda
Carmichael, Montgomery 23, 24, 129
Carter, Asa *see* Carter, Forrest
Carter, Dan T. 41
Carter, Forrest 40–42
cataloger's judgment 3, 13, 127, 128
cataloging objectives *see* Cutter's cataloging objectives
cataloging standards 1, 3, 14, 15, 16
Catholic Church 4, 22, 51
Chauncey Yellow Robe 26
Child Holocaust Survivors Group of Los Angeles 45
A Child of the Century 59
Child P.O.W.: A Memoir of Survival 72–73
Chou, Yi-Fen *see* Hudson, Michael Derrick
classification 13, 14, 16, 20, 128
Classification and Shelflisting Manual 13
The Clone 92
cloning 92, 93
Clum, John 38
Clum manuscript 38
Clutter family 87
Code of Ethics of the American Library Association 14–15

155

Index

Col. Crockett's Exploits and Adventures in Texas 4, 20–21
collating objective *see* Cutter's cataloging objectives
Confessiones 19
The Confessions 19
consensus 12, 19
controlled vocabulary 6–7, 13
Cooper, Dennis 115
Corliss, James R. 99
Cornerstone Magazine 44
Coulander, Harold 91–92
Coward, Charles 82
The Cradle of the Deep 27–28, 128
creative nonfiction 18, 87
Crockett, Davy 4, 20, 21
Cromwell, David *see* le Carre, John
cross-reference 7, 9–10, 105, 127–128
CSM *see Classification and Shelflisting Manual*
The Cult of JT LeRoy 117
cultural appropriation 106–107, 114, 123, 127
Cutter, Charles A. 14
Cutter's cataloging objectives 14

The Darkening Ecliptic: Poems 119–121
Darville, Helen *see* Demidenko, Helen
Davies, Dylan *see* Jones, Morgan
Defonseca, Misha 55–57
Demidenko, Helen 112–113
Denman, Thomas 30
Devil Worship: Exposing Satan's Underground 43
De Wael, Monique *see* Defonseca, Misha
Dewey, Alvin 89
The Diary of a Surgeon in the Year 1751–1752 29–30
Dillard, Annie 18
Dobbie Literary Award 114
Doessekker, Bruno *see* Wilkomirski, Binjamin
Don't Ever Tell see Kathy's Story
Doubled Flowering from the Notebooks of Araki Yasusada 122–123
Downing, Ronald 33, 34
Dreyfous, Leslie 48
Dumbartung Aboriginal Corporation 46–47, 108, 109
Dunne, John Gregory 111
Durack, Mary 108
Dylan, Bob 2, 101, 102

Eagle Speaker 25
Earp, Josephine Sarah Marcus 38, 39, 40
Eastwood, Clint 40, 41

Economou, George 97, 98
The Education of Little Tree 40–42, 128
Eggington, Robert 46
1877: Year of Living Violently 95
Elephant 116
The Embassy House 102–104
Emperor Constantine 4
Enola Gay 99
Eskin, Blake 55
evaluating objective *see* Cutter's cataloging objectives

fact-checking 11, 62, 78, 83–84
false identity *see* pseudonym
Famous All Over Town 10, 110–111
Fiction 8, 13, 16, 17, 105–107, 126, 127
Finch, A.L. 72–73
finding objective *see* Cutter's cataloging objectives
fixed fields 6, 7
"Flying Coffin" *see* "Spruce Goose"
Forbidden Love see Honor Lost: Love and Death in Modern-Day Jordan
Forrest, Nathan Bedford 41
Foucault, Michel 106
Fraginals, Vicki 47–49
Fragments: Memories of a Wartime Childhood 17, 45, 54–55, 129
FRBR *see* Functional Requirements for Bibliographic Records
Frey, James 3, 12, 17, 65–7, 128
Friedenberg, Richard 41
Friedman, Laurie 76
Friend, Tad 49
Fuhrman, Candice 46
Functional Requirements for Bibliographic Records 14
Fuoco, Joseph 99, 100

Galbraith, Robert *see* Rowling, J.K.
Gambino, Carlo 117, 118
Gambino, Michael 117–118
Ganzfried, Daniel 54, 55
genre 1, 2, 4, 9, 11, 13, 17, 18, 20, 83, 126, 128
genre/form headings 6, 7, 13, 127, 128
Geronimo's Bones: A Memoir of My Brother and Me 62, 63
Ghosts of the Titanic 99
Glass, Cathy 19
Glinski, Witold 34
Glovach, Linda 37
Go Ask Alice 20, 36–38
Godby, Jack 47–48
Golden, Arthur 106

Gone to Texas see The Rebel Outlaw: Josey Wales
Grabowski, Laura *see* Stratford, Lauren
granularity 16
Gray, Ernest 29–31
Greif, Gideon 53
Grey Owl 28–29
Groff, David 48, 49
Grosjean, Bruno *see* Wilkomirski, Binjamin
Guidelines for ALCTS Members to Supplement the American Library Association Code of Ethics 14–15
gun ownership 84, 94, 95

Haley, Alex 90, 91–92
The Hand That Signed the Paper 112–113
Harold's End 115, 116
Harris, Max 119–121
Harris, Michael 125
The Heart Is Deceitful Above All Things 115, 116, 117
heavenly tourism 80
Hecht, Ben 59
Heston, Charlton 94
Hillerman, Tony 106
Hiroshima, Japan 99
The Hoax 60
Holocaust Museum (United States) 54, 82
Holocaust survivors 4, 17, 18
Honor Lost: Love and Death in Modern-Day Jordan 95–97
The Honored Society 117–118
Houlahan, J. Michael 72–73
How We Decide 101, 102
Howard Hughes Medical Institute 57
Howard Hughes: The Autobiography: The Most Famous Unpublished Book of the 20th Century—Until Now 60
Hoyt, the Rev. William K. 22
Hudson, Michael Derrick 107
Hughes, Howard 57–59
Hughes Aircraft 57
Hughes Tool Company 57, 58, 59
Husseini, Rana 96

I Know You're Hurting 45
I Married Wyatt Earp 38–40
I Was There Too 53
IFLA *see* The International Federation of Library Associations and Institutions
Illustrated Life of Doc Holliday 39, 40
Imagine: How Creativity Works 2, 100–102, 128
In Cold Blood 3, 87–90, 128

Index

In His Image: The Cloning of a Man 92–93
indigenous Australians 108, 109, 114, 127
Ingrassia, Michelle 48
International Conference on Cataloguing Principles 14
The International Federation of Library Associations and Institutions 6, 14
International Standard Bibliographic Description 6
Irving, Clifford 57, 58–60
ISBD *see* International Standard Bibliographic Description

Jack Rivers and Me 109–110
James, Daniel 10, 110, 111,
Jansen, Sascha Weinzheimer 73
Jewish Quarterly literary prize for nonfiction 54, 55
Jihad! The Secret War in Afghanistan 9, 60–61
Johnson, Anthony Godby 47–50, 116
Johnson, Anthony Robert *see* Johnson, Anthony Godby
Johnson, Colin *see* Mudrooroo
Johnson, Kent 123–124
Johnson, Vicki *see* Fraginals, Vicki
Jones, Margaret B. 77–79, 128
Jones, Morgan 102–103
Jubilee 91
judgment *see* cataloger's judgment
Justice for Magdalenes 69

Kakutani, Michiko 19
Karavis, Andreas *see* Solway, David
Karsten, Lesley 49
Kathy's Story: A Childhood Hell Inside the Magdalen Laundries 67–69
Kaufmann, Walter 32
Kkhouri, Norma 95–97
Knoop, Geoffrey 116
Knoop, Savannah 116
Knyveton, John, M.D. *see* Gray, Ernest
Koolmatrie, Wanda 114
Kozol, Jonathan 54
Krakauer, Jon 70–71
Kristof, Nicholas 74, 76
Kweit, Konrad 52, 53

Labeling and Rating Systems: An Interpretation of the Library Bill of Rights 15
The Last Train from Hiroshima 85, 98–100, 128
Le Carré, John 4
Legros, Pierre 74, 75

Lehrer, Jonah 2, 100–102
LeRoy, J.T. 115–117
Levinson, Barry 50, 51
Levy, Oscar 31–32
Lewin, Leonard 10
Lewis, Damien 102, 103
The Life of John William Walshe, F.S.A. 23–24, 129
Lindgren, James 94
Little Boy (bomb) 99
Logan, Lara 104
Long, Sylvester Clark *see* Buffalo Child Long Lance
The Long Walk 33–34
Looking for Mr. Smith 33
Love Alone 47
Love and Consequences: A Memoir of Hope and Survival 77–79, 126, 128
The Love Poems of Marichiko 121–122, 128
Lowell, Joan 27–28

MacArthur, Gen. Douglas 72
Machine Readable Cataloging 6
Mächler, Stefan 55
Magabala Books 114
Magdalene Laundries 68, 69
Magdalene Sisters 68
Malarkey, Alex 79–80
Malarkey, Kevin 79, 80
Malley, Ern 119–121
Mam, Somaly 73–76
Man Midwife 30
The Man Who Broke into Auschwitz 80–82
Manne, Robert 112, 113
MARC *see* Machine Readable Cataloging
Marichiko *see* Rexroth, Kenneth
Markham, Frederick 23
Marks, Paula Mitchell 39
Maslin, Janet 65
Maupin, Armistead 48, 49, 116
McAuley, James *see* Malley, Ern
McChrystal, Stanley 71
McMartin Preschool 42–43, 44
Me and Good Mates 110
Memoirs 9, 10, 17–20, 127, 128
Memoirs of a Geisha 106
Michaelson, Johanna 44
Michelle Remembers 42–43
A Million Little Pieces 3, 11, 17, 19, 65–67, 128
Minnie A. Caine 27, 28
Misha: A Memoire of the Holocaust Years 55–57
Monette, Paul 47, 48
Monk, Maria 21–23
Monowitz *see* Auschwitz
Morgan, Marlo 45–47
The Morning Star 122
Mortenson, Greg 70–71
Motokiyu, Tosa 122, 123

Mowat, Farley 85–87; and subjective nonfiction 86
Moynihan, Michael C. 101, 102
Mudrooroo 108–109, 127
Murie, Adolph 85
Muscio, Inga 78, 79
Mutant Message Downunder 45–47
My Blue Checker Corker 110
My Friend Leonard 65, 67
My Own Sweet Time 114–115
My Sister and I 31–32

Nagasaki, Japan 99
Nasdijj 19, 62–64
Never Cry Wolf 85–87
The New Somaly Mam Foundation 76
Nietzsche, Elisabeth 31
Nietzsche, Friedrich 31–32
The Night Listener 49
Nilsen, Alleen Pace 36–37
nonfiction 4, 9, 10, 11, 13, 16, 17, 18, 83–84, 126, 128
nonfiction novel 3, 87, 88, 89, 128
North American Wolf Foundation 56
notes 13, 16, 107, 128; general 6, 7, 16, 129; source 6, 7; summary 6, 7
Nyoongah *see* Bibbulmun

O'Beirne, Kathy 67–69
Office of Indian Affairs 26
Olbermann, Keith 48, 49
The Oprah Winfrey Show 3, 12
Oprah's Book Club 3, 66
Osborn Associates 59
Ottaway, Mark 91
Owens, Terrence 115

Parini, Jay 35
Paris Principles *see* International Conference on Cataloguing Principles
The Password Is Courage 82
Patric, Jason 51
Pazder, Lawrence 42, 43
Pearman, Robert 88
Pellegrino, Charles 98–100
Pellegrino, Michael *see* Gambino, Michael
pen name *see* pseudonym
Pilgrims of the Wild 28–29
Plotkin, George David 32
poetry 8, 105, 106, 107, 119–125, 126, 127
principle of representation 14, 15
Proust Was a Neuroscientist 101
pseudonym 4, 7, 9, 10, 16, 41, 61, 105–107, 111, 113, 115, 121, 123, 126, 127
publisher 11, 12, 13, 17–18, 66–67, 83–84, 127

157

Index

Radley, Jack 110
Radley, Paul 109–110
Radzicki, Roma 76, 77
Rawicz, Slavomir 33–34
RDA see Resource, Description, and Access
Real People Tribe 45, 46
The Rebel Outlaw: Josey Wales (book) 40, 41
The Rebel Outlaw: Josey Wales (film) 40–41
Reed, Fred 125
Relin, David Oliver 70
Report from Iron Mountain 10
Resource, Description, and Access 3, 4, 13, 14, 15, 16, 105
Rexroth, Kenneth 107, 121–122
Rivera, Geraldo 43
The Road of Lost Innocence 73–76
Roberts, Gary L. 40
A Rock and a Hard Place 47–50
Rogers, Fred 48
Roots (book) 90–92
Roots (television series) 90
Rorvik, David M. 92, 93
Rose, Willie Lee 90–91
Rosenblat, Herman 76–77
Roth, Samuel 32
Rousseau, Jean-Jacques 19
Rowling, J.K. 126
Rules for a Printed Dictionary Catalog 14

Sabbagh, Amal al- 96
Saint Augustine 19
Santiago, Danny see James, Daniel
Saracen Island: The Poems of Andreas Karavis 124–125
Sarah 115–117
SAS see British Special Air Service
satanic ritual abuse 42, 43
Satan's Underground 43–45
Second Amendment 84, 93
Seltzer, Margaret see Jones, Margaret B.
Sessarego, Philip see Carew Tom

Sheridan, Michael 69
Sherrard House Hostel (Dublin) 69
SHM see Subject Heading Manual
Silence de l'Innocence see *The Road of Lost Innocence*
The Silent Enemy 26
The Singing Forest 52
Sleepers (book) 50–52, 127
Sleepers (film) 51
Slocum, the Rev. J.J. 22
Smith, Michelle 42–43
Smith, Perry 88–89
Smith, Richard Penn 4, 20–21
The Smoking Gun 11, 66
Snow, Karen 128
Solway, David 124–125
Somaly Mam Foundation 74, 75, 76
Sonderkommando 52, 53
Sparks, Beatrice 36–37
Speedie see LeRoy, J. T.
Spielberg, Steven 41
"Spruce Goose" 57
SRA see satanic ritual abuse
Stanton, John P. 46
Starnino, Carmine 124–125
Statement of International Cataloguing Principles 14
Steigerwald, Bill 35
Steinbeck, John 34–35
Stevens, J. Christopher 102
Stevenson, Philip 61
Steward, Walter K. 32
Stewart, Harold see Malley, Ern
Stoker 52–53, 81
stoker see Sonderkommando
Stone, William, Colonel 22
Stones into Schools 70–71
Stratford, Lauren 43–45
Stripped Naked 45
subdivision, form 7–8, 13, 16, 128
subject entries 6, 7, 8, 13, 14, 16
Subject Heading Manual 13
subject headings see subject entries
Suhrkamp-Verlag 54
Surgeon's Mate 30

Surviving with Wolves 56
Sylvester Chahuska Long Lance see Buffalo Child Long Lance

Talese, Nan A. 66
Terminator see LeRoy, J.T.
Three Cups of Deceit 70–71
Three Cups of Tea 2, 70–1
Titanic (film) 99
To Hell and Back: The Last Train from Hiroshima 100
Traveling Tongue see Morgan, Marlo
Travels with Charley 34–36

University of Arizona Press 39–40
University of New Mexico Press 41

Van Sant, Gus 65, 66, 116
variable fields 6, 7
veracity 3, 4, 10–11, 18, 19, 105, 126
Vidal, Gore 4, 9, 18,
Voices 36, 37

Walshe, John William 23–24
Waltzer, Kenneth 76–77
Watt, Donald 52–53, 81
Weale, Adrian 61
West, Duane 89
Wiesel, Elie 56
Wild Cat Falling 108–109, 127
Wilkinson Home for Boys 50, 51
Wilkomirski, Binjamin 45, 54–55
Willis, Linda 33–34
Willson, Laurel see Stratford, Lauren
Winfrey, Oprah 3, 66, 68, 76
The Wolves of Mount McKinley 85–86
women, of Jordan 96
Wyatt Earp's Tombstone Vendetta 20

Yad Vashem 53, 82
Yagoda, Ben 20
Yasusada, Araki 122, 123, 124